ESCAPE FROM AUTHORITY

JOHN H. SCHAAR

Escape from Authority

THE PERSPECTIVES OF ERICH FROMM

BASIC BOOKS, INC.
Publishers, New York

To my parents

We seek other conditions because we know not
how to enjoy our own; and go outside of ourselves
for want of knowing what it is like inside of us.
So it is no use raising ourselves on stilts,
for even on stilts we have to walk on our own legs.
And sitting on the loftiest throne in the world
we are still sitting on our behind.

—MONTAIGNE

Acknowledgments

My indebtedness to other writers is great, and I have tried throughout to give them their proper credit. Here I wish to thank those who helped directly in the making of the book.

To two of my colleagues, Professors Norman Jacobson and Sheldon S. Wolin, I owe debts which cannot be measured by a lean accounting of the specific contributions each made to the book. Very much of whatever is most worthy in the book came from them. Both read the manuscript carefully, criticized it frankly, and contributed many suggestions for its improvement. Many of the ideas that enrich my pages began in conversations with Professor Jacobson, and my book would be a duller thing without the spark given to it by his original and philosophical spirit. Professor Wolin shared with me his profound learning in political and moral philosophy, and his discerning intelligence saved me from some debilitating errors of fact and judgment.

Dr. Jacob G. Jacobson of the University of Colorado graciously consented to read the manuscript, even though he and I have never met. He clarified some of my conceptions of psychoanalysis and corrected some of my interpretations of Fromm.

I am also indebted to two graduate students in the University of California at Berkeley. Philip Chapman, my capable research assistant, worried about the book almost as much as I did, and tried hard to make it better. His frank and persistent criticism helped me to tighten my arguments and clarify my expression. Wilson C. McWilliams also read the manuscript and offered valuable suggestions for its improvement. His challenging intelligence stimulated me to modify a number of my pet formulations.

To my friend John Bourquin I owe a special word of thanks. He read the manuscript and contributed some valuable ideas to it. His keen sense of style trimmed a good many rough expressions from my pages.

My wife Karin endured my moods, improved my writing, and prepared the final index, all with skill and sympathy.

I am also indebted to Miss Francine Barban, who patiently and skillfully worked my ragged manuscript into an excellent typescript. Generous financial support from the Rockefeller Foundation gave me free time for work on the book.

Contents

ESCAPE FROM AUTHORITY

Prologue

Erich Fromm was born in Germany in 1900: he is, thus, very much a man of this century. As a young student in the splendid old universities of Heidelberg and Munich, he lived through the terrifying breakdown of culture which overtook the Germany of the 1920's. In the Berlin Psychoanalytic Institute he became a practitioner of psychoanalysis, the healing art which belongs peculiarly to the twentieth century. He studied and taught in the Frankfurt Psychoanalytic Institute, and in the Institute for Social Research of the University of Frankfurt. Uprooted by the Nazi terror, he came to the United States in the early 1930's. Since then he has taught at various colleges and universities here and in Mexico, and has written the books which make his name a prominent one in any serious discussion of modern social problems.

War, cultural chaos, psychoanalytic explorations, homelessness, totalitarianism—these are the epochal features of the world of Erich Fromm. He lives in a day when the sun has gone out of the human condition, and all his writing starts from the conviction that the life of Western man has

3

gone desperately wrong. This sense of urgency which pervades Fromm's work has made of it an ambitious system of social criticism. Few writers have attempted a fuller diagnosis of the social maladies of our time. But if Fromm's criticism runs deep, it is because his hopes run high. He thinks that man today has everything within his grasp—if he will but reach for it. In this, too, Fromm seems a man of the twentieth century, a century which has not known where to draw the bounds of human life. No writer has spoken more passionately for freedom and justice and love, nor made greater claims for the power of the human spirit. No writer has tried harder to teach men the way to freedom without loneliness, reason without rationalism, self-love without selfishness, authority without repression, religion without theology.

In his eager search for materials to support his case, Fromm has willfully and often violated the boundaries which increasing specialization has built around the separate fields of learning. He takes his materials where he finds them, and asks no questions about his right to them. From the beginning he has hunted in the unsettled lands where psychology, sociology, politics, philosophy, and religion meet, and sometimes clash. Nor has he hesitated to go to the utopians and the mystics, the "awakened ones," for inspiration and support, for they, like himself, were concerned above all with the meaning of goodness and the quality of human life.

Eclecticism contains both promise and danger: the promise of sweeping vision and synthesis; the danger of superficial scholarship and loose intellectual construction. If Fromm has not escaped much of the danger, he has achieved much of the promise, for at the heart of all his researches there is a compelling sorrow and a unifying vision. The sorrow is for Prometheus bound—man chained, isolated, suffering. The vision is of Prometheus unbound—man freed, his wounds healed, restored to strength; man in the image of God. All Fromm's work draws its meaning from this center.

This explains why Fromm can take freely from the social and psychological sciences and, at the same time, reject their relativistic orientation. Fromm insists that the sciences of man cannot be divorced from problems of philosophy and ethics. He believes, to adapt Kant's maxim, that percepts without ethical concepts are blind and impotent. For him, as for the Marx he admires, the task of philosophy is not merely to understand the world, but to change it. The passion and vision of Prometheus also explains Fromm's peculiar relations with psychoanalysis. Fromm's diagnosis of the modern condition is grounded in psychoanalytic premises and his discourse is usually carried on in psychoanalytic language, but his therapy is designed not so much to relieve individuals of their neurotic burdens, as to cure society. In Fromm's clinic, society is the patient. Like Marx and Rousseau, he believes that man is the victim of vicious institutions. Prometheus has been chained to the rock not by the angry gods but by an evil society. His freedom depends not upon mastering his own passions and humbling his own pride but upon the reform of society. Thus Fromm has undertaken with missionary intent the "research into the pathology of civilized communities" which Freud called for in one of his late works. If Freud is the Moses who showed the people the way out of the Egypt of their own passions, Fromm is the aspiring Joshua who would lead them into the promised land of the sane society.

The center of Fromm's work, then, is his conviction that our civilization relentlessly and systematically crushes and corrupts man's deepest needs and noblest powers. The

goal is the promised land of liberty and love. The body of
the work itself has three large divisions. The first is his
analysis of human nature and the human condition. The
second is his historical account of how modern society came
to be sick, together with his diagnosis of the sickness itself.
The third is his proposed cure, in which he communicates
his vision of the good life and drafts a sketchy constitution
for the good society.

There are several important features of Fromm's work
which the reader of this volume ought to keep in mind. The
first is that Fromm's pages are filled with ideas which are
plausible and deliciously attractive at first glance, but which
on closer view often turn out to be really astonishing in
their premises and disconcerting in their implications.
Fromm has the gift of putting profound ideas simply. He
has the knack of phrase, the ability to put his chief ideas
in polished and striking form. These talents lend his works
simplicity, a simplicity which is often deceptive; a simplicity,
I must suggest, which sometimes turns out to be superficiality. Fromm is sometimes blinded by his own dazzling
expressions. Caution is necessary not only to an appreciation of Fromm's work but also to an understanding of my
own method of discussing it. Time and again my argument
takes the form of reminding the reader that beneath the
clear and placid surface of Fromm's formulations lie restless and murky premises and implications, which he nowhere examines, and which the reader must therefore identify for himself.

Fromm is also something of a juggler. His system contains a large number of contradictory principles and concepts. It is remarkable how many of these would appear even
in a hasty listing: reason versus intuition; empiricism versus
mysticism; scientific versus philosophic method; detachment versus involvement; man as part of nature versus man

as the freak of nature; essential human nature versus social determinism; equality versus liberty; democracy versus aristocracy; communalism versus individualism. Fromm is forever juggling these incompatibles, trying hard to keep either side of the pairs from bumping into the other and knocking it out of the bounds of the system. When the performance succeeds, the effect is dazzling; when it fails, it is embarrassing. Sometimes Fromm conveniently shelves one term of one or another of his pairs while he displays the term which is more useful to his purpose at the moment.

What should be emphasized here is that Fromm's work is full of these incompatibles, and that he is forever bouncing from one side of a pair to the other. As a consequence, his work is tense and vigorous, full of movement and dare. As another consequence, any reader can find just about what he looks for in Fromm. But this same pervasive ambivalence of the work is also one of its most exciting features, for it stimulates the reader to try to reconcile the opposites and to make the hard choices which Fromm himself shies away from.

Failure to appreciate the inherent ambivalences of Fromm's work has weakened all the reviews and critiques of it that are known to me. Fromm has been called many names and made to stand for many things: Freudian revisionist, humanitarian Marxist socialist, bourgeois idealist, social scientist, liberal, humanist. He is all and none of these: the labels are not useful. Most misleading of all is the standard label, that of Freudian revisionist. It is certainly true that Fromm has carried on a one-sided argument with Freud for something over a quarter of a century, but an argument which embraces values Freud shunned, starts from premises he rejected, accepts types of evidence unknown to him, employs methods he denied, and leads to different conclusions on all the basic issues ought to be called what it is—opposition and not revision, revolt and not reform. Fromm is a revisionist of Freud in about the same degree, if not in the same direction, that the Prince of Darkness was a revisionist of the Prince of Light.

All of Fromm's ambivalences are resolved to his own satisfaction, I would conjecture, in some deep recess of his own inner convictions. This unifying conviction is nowhere made explicit in his writings, but I think it might be put in a form somewhat like the following: Erich Fromm believes that everything will come out right in the end, on some higher and as yet barely glimpsed plane, if man will only have faith in man. To say this is to say that Fromm is a moralist, a mystic, and a utopian. Yet that is only a way of putting the question of what Fromm stands for, and not a way of answering it.

Another feature of Fromm's work has already been mentioned, but it merits brief elaboration. Fromm is a social critic; in my judgment, a good one. He has made a full and serious analysis of our cultural and social crisis. His critique of the capitalist ethos, to take a single example, is keen and decisive. In a time when human nobility is powerfully threatened by an insensate materialism, Fromm reminds us that man may be the slave even while he thinks he is the master. In a time when society is looked on as a workshop for the production of the materials of consumption and destruction, and progress is measured by increases in the gross national product, Fromm insists that the only good society is the society whose product is good men. He has never wavered from the conviction that survival and comfort are merely animal and not human ends. All his books are about goodness. His work flows from the realization that beyond all scientific study of man and society, beyond all descriptions of cultural diversity and relativity, beyond all criteria of survival and efficiency, there looms the one important question: What is the good life, and by what signs shall we know the good from the bad? In an age which seems lost in its own instrumental knowledge, and in an age which takes as serious moral discourse the masked and pedantic complacencies of a Riesman and the banalities of a Peale, work such as Fromm's is worth a great price. It must not be forgotten, however, that a price must be paid for every healing doctrine. One of the purposes of this book is to estimate the price which must be paid for Fromm's.

The final feature of Fromm's work which needs to be mentioned here is its systematic character. His work is offered as something more than a series of reflections on man and society held together by a few major themes. Fromm has attempted a full system of moral philosophy, and he makes bold claims for the logical power of his system. His chief claim is that the system rests upon an objective and universal ethical base. When a writer forwards such a claim seriously, he deserves a serious reply. Therefore, and at the very outset, I examine some basic questions of logic and methodology in Fromm's thought. The reader may think I fiddle with formalities while the sane society burns, but a certain amount of such fiddling is necessary to an understanding of Fromm's system itself, together with its imperatives and its probable consequences. After this preliminary formal exercise, the essay moves on to the substantive questions.

These opening sentences suggest the sweep of Fromm's intention. His perspectives and achievements are what this essay tries to measure. Fromm is good at asking the right questions, even if he is not, as I shall argue time and again, so good at answering them. Over the course of his work, which extends from 1932 to the present, he has confronted most of the questions which must be dealt with by any man who would know his own ethical position and its responsibilities in this day. This means that an essay on Fromm is necessarily an essay in self-clarification. That suggests the dominant purpose, and in great part defines the character of the present study. I shall offer no full account of Fromm's ideas, for he has a wide and sympathetic public to whom his works need no introduction. Furthermore, he writes vigorously and clearly, so his ideas need no secondary exposition to make them intelligible. What I shall do is to ask some questions and offer some further reflections on Fromm's leading themes.

The major premise of the dialogue is that Erich Fromm is a man worth talking to. I urge the reader to remember that premise; otherwise, the impression will grow on him that I have forgotten it. Time and again in these pages I first praise Fromm, and then turn on him with critical intent. That is a risky procedure, both because it may appear that the praise is only the smile that opens the way for the thrust, and because Fromm always occupies the sympathetic position. In this day when man's fate seems bleak, one can go to Fromm for the gift of warmth and hope. To criticize him is to risk making oneself appear ungracious and ill-tempered, wanting in the human sympathies.

There is no way to avoid this risk, for as soon as one says that man is man and not God—a tautology which sometimes needs to be stated—he parts company with Fromm. He leaves the green and gentle land of Frommian perfection and enters a land of grays and arid stretches. Those who cross this terrain need prudence, authority, and discipline, as well as love and kindness and hope. I am morally convinced that to tell man he is perfect, as Fromm does, is to expose him to unnecessary dangers and excite him to catastrophic adventures. I am also convinced that the doctrine of perfection robs man of the nobility and grandeur which, precisely because they have been wrested from scarcity and affirmed in the face of despair, properly belong to the human estate.

I hope it will be clear that this is not a dialogue between an optimist and a pessimist, a yea-sayer and a nay-sayer. It is not my purpose to say no to man where Fromm says yes; and I have not taken it as my duty to point to the blemishes and scarcities of the human estate every time he points to its beauties and abundances. Along with Fromm, I mourn the condition of man and yearn for the noble city on the hill. I also agree with him that the indispensable thing is to keep searching for the lovelier and more noble life. Furthermore, I share the faith that man's estate can be better than it is. Any writer who today does not hold that view, it seems to me, hates mankind too much.

On all these fundamentals, we hold common ground. The difference between us is at bottom one of timing and location: we disagree on the questions of the probable location of the City of God, and on the best method of searching for it. Fromm puts God's City on that near hill, only ten miles away, easily visible from here. It seems to me, on the other hand, that God's City might better be put back in heaven, where it was before the eighteenth century. Located there, it is certainly harmless, probably beneficial, and possibly even true.

This approaches the ground which the dialogue will explore.

CHAPTER I

Foundations and Perspectives

Erich Fromm is a moralist. When we have his answer to the problem of good and evil we have struck the bedrock of his thought. Hence I shall approach Fromm through his theory of ethics, and I shall try to make my approach in the spirit of Aristotle's admonition that ethics is not an exact science. Therefore, he cautioned, a "rough outline of the truth" is all that can be achieved in ethical studies, and the man who demands more betrays his own shortcomings. "It is a mark of the educated man and a proof of his culture that in every subject he looks for only so much precision as its nature permits." [1]

Fromm wants his morals dignified by philosophy and supported by logic. That requires me to make another qualification. " 'Tis easy," wrote the most skillful of the skeptics, "for one of judgment and learning, to perceive the weak foundation even of those systems, which have obtained the greatest credit, and have carried their pretensions highest to accurate and profound reasoning." [2] Hume's remark applies with a special emphasis to ethical systems. No study is more vulnerable to the distortions of passion and parochialism. No study more easily falls victim to semantic confusions and lapses of logic. No study requires more knowledge of more kinds for its successful prosecution. For these reasons, no system is easier to criticize than a system of ethics. But Aristotle's maxim reminds us that it is foolish criticism that asks more precision of a subject than the nature of the subject can afford. The work of ethical system building is more like the work of a symphonist unfolding the possibilities of a theme than like the operations of a geometer drawing the consequences of his axioms. So one must bring to ethical discourse the spirit he must bring to any civilized conversation. Demand too many definitions, impose too many qualifications, and your companion will refuse to talk at all.

The Basic Position: Naturalism

Once upon a time, a man stepped from the communal caves, saw the pain of the life around him, and in his anguish and pride tried to force the universe to tell him why it must be so. Why must there be pain and suffering? Must man forever endure strife and misery? How can he make life happier and more noble? Moral philosophy still begins with these questions, and one cannot be certain that it has gone much beyond the answers given by the earliest questioners. Each new writer on moral subjects enters a rich and subtle conversation with the past. In this conversation, advancement of understanding seldom occurs by leaps of discovery. It occurs, rather, by making modest additions to the stock of the past, by the slow refinement of old ideas, by the expression of inherited conceptions in new terms, and by the extension of old meanings into new situations.

So it is with the basic question of moral philosophy,

the question of the origin and nature of evil and suffering. After centuries of talk, there are still only two main answers (I deal here with ideal types) to this question. They are supernaturalism and naturalism. Fromm has tried to find a way between them, which he calls normative humanism. The main claim of normative humanism is that while its norms are made by man they are still universal and objective. In order to see more clearly where Fromm's proposed middle way leads, we must first look at the paths on either side of it.

The supernaturalist sees all creation as radically imperfect, tinctured with corruption and viciousness. As part of nature, man shares its imperfections. But he also strives for the realm of perfection beyond nature. He may never reach this realm, but only to the degree that he struggles toward it will his life be good. Supernaturalism is profoundly pessimistic, for its premise of the imperfection of created being compels the conclusion that evil and suffering cannot be conquered in this life.

The major premise of naturalism is that nature is in itself complete, inferior to no supernatural realm. Man as part of nature is also in himself whole and complete. In strict terms, the naturalist can talk only of pain and pleasure. Pain is the frustration of a creature's needs, and pleasure is their satisfaction. It is, again speaking strictly, logically impossible for the naturalist to say that pleasure is "better" than pain, or that pain is better than pleasure. It is equally impossible for him to say that one pain or pleasure is better than another. In short, naturalism cannot talk of good and evil for these are terms of moral judgment, and the naturalist admits no realm of being and meaning outside nature by which nature can be judged.

Although the naturalists cannot logically claim the categories of good and evil, practically every naturalist has smuggled them into his system under the cover of a small prefix. The naturalist first introduces the notion of the *un*-natural, and then goes on to identify good with natural and evil with unnatural. Pain, which is now evil, is the result of unnatural transgressions of nature's laws. These transgressions flow not from any evil inherent in man, but from man's ignorance of the true laws of nature or from his misguided efforts to change them through social action.

In most systems of naturalistic thought, society is the great corrupter of man. Man is naturally good, but society, which is artificial, corrupts him. To overcome evil, we must understand nature's laws and we must organize society on natural principles. Only evil can flow from attempts to tamper with nature without understanding her laws. Evil flows from ignorance. Good flows from a life lived in a society fashioned after nature. This is why the injunction of naturalistic social philosophers has always been to simplify: overthrow false customs, break down artificial restraints, study nature's plan—which reason can make lucid—and model society after it. Then society too will be perfect. This injunction was as central to the thought of the optimistic *Philosophes* of the eighteenth century as it was to the more pessimistic Social Darwinists of the nineteenth. Both thought perfection would follow directly upon the ordering of society on natural principles.

The history of naturalism shows two main tendencies, one optimistic and the other pessimistic. Sometimes the difference in mood stems from the philosopher's whole view of nature. Thus, the pessimistic Social Darwinists held that pain and suffering are in the constitution of nature, and that nothing man could do would alter the grim fact that only the fit survive, and that they do so by deadly struggle against the weak. On the other hand, optimistic writers (Kropotkin was a prime example, as F. M. Ashley Montagu still is) argue that love and mutual aid are as much a part of nature's plan as are struggle and survival of the fittest. Or the difference in mood can stem directly from the philosopher's view of man. Here Freud has set forth the most thoroughgoing pessimism. His view that the taint was in man himself left little hope for measures of social amelioration. Pain is the price we pay for civilization. Pay it we must, however, for without imposed restraints man is only the most capable of the beasts of prey. "*Homo homini lupus;* who has the courage to dispute it in the face of all the evidence in his own life and in history?" [3]

As a philosophy, then, naturalism means two things. First, nature is complete in itself and inferior to no other realm. Man is immersed in nature and subject to all its laws. Naturalism is, in the second place, a theory of morals based upon the notion that what is natural is good and what is unnatural is evil. The distinction between the natural and the unnatural is introduced to bridge the gulf between pleasure and pain, which are descriptions of physical states, and good and evil, which are descriptions of moral states.

Before moving on to Fromm's humanism, it will be useful to summarize the main differences between naturalism and supernaturalism on the problem of good and evil. The chief difference is clear. The naturalist thinks evil flows from attempts to stifle nature, to violate her. These attempts in turn flow from man's ignorance of nature's laws and his translation of that ignorance into social institutions. It follows that in the naturalistic perspective the creative dialectic of human life is the struggle between man's desire to follow nature and society's tendency to violate nature and to suppress or corrupt man's natural needs. The supernaturalist thinks that nature itself is imperfect, and evil is inherent in its constitution. Man does evil because it is in him as a part of nature to do so. In the supernaturalistic perspective, the creative dialectic is man's struggle to overcome the imperfections of the City of Man and climb toward the perfections of the City of God.

The label humanistic has been applied to many different men and ideas, but all the meanings are variations on one theme, which is man as the measure of any view of the world. The humanist puts man at the center, in a realm uniquely his own. Just as the humanist resists all efforts to drag man down into nature's realm, so does he refuse to see man humiliated before a transcendental tribunal.

Fromm explicitly holds this view. His first book flies the proud emblem drawn from Pico's *Oratio de Hominis Dignitate:*

> Neither heavenly nor earthly, neither mortal nor immortal have we created thee, so that thou mightest be free according to thy own will and honor, to be thy own creator and builder. To thee alone we gave growth and development depending on thy own free will. Thou bearest in thee the germ of a universal life.[4]

In his major work on ethics, he again affirms his allegiance to the camp of the humanists. "The humanistic position is that there is nothing higher and nothing more dignified than human existence." [5]

As a humanist, Fromm says that "only man himself can determine the criterion for virtue and sin, and not an authority transcending him." [6] What is this criterion? "*The aim of man's life* . . . is to be understood as *the unfolding of his powers according to the laws of his nature.*" Put another way, "*good in humanistic ethics is the affirmation of life, the unfolding of man's powers. Virtue is responsibility toward his own existence. Evil constitutes the crippling of man's powers; vice is irresponsibility toward himself.*" [7] In short, the good for man is that which aids his growth "according to the laws of his nature." Evil is the "crippling of man's powers."

How can one distinguish factors which aid man's growth from those which stunt it? The answer follows quickly. "The decision as to what is good and bad has to be made on the basis of our knowledge of man's nature and the laws which govern its growth." [8] We must discover the basic needs of man, needs which are inherent in human nature and the human condition, and then it is easy to see that fulfillment of these needs constitutes good and their frustration evil.

By this point it is clear that Fromm's humanism is really naturalism in disguise. The naturalistic core shows through in his conception of good and evil. Naturalism, to repeat, regards goodness as inherent in nature and evil as the result of deviations from nature. Evil is the frustration of natural needs and good is their gratification. Usually society is indicted as the frustrating agency. This is precisely the form Fromm follows in his treatment of the problem of good and evil. His use of the label "humanism" clouds but cannot conceal the basic point, which is that man himself does not in any real sense *make* the "criterion for virtue and sin," but only *discovers* it in his own "nature and the laws which govern its growth."

Fromm deviates from earlier naturalism in just one respect. He departs from the naturalistic thesis that man is qualitatively no different from the other animals. Man has psychological needs peculiar to himself, shared by none of the other creatures. Whereas the earlier naturalists believed that utopia would flower when all man's physical needs were met, Fromm postulates certain psychic needs which must be satisfied if man is to achieve a fully human life. Coming as it does from a psychoanalyst, this occasions no surprise. But the sources of Fromm's psychic naturalism lie elsewhere than in his own psychoanalytic training. He, after all, lives with the rest of us in the first years of the Brave New World. As the problem of production comes closer to final solution and the age of abundance begins, we have tasted the fear that comes with the realization that easy gratification of the physical needs may be the shortest path to the loss of moral selfhood. What matters at this point, however, is that Fromm shares with earlier naturalism the formulation of the problem of good and evil as a problem of the satisfaction or frustration of needs. If support for this conclusion were needed, it could be found on every page of *The Sane Society*. That whole work is a passionate indictment of modern, industrialized, urbanized society on the ground that it frustrates all the needs that are unique to man and crushes all the powers that are the glories of man.

In the development of both Capitalism and of Communism as we can visualize them in the next fifty or a hundred years, the process of automatization and alienation will proceed. Both systems are developing into managerial societies, their inhabitants well fed, well clad, having their wishes satisfied . . . , automatons, who follow without force, who are guided without leaders, who make machines which act like men and produce men who act like machines. . . .

This alienation and automatization leads to an ever-increasing insanity. Life has no meaning, there is no joy, no faith, no reality. Everybody is "happy"—except that he does not feel, does not reason, does not love.

In the nineteenth century the problem was that God is dead; in the twentieth century the problem is that *man is dead*.[9]

What Fromm calls humanism, in short, is not so much a third way between naturalism and supernaturalism as it is a heresy within naturalism. Hence his theory of good and evil inherits all the difficulties naturalism has always had with this problem. I shall mention three of them. All three stem from the attempt to translate empirical observations into moral imperatives.

The first is the naturalistic fallacy, or the fallacy of heterogeneity. It is hardly necessary to rehearse here Hume's undermining of the logical bridge between fact and value, or G. E. Moore's demolition of it. I shall only offer a few remarks in support of those who still try to make the crossing.

It is much too easy to say that value is independent of fact, and let it go at that. Value is of course logically independent of fact, but in the world where men live the two always come together. In this world, as Dewey insisted, you are always confronted with value-facts and fact-values. To cut off inquiry at the point where fact and value can be logically distinguished is to stop just where the tough and worthwhile problems of social thought begin. It is as true and useful to say that value and fact are independent as it is to say, for example, that reason and civilization are independent, or that justice and law are. It is important to recognize that justice and law are not the same, but it is equally important to recognize that justice is at every moment to some degree embodied in law, just as reason and the ideal are at every moment to some degree embodied in a living civilization. Justice is not exhausted in law, nor reason in civilization, but justice and reason are always to some degree embodied in law and civilization. The firmest facts of social experience are always presented to us as value-facts. To understand this is to take the first necessary step toward understanding how social philosophy must deal with social relations. Social philosophy, which is always critical, must take reality as it comes, and it always comes as a blend of fact and value. To expose the naturalistic fallacy, and stop there, is in effect to deny the possibility of social philosophy, or to render it trivial.

On the other hand, from the point of view of social philosophy the naturalistic fallacy is more than a "mere" error of logic. From the Sophists forward, social theorists have recognized that the polity is something more than a natural growth, something more than a subsystem of the larger system of nature. In fact, social philosophy does not begin until men are able to grasp the discontinuity between society and nature and to understand that society is not a mere extension of nature but an independent realm of being which follows its own laws. There is an element of human will and art in society which is lacking in nature. Society, it might be said, is artificial, a product of human design and fabrication. Thus naturalism errs when it attempts to make society flow from nature, or when it tries to absorb fact into value by a natural process. This is an error whose consequences are greater than the consequences of the logical error which naturalism contains. As will be shown later, it is an error which weakens Fromm's ethical theory.

The second weakness in the naturalistic position flows, like the first, from the translation of empirical categories into the language of morals. The analysis will be easier if we return for a moment to familiar ground.

Simple naturalism knows only pleasure and pain. Pleasure is a state of feeling induced by the satisfaction of needs. Pain is a state of feeling induced by the frustration of needs. The naturalistic theory of morals, however, must distinguish between pleasures and pains which are natural and those which are unnatural. Only the former are good, while the latter are evil. Thus, some miseries, for example those caused by the operation of the natural laws of struggle for existence and survival of the fittest, are inherent in the order of nature and therefore good. Any attempt to reduce these miseries by social legislation might create, if only temporarily, pleasures for some men which would be bad because unnatural. Furthermore, regulatory attempts might ultimately lead to a condition of greater miseries, as a result, say, of the continued existence and reproduction of defective persons. All the pains of this new state of increased misery would be bad, because they would be unnatural; that is, they would result from attempts to violate natural principles. So the problem becomes more and more involved, the distinctions more and more elaborate.

What is important here is that a naturalism of the type Fromm holds permits him to say what is good only when he can say what is natural, for one's knowledge of the good is a direct function of his knowledge of nature. It follows that the naturalist can state with confidence what the good is only when he has complete knowledge of nature. This is a basic weakness of the position. In Fromm's work this difficulty is magnified by his "humanism." Fromm rests his theory on needs and qualities specific to human nature. Therefore, if he is to make his case persuasive, he must have full knowledge of the laws of human nature. Such knowledge is just not available to us. Will it ever be? Shall we ever force the secret of that being Pascal called the Incomprehensible Monster?

I would hesitate to apply the argument of the foregoing paragraph to most writers on ethical subjects because at bottom the argument itself is not satisfying. Carried to the end, the argument requires that we know everything before we can say anything meaningful, a requirement capable of killing any conversation. So I would not apply this argument in its absolute form to any writer, and I would hesitate to apply it even in a modified form to a moderate writer, a writer who makes modest claims and mild demands. But that is just the point here. Fromm is not a moderate writer. He makes sweeping claims and huge demands. He claims full knowledge of the conditions of the good life, and criticizes every feature of modern society on moral grounds. He proposes revolutionary changes which will bring about the social order in which all shall live the good life, and insists we are doomed unless we make the changes he proposes. Fromm, in short, is a revolutionary and a utopian. When such a writer calls knowledge virtue, we must examine the scope and quality of his knowledge very carefully. That is all the foregoing argument is intended to do—to invite the reader to ask whether Fromm, alone among ethical writers, has really found the final and full knowledge of the good life or whether his knowledge, like that of all other writers, is something less than perfect. Let me, symbolically, distinguish between human and divine knowledge, and caution moralists to remember that they have gained only the former, even while they aspire toward the latter. This is absolutely necessary to my discourse, for I cannot proceed on the basis that disagreement with Fromm is disagreement with God.

The third difficulty is more like the first than the second, but to explore it fully would lead us across large spaces and we would finally have to come to the gloomy terrain of theology. Lacking the skill and courage for that, I shall try just to expose the center of the problem without exploring its subtleties.

Every naturalistic theory of morals contains within itself the seed of its own logical undoing. A theory of morals may hold that good and evil exist in no other way than in name only, that is, in no objective way; or it may hold that absolute good is not a valid directive principle in human life. A theory that accepts either of these premises must reject both naturalism and supernaturalism. But Fromm wants a theory of morals which is objective, and he insists on the universality of the human needs which must be met, and therefore on the absoluteness of the standard one uses to judge the degree to which they are being met. Fromm both insists on the reality of evil and assumes a tension between evil and perfection. No naturalistic framework can contain both these desires, for it is inconsistent to hold both that evil is real and that nature, including human nature, is without it. The point can be put another way. If nature is complete in itself and inferior to no other realm, then everything that exists in nature is natural. Fromm asserts that evil exists. Therefore, evil is natural. Since what is natural is good, it follows that evil is good—which is absurd. In short, a moral theory which admits the existence of evil can locate the standard of perfect good only outside nature. On this one score, supernaturalism is a more logically satisfying doctrine than naturalism.

But one cannot go beyond that and accept supernaturalism. It has its own difficulties, which are hard enough to put off any mere logician. Even if we could discover Plato's transcendental realm of pure ideas, or even if we could follow the proofs for the existence of a divine norm-giver, our problems would have just begun. How shall we, who are by nature finite and mortal, gain knowledge of a being who is infinite and immortal? We could never confidently assume with Descartes that such a being would not deceive us. And even though our whole salvation depended exclusively upon following His word, we—even the wisest and most sanctified among us—could never be quite sure just what the word commanded. "Let us hear the conclusion of the whole matter: Fear God, and keep His commandments: for this is the whole duty of man." [10] Job, a man who was "perfect and upright and one that feared God, and eschewed evil" [11] followed the Preacher's word, and was afflicted. Logic will not bring one to accept the supernaturalist position. It must be embraced with reasons that the reason knows not of.

Objectivity

The loquacious Socrates was enjoying another of his endless talks with a few companions. This time the subject was justice, and Socrates was adeptly leading his friends here and there among the definitions when Thrasymachus interrupted. Enough of this amiable nonsense, he protested, all the high talk of philosophers must at last come down to one conclusion: justice is nothing more than the interest of the stronger. Socrates accepted the challenge and the argument was joined.

Socrates argued that justice or, more generally, the good exists independently of human desire and opinion, and that its nature can be ascertained by reason. When two people disagree about the nature of justice at least one of them is in error in exactly the way in which one can be in error on a question of fact. Plato, or his spokesman Socrates, believed he could prove that his ideal republic was good and that the idea of justice upon which it rested was an objectively valid idea. Thrasymachus held that the notion of proof or disproof did not apply to ethical concepts. Either you like Plato's ideal state or you do not, Thrasymachus said in effect, and only if you like it, is it good for you. If you do not like it, it is bad for you. If one powerful faction in the state likes it and another does not, and if both factions feel intensely about the matter, there is no way to decide the issue between them except by force. The faction that prevails will organize the state according to its own interests and desires. Hence what is called justice is no more than the interest of the stronger.

Socrates never lost an argument. His conception of himself as the only man in Athens who knew he knew nothing gave him the advantage in any contest, for his was the easy task of demolishing his opponent's position without really having to defend a position of his own. In the ensuing carnage, Socrates' position always seemed to be the only one standing; and because it remained standing the listeners took it as proven. That is an effective way to win a victory in debate, but not to keep it. Plato's sense of the dramatic compelled him to express Thrasymachus' arguments vigorously so that the inevitable defeat would be all the more complete. It is doubtful, however, whether Plato really appreciated the great power of the arguments he let Thrasymachus speak: Socrates' replies seem like mere sallies, annoying but not damaging. In any case, the question between Socrates and the Sophist, which is the fundamental question in ethics and politics, is still open.

Fromm frames the question fairly: "Must we then give up objectivity if we choose humanism? Or is it possible to establish norms of conduct and value judgments which are objectively valid for all men and yet postulated by man himself and not by an authority transcending him?" * Fromm's answer is an old and still interesting one.

---

* *Man for Himself*, p. 16. Incidentally, that phrase, "an authority transcending him," is one Fromm often uses to distinguish between the source of norms in humanistic and authoritarian ethical systems. He accepts the notion that if we can establish the existence of a supernatural norm-giver, we have settled the question of objectivity in ethics. That is not the case. Let us say with the theologians that God determines what is good and bad; hence, the man whose will is in harmony with God's, and who obeys His commands, is good. This only introduces the problem. Theology must say that God can determine good and evil because He is good, and thus knows good from evil. But to say that God is good implies a standard of goodness independent of God's decree. That takes us back where we started from—to the search for the meaning of goodness.

An art, say medicine or bridge building, is an activity requiring specific knowledge and skills. Part of the knowledge which goes to make up an art is theoretical and part of it is practical. By these terms we mean only the commonplace distinction: a theoretical science aims to discover certain facts and principles about the way the world runs; an applied science uses this theoretical knowledge to accomplish desired ends. Thus in the arts we in effect deduce from our theoretical knowledge practical norms about how a thing ought to be done. In this context, ought is determined by scientific knowledge of facts and principles. Of course, one pursues an art only after he has decided that the aim of the art is one he wishes to achieve. Every art or applied science is based on the premise that the end of the activity is desirable. We can say, then, that an art includes three elements: (1) a body of theoretical knowledge; (2) a body of practical norms deduced from the theoretical knowledge, plus a body of skills which grows with experience; and (3) an axiom that the end of the art is desirable. The practice of medicine rests on the axiom that it is desirable to control disease and improve health. The medical arts also include a body of pure or theoretical knowledge about human physiology, anatomy, chemistry, and so forth. Finally, the practice of medicine includes a body of practical norms based upon this theoretical knowledge plus certain skills such as bandaging, surgical techniques, and the like. The practical norms of medicine are strictly objective. They are of the following form: If you want to cure a person of a certain disease then you must perform certain operations on the victim and administer certain medicines to him. If you do not wish to cure the person, then the knowledge and skills of medicine are useless and irrelevant—unless you want to kill him.

Living, like medicine, is also an art requiring specific

knowledge and skills. Part of this knowledge is theoretical or pure knowledge about the nature of man; and part of it consists of practical norms deduced from the theoretical science of man. We shall call these practical norms ethics. Achievement in the art of living, as in any other art, is proportional to one's theoretical knowledge and to his skill and practice in deducing norms from this theoretical knowledge and applying them to the conduct of his life.

The art of living differs from the other arts in two ways. First, in this art man is both artist and material, both physician and patient. Secondly, the axiom underlying the art of living differs from the axioms underlying all other arts in that it is objectively valid; that is, it is inherent in man's nature and is not the result of a subjective value choice. We can imagine a culture which does not wish to control disease or build bridges, but we cannot imagine one in which people do not desire to live. "The drive to live is inherent in every organism, and man cannot help wanting to live regardless of what he would like to think about it. The choice between life and death is more apparent than real; man's real choice is that between a good life and a bad life." [12] The axiom underlying ethics, or the art of living, inheres in the nature of life itself.

Since ethics consists of the body of practical norms for achieving excellence in the art of living, ethical rules must be based on the nature of life itself. Now, it is the nature of life to preserve its own existence. Thus we can say, metaphorically, that the first duty of an organism is to be alive. To be alive is a dynamic concept. "*Existence and the unfolding of the specific powers of an organism are one and the same.* All organisms have an inherent tendency to actualize their specific potentialities." [13] Therefore, the aim of man's life is the unfolding of his powers according to the laws of his nature. Since each person is a unique blend of character and temperament, passions and talents, he can "live" only by realizing his individuality, by becoming the individual he potentially is. Since to live means to actualize one's potential, it follows that the good is that which aids in the unfolding of one's powers and evil is that which cripples one's powers. This is an objective norm because it is based on the nature of life itself. Therefore humanistic ethics, which sees good as the affirmation of life, can be objective because it is based on scientific knowledge of human nature and the nature of life, and because the axiom on which it rests is inherent in life itself and is not the subjective choice of a man.

In summary, Fromm thinks there is an objective standard of good and he thinks he has found it. The good is to be judged by the criterion of enhancement of life: whatever aids a person to actualize his potential is good; whatever cripples life and thwarts the life-urge is bad. This is the lever with which Fromm hopes to move the human world toward sanity.

The argument is not convincing. First, we cannot easily grant what Fromm most wants us to grant; namely, that "the drive to live is inherent in every organism . . . [and] the choice between life and death is more apparent than real . . . [so] man's real choice is that between a good life and a bad life." It will not do to say, as Fromm says, in a footnote, that "suicide as a pathological phenomenon does not contradict this general principle." [14]

Hamlet's question is as real as Fromm's, and prior to it. Only a very hardened or busy or comfortable man could fail to see that he faces this question every day. There are many ways of refusing to live, and suicide is only the most obvious of them. The whole tenor of Fromm's thought shows that he basically appreciates this, but that he set it aside while he was trying to build an objective foundation for ethical norms. He set it aside only at the expense of an inconsistency in his thought. If we take seriously the notion that existence is the same as unfolding one's powers, it follows that the man who does not unfold his powers is in effect already dead, or dying. For that man, suicide is just a public announcement of an already accomplished private fact. Furthermore, and disregarding all considerations of motive and circumstance, the fact that there are suicides shows that the inherent drive to live which Fromm speaks of can be overcome by other forces. The most we can accurately say is that the organism has a drive to live under certain conditions.*

The moral meaning of suicide is not exhausted by calling the act pathological. Under certain circumstances voluntary self-destruction is the highest affirmation of life; not of one's own life, perhaps, but of another's. Giving one's own life so that another might live is under certain cir-

---

* There are other, more technical, criticisms to be made of these Frommian ideas. I am not competent to evaluate such arguments, but I can at least suggest them. First of all, the vague notion of the "instinct of self-preservation" is rapidly disappearing from psychology. (See Anne Roe and George Gaylord Simpson, eds., *Behavior and Evolution* [New Haven: Yale University Press, 1958], p. 184.) Secondly, modern biology is transferring its attention from individuals to species and is beginning to employ statistical concepts in its study of life processes. This means that the older clichés of struggle for existence and survival of the fittest, along with Fromm's closely related notion of the drive toward self-preservation, must be reformulated in terms of populations rather than individuals, and in terms of differential reproduction rather than self-perpetuation. Thus: "The clichés of struggle and survival, even for the professional biologist, have focused attention on secondary aspects of the historical process whereby genetic information accumulates. They have focused it on individuals—and it should be on populations; they have focused it on the avoidance of death (perpetuation of the individual)—and it should be on reproduction (perpetuation of the genotype)." (*Ibid.*, p. 397.) From this newer perspective, Samuel Butler's mocking maxim "a hen is only an egg's way of making another egg" turns out to be good biological theory. In a sense, the developed individual organism is only a vehicle for its genotype: the hen is the tool of the egg; men and women are nothing more than the vehicles of sperm and ova. This casts a baleful light on Fromm's drive of the organism to realize itself.

cumstances the fullest act of freedom and the supreme expression of love. "Greater love hath no man than this. . . ." Or one may give his life for a cause or in obedience to duty. It is a cold heart that cannot thrill to the memorial the Spartans erected for their three hundred who died at Thermopylae: "Go, way-farer, bear news to Sparta's town, that here, their bidding done, we laid us down."

Even if Fromm's assumption about the urge to live were granted, there would still be a difficulty in his argument. Fromm's argument comes down to an effort to incorporate "living well" into the "drive to live." He tries to make "living" mean the same as "living well." To put it another way, he tries to amalgamate to the drive to live a hierarchy of styles of life. Then he will have a situation where death is at one pole and a certain style of existence, which he calls the productive orientation, at the other. All other ways of existence can be assigned positions along the range between the two, with those closer to the top being more "alive" than those below them. Socrates dissatisfied is more alive than Apeneck Sweeney satisfied. Fromm has to avoid a simple opposition between the physiological states of life and death, where styles of life are irrelevant, and show that living and living in a certain way are the same. The hierarchy of life-styles and the drive to live must be fused or the argument falls, for if the life-urge itself does not contain a standard of value, then the standard must be either arbitrary or transcendental.

The whole argument rests on one sentence: "*Existence and the unfolding of the specific powers of an organism are one and the same.*" The sentence is by no means self-evident. Further, it may not be (is not?) susceptible to proof or disproof. At the very least, we must require Fromm to persuade us of its truth, and this he does not do. The most he offers is some vague passages from Aristotle, but the Philosopher's authority does not determine the issues. The passages cited from Aristotle rest upon a subtle set of concepts in which normative and empirical categories are already mixed, and upon an essentialist metaphysic whose claim to belief is at best questionable.[15] More of that later.

In summary, Fromm's attempt to show that the logical status of ethical judgments is the same as that of empirical judgments is unsuccessful because the whole case rests upon the assertion that living is the same as living well. He tries to avoid a simple opposition between the physiological states of life and death by fusing to the drive to live a hierarchy of styles of life, but no amount of research or argument will alter the fact that the question of whether an organism is dead or alive is an empirical question, while the question of whether an organism is living well or poorly is an ethical question.

This ends my treatment of the basic questions of logic in Fromm's ethical theory. With that, the way is prepared for a first view of some of the substantive matters he takes up. What follows is by no means exhaustive. It is only an effort to introduce some of the dominant themes in Fromm's work which stem directly from his theory of ethics and his conception of human nature. Fromm's heroes in the tradition of humanistic ethics are Aristotle, Spinoza, and Dewey. All three of these writers shared two fundamental convictions. The first is that only man himself and not some authority over him can determine the criterion for virtue and sin. The second, as was stated above, is "that 'good' is what is good for man and 'evil' what is detrimental to man, the sole criterion of ethical value being man's welfare." Now, if the norm giver is to give himself good norms he must know who he is and what he needs. If good is what is good for man, it follows that in order to know what is good we must first know man's nature. Ethics rests upon psychology. If we can build a "model of human nature" which will describe man's basic needs and qualities, we can then determine what is good or bad for man.

This notion of a theoretical science of human nature presumes that its object, man, exists. Now, nobody has ever seen man, though much has been written about him. Man is not a fact but a mental construct. As de Maistre insisted, when he looked around him he saw always and everywhere Frenchmen, Englishmen, Spaniards, but never and nowhere "man." Man, he thought, was nothing other than the imagination of disturbed *Philosophes*.

How can the student of psychology move from men to man? Fromm has two very different answers to this question, though he seems not to realize how different they are. The first is the approach to man through an empirical science of man. The second approaches man through a philosophical analysis of the human condition and the psychic needs which stem from it. In the following pages I shall briefly discuss each.

The Science of Man

The science of man is inductive. Fromm thinks we can come to man by observing the reactions of men under varying conditions and then from these observations we can make inferences about the nature of the being that reacts. In this way it is possible "to infer the *core* common to the whole human race from the innumerable *manifestations* of human nature, the normal as well as the pathological ones, as we observe them in different individuals and cultures." [16] Once this core is identified the science of man has completed its task and the student of ethics can begin his.

This sound empirical canon would seem to call for

few changes in present conceptions of the social sciences. At most, it would ask the social scientist to pay a little less attention to the factors that act on men and a little more to the being who reacts. It would ask the scientist to design his studies so as to permit him to draw inferences about why an individual or a group reacted in a certain way to certain conditions. Presumably, from enough such observations there would one day emerge a scientific portrait of man.

Fromm concedes, however, that "our knowledge of man is still so incomplete that we cannot yet give a satisfactory definition of man in a psychological sense." [17] Given this state of affairs, how can we be sure a common core of human qualities exists? Fromm argues that the very fact that there is human history supports the postulate of the common core:

> Man is not a blank sheet of paper on which culture can write its text; he is an entity charged with energy and structured in specific ways, which, while adapting itself, reacts in specific and ascertainable ways to external conditions. If man had adapted himself to external conditions autoplastically, by changing his own nature, like an animal, and were fit to live under only one set of conditions to which he developed a special adaptation, he would have reached the blind alley of specialization which is the fate of every animal species, thus precluding history. If, on the other hand, man could adapt himself to all conditions without fighting those which are against his nature, he would have had no history either. Human evolution is rooted in man's adaptability and in certain indestructible qualities of his nature which compel him never to cease his search for conditions better adjusted to his intrinsic needs.[18]

Certainly it is true that history is a record of the reactions of men to the conditions of their lives, but our present understanding of the record will not permit us to say much more than that. We can learn from history that men have reacted in a fantastic variety of ways. We cannot go on to say that this variety of reactions proves the existence of a common core of human needs and qualities and that if the environment does not fulfill these needs man will struggle to change it until it does. History's lesson is not that plain.

> Think now
> History has many cunning passages,
>   contrived corridors
> And issues, deceives with whispering
>   ambitions,
> Guides us by vanities. Think now
> She gives when our attention is
>   distracted
> And what she gives, gives with
>   such supple confusions
> That the giving famishes the craving.[19]

Fromm rests his case on the possibility of a science of man which will build a true model of human nature. He admits that such a science does not yet exist. Therefore, it would appear that Fromm is duty bound to undertake the scientific researches into the nature of man which he himself calls for. He does not. Far from restricting himself to the empirical procedures of the sciences, Fromm is in fact rather impatient with them. He has a model of man, to be sure, but it is not a model built by scientific procedures. It is a picture drawn from the writings of certain philosophers, moralists, and religious teachers. Fromm's real answer to the questions, how do we know a common core of human qualities exists, and, if it does exist, what are its contents, is a philosophic position rather than a scientific conclusion.

The appeal to "science" merely clutters Fromm's case

and confuses his arguments. Let me illustrate this point with two examples. The first will show that he thinks all the features of man's nature prerequisite to a system of ethics have already been discovered and, therefore, a science of man is superfluous. The second will show that in his view no merely scientific method will ever uncover the essential secrets of man's nature.

Example one. Throughout his work Fromm has tried to develop a concept of the good life, or mental health, which is based on the inherent traits of human nature and which is the same for all men everywhere. At one point he offers a full definition of this concept of mental health, and immediately after the definition makes this comment:

> This concept of mental health coincides essentially with the norms postulated by the great spiritual teachers of the human race. This coincidence appears to some modern psychologists to be a proof that our psychological premises are not "scientific" but philosophic or religious "ideals." They find it difficult, apparently, to draw the conclusion that the great teachings of all cultures were based on rational insight into the nature of man, on the conditions for his full development. This latter conclusion seems also to be more in line with the fact that in the most diverse places of this globe, at different periods of history, the "awakened ones" have preached the same norms, with none, or with little influence from one upon the other. Ikhnaton, Moses, Kung Futse, Lao-tse, Buddha, Isaiah, Socrates, Jesus have postulated the same norms for human life, with only small and insignificant differences.[20]

Leaving aside all the questions this passage raises for a student of intellectual history, it is sufficient to say that whatever other methods of research the "awakened ones" may have used to achieve their "rational insight into the nature of man," they did not use the methods of modern empirical social science. I am arguing not that something should be excluded from science *because* it was stated in some other context by a "great spiritual teacher," but that, for Fromm, the findings of the great spiritual teachers are quite enough.

Example two. In one of his occasional essays Fromm has argued a position that makes scientific knowledge of man not superfluous but inadequate.[21] "Complete rational knowledge is possible only of things," he writes, for things can be dissected without being destroyed, but man is not a thing and to dissect him is to destroy him. Psychology can help us remove the illusions we have about ourselves and others, so in this sense psychology can teach us what we are not, but it can never teach us what we are. Fromm states the thesis emphatically:

> Psychology can show us what man is *not*. It cannot tell us what man . . . *is*. The soul of man, the unique core of each individual, can never be grasped and described adequately. It can be "known" only inasmuch as it is not misconceived. The legitimate aim of psychology . . . is the *negative*, the removal of distortions and illusions, *not the positive*, full, and complete knowledge of a human being.[22]

In the last analysis, man's mystery is not accessible to thought but can be grasped only through love. And what is known by love cannot be told in words.

> Love is active penetration of the other person in which my desire to know is stilled by union. In the act of fusion I know you, I know myself, I know everybody—and I "know" nothing. I know in the only way in which knowledge of that which is alive is possible for man—

> by the experience of *union*, not by any knowledge our
> thought can give. The only way to full knowledge lies
> in the act of love; this act transcends thought, it tran-
> scends words.[23]

That is the language of mystical religion, not of empirical
science.

These comments about the nonscientific character of
Fromm's work are not to be read as denials of its value.
They are intended only to show that he is not consistent
on this point, that while he often appeals to "science," the
basic presuppositions and intentions of his work have very
little to do with science. Modern social science studies how
men live and what they do. Perhaps when we have collected enough behavioral data and observed enough connections among them we shall have the measure of man
himself. That may happen, but it will surely take too long
to please Fromm, for he is a man in a hurry.

Most of the work and method of modern social science
is simply irrelevant to Fromm's purposes. The methods of
modern social science are designed to collect and analyze
public data—data about births, education, income, status,
political opinions, occupations, role performance, religious
affiliation, and the like. The main question a person with
Fromm's interest must ask about such data is not whether
they are correct, or whether connections can be observed
among them, but what *order* or *level* of life they chart. In
Fromm's view, man is a being of infinite depths and subtleties. He is the being who can conceal himself from others
and himself. The least important things about a man are
the public things, and it is the public things that the
methods and practitioners of social science are equipped to
deal with.

This is not to suggest that such a social science is useless. Far from it. If your purpose is to control men, to shape and guide the outward forms of life and the course of events, then this is the most useful knowledge you can have about men. But if your purpose is to understand the deepest wishes and beauties of a human life, or if your purpose is to learn the meaning of love and nobility, or if it is to learn about the grace of charity and the virtue of dignity, then such knowledge is all but useless. Worse than that, it may be destructive, for it inclines us toward the belief that when we know the public facts about a man we know all there is to know. It teaches us to believe that we can reduce man to an object of scientific curiosity, a specimen for our observations and experiments, and still have man intact. Somehow, it has become possible for the social scientist to forget that the only way to understand another human being is to approach him through care and love. To reduce another to an object is by that very act to rob him of his humanity and to close the door between you and him.

Given some such premise as this, which I think underlies Fromm's work, he is bound to look elsewhere than in the literature of social science for an understanding of man. Specifically, he has read the classics of philosophy, literature, religion, and mythology in a spirit which is rapidly disappearing from social science. The social scientist is coming increasingly to regard such works as data in the history of ideas, or as objects to be understood by the methods of the sociology of literature, or as "merely" esthetic experiences which ought to be strictly distinguished from scientific and useful knowledge about man and society. At most, the social scientist might mine these sources for scientifically testable hypotheses. Fromm's whole work shows how differently he regards such materials. He cites them not as illustration but as deepest truth. He reads them not for pleasure but for wisdom. It is easy to see why. Fromm distinguishes sharply between the public and the private sectors of a man's life. He argues that one man can discover another only through an extraordinary act of creative love and union. It follows that if we want knowledge of the inner life of man we must go not to the standard or common observer who employs the methods of social science but to the rare and special observer who employs the methods of the poet, the lover, or the artist. William James once remarked that the broadest gap in nature is the gap between two minds. To leap that gap requires the extraordinary strength of the poet and the mystic, not the strength of the ordinary social scientist using the ordinary methods of social science. Hegel wrote that "A hero is never a hero to his valet; and that is not because the hero is not a hero, but because the valet is a valet." Ordinary men see ordinary things in other men. Only an extraordinary man can see the extraordinary things in other men, or tell us how wonderful and extraordinary the apparently ordinary things really are.

This is to argue that social science is limited in its possibilities and ought to be limited in its claims. It is to argue, concretely, that to treat the works of Shakespeare, or Goethe, or Spinoza as on a level with the latest treatise in behaviorist psychology is to misunderstand both. The plays of Shakespeare, the sermons of Christ, the poems of Goethe are not reports to be checked for their verisimilitude, not mines where hypotheses lie, not papers to be read and judged as the teacher grades an undergraduate blue book. They are rare and wondrous works of genius whose meanings may be ultimately inaccessible to most of us. Our proper attitude toward them is an attitude of respect, of appreciation, of earnest attempt to understand. If we treat them as examinations to be graded by our standards we diminish them. If we mine them for hypotheses we destroy them.

This is to argue that rule and method cannot replace genius. In the view of Fromm, the order of knowledge achieved by the social scientist will never replace the order of knowledge which belongs to the awakened ones. In the end, Fromm's call for a science of man comes down to the conviction that man is the center of the universe, and to the thesis that if we are to advance in the moral studies we must lay the ground for the advance in an understanding of man. Thus far and no farther could Fromm agree with Hume:

> Here then is the only expedient, from which we can hope for success in our philosophical researches, to leave the tedious lingering method, which we have hitherto followed, and instead of taking now and then a castle or village on the frontier, to march up directly to the capital or center of these sciences, to human nature itself; which being once masters of, we may every where else hope for an easy victory. . . . There is no question of importance, whose decision is not compriz'd in the science of man; and there is none, which can be decided with any certainty, before we become acquainted with that science. In pretending therefore to explain the principles of human nature, we in effect propose a compleat system of the sciences, built on a foundation almost entirely new, and the only one upon which they can stand with any security.[24]

That "march up to the capital" will be made not by the battalions of social science but by the small band of the "awakened ones."

I have tried to establish two conclusions: (1) no science of man exists in the sense that Fromm has in mind; and (2) the prevailing methods and concerns of modern social science make of it a thing that is, at best, of small use in laying the base for an ethical system of the kind he wants to build. Fromm's appeal to "science" is a foreign element in his argument. Fromm does have an image of human nature, and he does set forth a panel of basic human needs which must be satisfied if life is to be good, but this common core, this model of human nature, is not a construct inferred from empirical-scientific observations of human behavior. It is, rather, based upon a philosophical analysis of the human condition. Here is the root of Fromm's system of ethics. It remains true that our "decision as to what is good and bad has to be made on the basis of our knowledge of man's nature and the laws which govern its growth;" [25] but this knowledge rests not upon an empirical study of human behavior but upon a philosophic analysis of man's needs as they stem from the conditions of his existence. *"The archimedic point of the specifically human dynamism lies in this uniqueness of the human situation; the understanding of man's psyche must be based on the analysis of man's needs stemming from the conditions of his existence."* [26] In the following section I shall set forth Fromm's analysis of the human situation and his description of the needs that arise from it.

The Freak of the Universe

"Behold the fowls of the air: for they sow not, neither do they reap, nor gather into barns; yet your heavenly Father feedeth them. Consider the lilies of the field, how they grow; they toil not, neither do they spin: And yet I say unto you, That even Solomon in all his glory was not arrayed like one of these." [27] The fowls of the air and the lilies of the field do not live; they are lived. Absorbed in nature, they are governed by her laws, which they can neither understand nor question. They live in harmony with nature, equipped by her to meet the conditions she imposes. The animal's inherited biological equipment makes it a fixed and unchanging resident of nature's kingdom, to which it must adapt, or from which it must disappear.

And then, at some point, the great chain is broken. The "freak of the universe" appears.[28] Life becomes aware of itself and makes demands on itself. The birth of this new organization of life took tens of thousands of years, but with its achievement nature has found her master. Man is still part of nature and subject to her laws, but he stands erect and with his mighty brain grasps nature in his thought and bends her to his will. But reason, which is man's glory, is also his curse, for it has driven him from the garden and made him the eternal wanderer.

> Self-awareness, reason and imagination disrupt the "harmony" which characterizes animal existence. Their emergence has made man into an anomaly, into the freak of the universe. He is part of nature, subject to her physical laws and unable to change them, yet he transcends the rest of nature. He is set apart while being a part; he is homeless, yet chained to the home he shares with all creatures. Cast into this world at an accidental place and time, he is forced out of it, again accidentally. Being aware of himself, he realizes his powerlessness and the limitations of his existence. He visualizes his own end: death. Never is he free from the dichotomy of his existence: he cannot rid himself of his mind, even if he should want to; he cannot rid himself of his body as long as he is alive—and his body makes him want to be alive.[29]

Unable to restore the primal union with nature, man must always go forward. He must solve the mystery of himself and find the meaning of his own existence. Driven by

a craving for an absoluteness which can overcome his loneliness, he must restlessly struggle to build by reason and will
a new community which will lift the curse which separates
him from nature, his fellow man, and himself. The long
birth goes on. Man, the race as well as each individual, must
continue to seek solutions to his existence. Each step forward is painful, but a step backward is even more painful:

> We are never free from two conflicting tendencies: one
> to emerge from the womb, from the animal form of
> existence into a more human existence, from bondage
> to freedom; another, to return to the womb, to nature,
> to certainty and security. In the history of the indi-
> vidual, and of the race, the progressive tendency has
> proven to be stronger, yet the phenomena of mental
> illness and the regression of the human race to positions
> apparently relinquished generations ago, show the in-
> tense struggle which accompanies each new act of
> birth.[30]

Fromm believes that we shall never understand man if
we try to reduce all his passions and strivings to instinctual-
biological drives. Nor shall we come closer to him if we see
him merely as a product of society. An understanding of
man must start with an understanding of his existential condition. The disharmonies of man's existence arouse in him
passions and strivings which are uniquely human, which
transcend his animal origins. The existential condition imposes needs which must be filled if the individual is to remain sane and grow. Any social arrangement which fails
to fulfill these needs cripples man and will ultimately be
overthrown by him. Fromm's own words are the best summary of the point: *"The necessity to find ever-new solutions for the contradictions in his existence, to find ever-
higher forms of unity with nature, his fellowmen and*

himself, is the source of all psychic forces which motivate man, of all his passions, affects and anxieties." [31]

What are these basic needs and passions which stem from the human condition and which must be fulfilled if man is to remain sane and grow to his full stature? Once these are set forth, we shall know concretely Fromm's conception of good and evil, for good is the satisfaction of these needs and evil is their frustration.

The concept of basic needs which stem from the human condition has taken on increasing importance in Fromm's work. The idea did not appear in the early German articles of 1932 and 1934. Fromm seemed more concerned there to sociologize Freud than to present his own positive conceptions of human nature and social process. *Escape from Freedom* marked the first important discussion of the idea, but Fromm treated only one psychic need at length (the "need to be related to the world outside oneself, the need to avoid aloneness"),[32] and he treated it more in terms of "human nature" than in terms of the "human condition." Perhaps this can be explained by two factors: first of all, he probably had not yet worked out the full list; secondly, in that book he was specifically trying to show that the individual could not tolerate the "empty freedom" of modern society because it violated the need for relatedness. Furthermore, *Escape from Freedom*, and I think its commentators have not adequately pointed this out, vacillated between a thoroughgoing social determinism, a view which sees man as a creature of social forces, and the view that there is a basic human nature which is the same always and everywhere. Apparently, Fromm had not yet seen his way through to a clear position on this basic question.

Man for Himself (1947) marks an important step forward. Here Fromm presented his first full discussion of the "human situation" and made his first comprehensive argument for the existence of a normative human nature and for basic needs rooted in the conditions of man's existence. But he still offered no full panel of the needs themselves. That did not appear until *The Sane Society* (1955), which first repeats the argument of *Man for Himself,* and then goes on to present a full discussion of the basic needs. The appearance of the list in this volume is probably due to the fact that Fromm was specifically undertaking a full criticism of the social order. For that task, he needed a standard by which to judge the goodness of a society, and the degree to which the society filled the basic needs became the standard. In any case, what matters is that Fromm has consistently moved away from social determinism toward the position that there is a basic human nature with basic needs stemming from the existential condition.*

---

* Compare these two statements, the first from *Escape from Freedom,* p. 12, the second from *The Sane Society,* p. 67. "Although there are certain needs, such as hunger, thirst, sex, which are common to man, those drives which make for the *differences* in men's characters, like love and hatred, the lust for power and the yearning for submission, the enjoyment of sensuous pleasure and the fear of it, are all products of the social process. The most beautiful as well as the most ugly inclinations of man are not part of a fixed and biologically given human nature, but result from the social process which creates man. . . . Man's nature, his passions and anxieties are a cultural product. . . ." "The great passions of man, his lust for power, his vanity, his search for truth, his passion for love and brotherliness, his destructiveness as well as his creativeness, every powerful desire which motivates man's actions, is rooted in this specific human source [i.e., in the conditions of the human situation]. . . ." Fromm's recent work all revolves around the concept of existential needs. Thus, *Psychoanalysis and Religion* (New Haven: Yale University Press, 1950), is basically a long discussion of how man has tried to fill one of the basic needs (the need for a framework of orientation and devotion) through religion. *The Art of Loving* (New York: Harper, 1956), is a treatment of the only productive way of solving another of the basic needs, the need for relatedness. *The Forgotten Language: An Introduction to the Understanding of Dreams, Fairy Tales and Myths* (New York: Grove Press, 1957), rests on the premise that all men share a common "forgotten language," and that this language expresses the universal concerns which arise from the human situation. The only book which does not fit this pattern is *Sigmund Freud's Mission: An Analysis of His Personality and Influence* (New York: Harper, 1959). This book culminates a criticism

Since *The Sane Society* contains the fullest treatment
of the basic needs, my exposition will follow it.[33] Fromm
postulates five basic psychic needs. The first is the need for
relatedness. Man has lost his primal union with nature.
Having reason and imagination, he knows that he is alone,
cut off, his birth and death accidental happenings in an
indifferent world. Man cannot bear this state of being and
must strive to build ties with his fellows which will replace
the instinctual ties he has lost. "The necessity to unite with
other living beings, to be related to them, is an imperative
need on the fulfillment of which man's sanity depends." [34]

As with all the other basic needs, the need for relatedness can be satisfied in various ways. A person can try to

---

of Freud which began in 1932 and has run through all Fromm's work. The
doggedness of the assault on Freud suggests that man may have another
basic need which Fromm will not admit—the need to have an enemy. The
crusade against Freud accomplished, Fromm has returned to the basic human
nature thesis in his latest essay, "Psychoanalysis and Zen Buddhism," which
appears in D. T. Suzuki, Erich Fromm, and Richard De Martino, *Zen
Buddhism and Psychoanalysis* (New York: Harper, 1960), pp. 77–142.

It is interesting to speculate on the reasons for Fromm's changing position
on the question of essential human nature versus social determinism. Perhaps the change can be accounted for in terms of an increasingly strident,
almost frantic, optimism in his work. In *Escape from Freedom*, I would
conjecture, Fromm proposed a heavily social deterministic thesis as an antidote to Freudian pessimism. In the later works, he had to re-design human
nature with the optimism built right into it, because what now threatened
man was not Freudian pessimism but insane societies. Fromm's optimism
has stayed about the same, but the enemies of optimism have changed.

What is even more interesting is that the whole undertaking may have
been an unnecessary one because, from a certain angle of vision, it appears
that Fromm's optimism need not have moved him away from Freud. Freud,
to be sure, was explicitly a pessimist. Still, he performed the dazzlingly optimistic feat of affirming that, despite the deep biological bases of the instinctual drives, a man could transcend them by lying on a couch and
confronting them in the company of another, specially trained, person.
Whereas Fromm must call on social reform to achieve this conquest, Freud
put it completely within the power of the individual, implying thereby an
unspoken postulate of inherent, unconscious productive potential, which
looks much like the same optimistic premises which Fromm has struggled
to achieve.

become one with the world by submitting to some outside force—a person, an institution, a cause, a group. He overcomes his separateness and powerlessness by merging with something greater than himself and finding his own meaning in it. In this way, one does find the courage to be, but only "to be as a part," as Tillich calls it. Or one can achieve union by having power over the world, by establishing dominion over others and making them a part of oneself. Both these types of relatedness are symbiotic. They entail the loss of freedom and integrity for all persons caught in them.[35]

Only one way of relatedness can satisfy man's need to unite with the world and at the same time enable him to retain his own freedom and develop his own individuality. That is love. Love is giving, not giving up, but giving as the highest expression of joy, wealth, and power. The one who loves gives the most precious gift he has—himself, his joy, sorrow, knowledge, respect. This giving enriches both giver and receiver. He who gives brings to life something in himself. The gift in turn enhances the receiver, who now in his abundance returns it manifold. So the two together have brought something new to life, each by giving of himself. "In the act of giving something is born, and both persons involved are grateful for the life that is born for both of them." [36] There are many ways of love—motherly love, brotherly love, erotic love, self-love, love of God—but all are an active giving, and all have at the center a cluster of attitudes toward the loved one: care, responsibility, respect, and knowledge.[37] The great mystery of love is that it is the only form of relatedness in which the person experiences union and yet retains his own individuality and independence. Thus love is the only productive resolution of the need for relatedness.

The second psychic need is the need for transcendence.

Man is brought into this world without his consent and taken from it against his will. He is the creature and ultimately the victim of a fate that acts arbitrarily and does not ask for his opinion. But man will not tolerate this passive role of the creature. He will not permit his destiny to be decided by the cosmic dice-throw. He is driven by a basic urge to transcend his creatureliness, to go beyond himself and his fate.

The need for transcendence can be met in either of two ways. First, man can become a creator. "In the act of creation man transcends himself as a creature, raises himself . . . into the realm of purposefulness and freedom." [38] But if man cannot create, then he will destroy. The act of destruction, like the act of creation, sets man above life, gives him power over it, and thus enables him to transcend the role of the creature.

Fromm will not give over the world and the soul to Eros and Thanatos. He will not make of the human spirit a battleground where love and hate, creativeness and destructiveness, solidarity and repulsion struggle for supremacy. Fromm holds that creativeness and destructiveness are not two hostile forces or principles each with its own realm and resources. Rather, they are alternative ways of meeting the need for transcendence, and there is a struggle between them only in the sense that "the will to destroy must rise when the will to create cannot be satisfied." [39] Creativeness is the primary potentiality and destructiveness is secondary, appearing only when man's inherent urge to fulfill all his potentialities is thwarted. If the human urge to grow and ultimately to transcend itself in the act of creation is blocked, then the dammed up powers break through in destructive forms. Following Spinoza, Fromm holds that *"destructiveness is the outcome of unlived life."* [40]

This is the heart of Fromm's conception of good and evil. Man is not basically evil. He becomes evil or does evil only if the conditions needed for his growth are lacking. Evil as such has no independent existence. It is only the absence of good or the result of the failure to realize the full potential of life, which is the good. Fromm, in short, rejects all dualisms in the field of ethics and psychology and asserts that man is basically good.

The rejection of Thanatos is the very center of Fromm's thought. It is surely the fountain of the profoundly Erotic quality of his own thought, and it is almost surely the basic reason behind his rejection of Freud. Time and again in this essay I shall suggest that while this gives Fromm an outlook which is warm, generous, and sympathetic toward all mankind, it also blinds him to whole dimensions of reality and makes his view of society and of human nature seem narrow in comparison with the richer, more varied, more realistic view which is provided by a psychology which recognizes the forces of repulsion and conflict to be as real and as important as the forces of attraction and union.

The third basic need is the need for rootedness. Man's severance from his home in nature is fraught with pain and danger. He can dispense with the natural roots only insofar as he finds new human roots. Thus man is driven to build a human home which can replace the lost natural home. This human habitation can be built on either of two principles: incest, which is the illicit worship of and desire to merge with one's own blood, soil, and clan; or brotherliness, which is the affirmation of all others as equally sons of man and as equally entitled to love and justice. Only brotherly rootedness can fulfill the need for roots in a productive and fully human way. In our time, nationalism, state worship, and racism are all regressions to incestuous fixations and all deny the full use of man's productive powers.

Only when man succeeds in developing his reason and love further than he has done so far, only when he can build a world based on human solidarity and justice, only when he can feel rooted in the experience of universal brotherliness, will he have found a new, human form of rootedness, will he have transformed his world into a truly human home.[41]

The need for identity is the fourth basic need. Man is the creature who must know who he is. He must be able to sense himself as both author and object of his actions. The only satisfactory solution to this need is the development of a fully individuated personality which knows itself as the center and subject of its own being. Very few men achieve this goal. Most men find substitutes in identification with a nation, religion, occupation, class, or status. Herd conformity becomes the chief way—an illusory one—of achieving a sense of identity. Descartes' "I think; therefore I am," has become "I belong; therefore I am."

The fifth and final need is the need for a frame of orientation and devotion. Having reason, man has to make sense of the world about him. He must orient himself and this he can do only by converting the blooming, buzzing confusion of raw impressions into meaningful patterns. Since man is not merely a disembodied intellect but a being who wills and feels and desires, his system of orientation must also include some "object of devotion which gives meaning to his existence and to his position in the world." [42] The basic requirement is for *some* frame of orientation and devotion. Without that, man goes insane. But beyond that the system of orientation must be rational and objective, based on a sound knowledge of self, nature, and society. Without that, man's happiness and serenity, if not his sanity, are at stake. Like all the other basic needs, this one must be satisfied if man is to remain sane, but it can be satisfied in ways which contribute to happiness or in ways which contribute to unhappiness. Only a frame of orientation and devotion based on reason and objective knowledge will contribute to happiness.

This analysis of the human condition and the psychic needs stemming from it is the foundation of Fromm's social criticism. He measures the happiness and virtue of an individual by the degree to which the person has fulfilled the basic needs in a productive way. He judges the worth of a society by the degree to which it helps the individual satisfy the needs. A careful look at the scheme now will ease the way for later discussions. In the following pages I shall first mention a few logical and terminological difficulties in the analysis, move on to expose the hypothesis that underlies it, and then discuss the view of human nature which it contains. This will lead into some remarks on the larger social and ethical implications of the analysis.

It is clear at the outset that Fromm did not find the five needs by following the method of his own proposed science of man, that is, by observing the reactions of men to varying situations and from these observations inferring the core qualities of the being who reacts. He found them in the pages of a number of philosophers and moralists and in his own brief philosophical analysis of the human condition. They are philosophical postulates, not empirical findings. That does not destroy the value of the constructs, but it does remove them to a realm beyond the reach of "merely" scientific and empirical criticism. A discussion of this part of Fromm's work must take its terms from logic and esthetics.

The notion of the existential dichotomy or contradiction is very important to Fromm's thought. As will be shown later, it is the base of his theory of biological-moral progress. Yet, what he means by the term is never quite clear. What is the source of existential dichotomies? Fromm says they are a result of the emergence of reason. He also says they come from the split between the human and the animal parts of man's nature. What are the existential dichotomies? The fundamental one is that between life and death. Another is that between man's drive to realize all (not just his own) human potentialities and the brevity of his life. It is evident that dichotomy or, as Fromm also calls it, contradiction, has many meanings, not all of which are clear. What can it mean, for example, to say that there is a contradiction between the fact that man wants to but cannot return to the passionate animal state and the fact that he feels driven to use his reason to master nature and build society? The fact is, some men have returned to the animal state, and others have never left it. Finally, to say that man must use his reason sounds less like a contradiction than it does like a part of the definition of human nature.

Fromm's basic meaning here will become clearer, I think, if his passages on the development of a brotherliness and a framework of orientation and devotion based on "reason" are translated from the language of dichotomies into the language of commitment. This translation can be made with confidence because in his latest essay Fromm makes fully explicit a theme which has been powerful, but implicit, in his thought from the very beginning. For Fromm, the basic question of life is: "How can we overcome the suffering, the imprisonment, the shame which the experience of separateness creates; how can we find union within ourselves, with our fellow man, with nature?" [43] He then relates various attempted answers to this question and discusses various impediments to its solution. Among the latter, he mentions "intellectual knowledge," the vice of which is that it deludes a man into thinking that *he* grasps reality, while in fact it is not his whole self but only his "brain-self" which grasps it. This kind of knowledge, which is "more widespread and intense in modern culture than it probably was at any time before in history," takes man ever farther away from himself, from his fellows, and from nature. If there is any doubt as to just what is at stake here, Fromm dispels it with an incisive phrase: "The cerebrating person is the alienated person. . . ." [44]

Put the two notions together—the basic problem of life is the achievement of union; the cerebrating man is the alienated man—and it becomes clear that for Fromm the "original sin," the force which has driven man from the garden and made him a wanderer, is reason itself. Reason corrupts because it separates man from himself, from his fellows, and from nature. We must learn to perceive and relate to the world "beyond the fold of reason." Fromm may explicitly affirm that man must "go forward" to a new harmony based on reason, but it is clear that the deeper thrust of his thought urges us "backward" to a state before reason. This, I think, is the real meaning of his theory of progress. It is a kind of great circle theory of progress; or, as Koestler calls it, the theory that history progresses by the "law of detours": we can only go forward by first going back. "Forward to Yesterday," as the Southern Senator put it in a recent Broadway musical.

The confusions of the existential dichotomies are compounded by the introduction of "historical dichotomies." [45] As distinguished from the existential variety, these dichotomies are man-made and soluble. They result from a shortage of courage and wisdom. Fromm provides two examples: the institution of slavery in ancient Greece, and the modern contradiction between an abundance of technical means of production and the incapacity to use them exclusively for peace and public welfare. If Fromm means to say only something like "it is unfortunate that we use some of our economic facilities for military rather than for peaceful purposes," then his formulation is at least understandable: he is expressing a preference for one set of goals over another. But it is not enough just to assert the preference, and to imply that men who disagree lack courage and wisdom. On the other hand, if Fromm means to say that there is something inherent in the structure of an advanced industrial economy that leads it to produce for war rather than for peace, he has a very big job of analysis on his hands before we can accept the thesis. I think this latter position is in fact the one Fromm holds, for it is consistent with his Marxist orientation: just as the Greeks needed slavery to run their economy, so does advanced capitalism need military production to maintain itself. This may clarify Fromm's view, but it does not make it compelling, for the Marxist argument on this point suffers from a number of defects, most of which are so well-known that they need no statement here.

What is the relationship between historical and existential dichotomies? It may be a little closer than Fromm would like to think. Existential dichotomies compel men to action. This action can take place only on the stage of history. So the existential dichotomies cause the historical dichotomies, in the sense that they compel men to the actions which produce historical dichotomies. Seen in this light, it is not so easy to say that the historical dichotomies can be annulled if we apply enough courage and wisdom to them, for a shortage of courage and wisdom is part of the very definition of the human condition. Man is limited. He makes mistakes. This conclusion is implicit in Fromm's analysis, but he dare not accept it. To do so would bring down the utopian aspirations of his thought.

In summary, while it is difficult to attach any clear and

decisive meaning to the concept of dichotomy in Fromm's thought, it is easy to find ambiguities in his usage of the term. This conclusion will become relevant when we consider his hypothesis of biological-moral evolution.

The final logical difficulty I want to consider is not a new one with Fromm. Here, as throughout his ethical theory, he is blind to the dangers involved in moving from is to ought. Even if we assume that the needs he describes are genuine empirical findings, it is still logically impossible to leap from the discovery of such needs to the conclusion that they *ought to be fulfilled in a certain way.* We can at most conclude that they *must be filled in some way* if the organism is to survive. That Fromm could have overlooked the implications of this difference is mildly surprising when a moment's reflection will show that the difference itself is woven into the very fabric of his system. Thus, he tells us that there are at least two ways of fulfilling each need. The need for relatedness, for example, can be fulfilled symbiotically or lovingly. The need for transcendence can be filled by destroying or by creating. Either way will do to satisfy the need itself. Fromm argues that only one way will lead to "happiness" or "mental health," but no amount of research will dissolve the fact that a notion of happiness or mental health is a moral concept, not an empirical one. All we know empirically is that the needs can be satisfied in different ways. We may prefer one way to the other because we believe it contributes to happiness, but the meaning of happiness remains normative, not empirical.

Beneath Fromm's analysis there lies a remarkable hypothesis. Perhaps assumption would be the more accurate word, for Fromm nowhere argues or even fully states the concept, although it has become of growing importance in his work. This daring assumption glimmered through *Escape from Freedom* but it has grown in power and clarity until it lights the whole structure of *The Sane Society*. Fromm asserts that there is moral progress. Of course, this in itself contains nothing remarkable for the thesis of moral progress has been often argued; and if Fromm's advocacy of the notion is daring, it is so only in the sense that it takes a lot of innocent courage to talk like Condorcet today. Fromm, however, gives the old notion a new twist: he argues that moral achievements become transformed into biological imperatives, so that his hypothesis of moral progress is really a hypothesis of moral-biological progress. The notion can be developed in a few paragraphs.

Fromm believes that as man has moved through history he has come closer and closer to a full conception and realization of the sane and happy life. Further, he believes that as history progresses each generation incorporates into itself every advance toward freedom and productive fulfillment of the basic needs made by previous generations. This incorporation is of such a nature that if man tries to deny the advances and return to a previous stage the consequences will be pathological. Here is the fullest statement of the thesis:

> We have reached a state of individuation in which only the fully developed mature personality can make fruitful use of freedom; if the individual has not developed his reason and his capacity for love, he is incapable of bearing the burden of freedom and individuality, and tries to escape into artificial ties which give him a sense of belonging and rootedness. Any regression today from freedom into artificial rootedness in state or race is a sign of mental illness, since such regression does not cor-

respond to the state of evolution already reached and results in unquestionably pathological phenomena.[46]

On the surface, this is similar to Freud's characterization of individual neurosis as a fixation at or a regression to an earlier state of psychic development than the one the person ought now to be in. Fromm appears to apply this concept to the whole human race. He seems to be saying that any society which reverts to or lingers at a stage of cultural evolution which the race has already passed through is sick. To say no more, this notion is very dubious. What shall we make of all of Toynbee's "arrested civilizations"? Can we call them sick because they have achieved a stable response to the challenges of their environment and have stopped at that? What shall we make of the overwhelming fact of diversity of cultures within the world? Fromm really seems to assume a perfect communication among all peoples during all of history—an assumption too wayward to discuss. In addition, what shall we make of the fact of diversity among groups even within one society? Shall we describe as pathological the position of, say, the peasants of Provence because they have not achieved the level of civilization of the Existentialists of Paris? Can we be really sure that the Existentialists, with all their resolve to face up to freedom, are less pathological than the peasants, with their incestuous ties to the land?

Good sense can be made of this notion of moral regression when it is translated into different terms and applied within the confines of one culture. For example: I think even the staunchest cultural relativist would be willing to say that an act of cannibalism performed by a citizen of the United States could be meaningfully described as regressive—although Mr. Tennessee Williams might not be entirely willing to apply the label, at least not to Southerners. But this is a regression within a specific culture, and can be measured as a movement "backward" from the norms which parents teach their children in that culture. The Supreme Court, in the case of *Reynolds* vs. *United States*, banned the practice of polygamy as regressive and repugnant, and for that reason subversive of good morals. Some Mormons by no means agreed with the judgment; and now and again the agents of the law rout from his settled ways in the Utah backcountry some patriarch who still has the courage of his convictions. All I mean to say is that the cases quickly approach the borderline, even within the confines of one society. There seems to be no warrant either for Fromm's arrangement into a moral hierarchy of all the social practices of all the peoples in the world, or for his easy assumption that progress can be measured by movement along this empirical-normative scale.

When an intelligent writer suddenly seems to say obviously unintelligent things, we ought to be ready to admit that we have not understood him. So it is here. Fromm's evolutionary concept is not, I think, properly analogous to Freud's characterization of neurosis, even though Fromm himself uses this analogy. The notion is more like Bergson's creative evolution than it is like Freud's developmental concept of the neuroses. Bergson, in richly metaphorical language, postulated life itself as a great force, a vital impulse, which had been set down once and for all at the beginning of the world, and which has been struggling ever since to express its full capacities. Bergson thought evolution could not be explained by the principle of adaptation to the environment, but must be understood as truly creative. A vital impulse to action has existed from the beginning and has been ceaselessly striving to fulfill its own demands. We cannot know beforehand, however—nor can the impulse itself know—just how the demands of the impulse will be satisfied. Thus both mechanistic and teleological explanations of evolution are inadequate. The important thing is that the vital impulse creates real novelty, and that once a height has been taken there can be no retreat without crippling the life force. Evolution is irreversible.

Fromm's views are strikingly similar to Bergson's, though his terminology is different. Like Bergson, he draws the essential distinctions first between life and nonlife, and then within life itself, between instinct and reason (Bergson calls the latter intellect). Fromm's account of imagination and self-awareness, the capacities which make it possible for man to be an object to himself, is very much like Bergson's account of intuition, which is instinct conscious of itself, disinterested, and able to reflect upon its own nature and thus to change it. Fromm holds that only among the base animals does adaptation adequately account for evolution while with man, reason and imagination set up their own demands which cannot be known until they are expressed, but which must be met, and which have a dynamism of their own. Fromm also holds that the evolutionary process is irreversible.

But there are two important differences. Fromm's metaphysic is teleological. Life unfolds its own inherent potential: the future is implicit in the past. Secondly, he applies this evolutionist paraphernalia explicitly to the psychic and cultural spheres. Fromm's evolutionary hypothesis asserts that each generation incorporates all the advances toward freedom and psychic maturity which were gained by past generations. Any regression has pathological effects. The implications of this are astonishing. If Fromm's hypothesis is correct, it means that cultural advances are permanently registered in the psyche, and any retreat results in pain and the crippling of life. Put another way, the assumption would suggest that the highest cultural achievements (that is, movement toward freedom and psychic maturity) of one generation become something like moral-biological imperatives for the next. This capacity to convert cultural achievement into biological imperative is a capacity of the human organism itself. Fromm gives us a fateful choice: either we go forward with the whole force of our biological equipment with us; or we go back, with all of it against us.

It is interesting to compare Fromm and Freud on this matter. In Freud's view, the instinctual forces are always waiting to strike against civilization and return to the "state of nature." He offers us civilization at the price of instinctual renunciation and neurosis. In Fromm's view, regression to a lower biological-moral level is itself the great cause of neurosis. He offers us civilization only if we unleash all the vital powers of man and give them total freedom. For Fromm, the highest state of civilization means the unrestrained expression of all man's capacities, as in the "state of nature." The difference between Freud and Fromm on this question of civilization and its discontents is absolute. It cannot be explained away by calling Fromm a Freudian revisionist.

What can be said about Fromm's audacious concept of moral-biological evolution? Very little at all, I think, and nothing by way of proof or disproof. We have spared Fromm the embarrassment of saying silly things only by making him say unverifiable things. But he does make, or clearly imply, the unverifiable statements I have attributed to him. The ideas I have suggested are consistent with the whole of his ethical theory and social criticism. More than that, they are basic to the rest of his work, for he rests his case for the existence of moral powers in man and for the view that mental health requires a constant unfolding of the potentialities of the self on this assumption that cultural achievements become incorporated into persons and function as psycho-biological forces.

Universal Man and Unique Individual

Fromm is no exception to the rule that every social reformer starts with an implicit or explicit image of man. Nor is he an exception to the rule that those who paint the portrait of man never paint him whole but always highlight some of his features and shadow others. Anyone who studies these portraits must conclude that what the painter usually does is to seize upon some limited portion of the whole content of experience and take it for the whole, a procedure which comes down to saying that some parts of experiences are more real than, or superior to, others. The logic may be weak but that has not saved it from steady employment. It is also clear that the portion of experience which one selects to make up his portrait is usually a reflection of his own social and personal values and experiences. Marx gave away the show when he observed that Bentham, who pretended to put the normal man at the base of his ethical theories, had in fact found only the English shopkeeper.

Fromm at least does not do that. His man does not exist. Fromm looks at the masses around him and sees automatons, men living in spiritual poverty yet only vaguely aware of their misery. He sees men alienated from themselves, their fellows, and their society. He sees legions preparing for an insane war even while they indulge in orgies of consumption in a vain effort to fill the hollowness and boredom of their meaningless lives. But when Fromm comes to draw his portrait of "real" human nature he no longer sees such crippled men. Perhaps more accurately, he sees the cripples as men in the fallen state, while with his artist's eye he sees men reborn erect and tall, intact, strong in reason and united by ties of brotherhood with all mankind. He sees men able to love and create, able to make of their own lives works of art. It would not be wrong to say that Fromm's model of man is copied after the lives of small children (pre-Freudian), romantic artists, and a few great teachers. Fromm thinks this man is more real than the crippled man, for the crippled man is only a hateful distortion of man as he potentially is and ought to be.

We cannot say that this vision is wrong, but only that it is partial. Fromm has taken a part of the whole of experience and called it more real than the rest. He has taken one kind of man and seen him as genuine, while all the others are false.

An example of the method Fromm uses to divide experience into the real and the less real can be found in his treatment of the ways of fulfilling the "need for transcendence." The need can be filled creatively or destructively, but creativeness is the primary potentiality. Destructiveness is what Fromm calls a secondary potentiality. It appears only when creativeness has been thwarted. It is the outcome of unlived life. By this easy use of words, Fromm shows that hate, envy, cruelty, pride, selfishness, and all the other destructive passions are somehow not really real. They are only secondary qualities, perverted expressions of the energy of a being who is naturally loving, creative, generous, and reasonable.

This is unconvincing because it rests upon an essentialist conception of the self which Hume discredited and which no later writer has been able to restore to philosophical respectability. This is such an important component of Fromm's thought that I shall backtrack briefly to set the problem in context.

Fromm believes there is a definable human nature. He further believes that each member of the race has a unique self, even though many members have lost touch with theirs. If someone violates his self or loses it, he becomes sick. If he lives in such a way as to realize its full potentialities, he remains healthy. Starting from the premise that something called the self or soul exists, Fromm reaches the conclusion that the good is synonymous with the fulfillment of the soul's needs and the realization of its potentialities. Fromm wants to return to the "tradition in which psychology as the study of the soul of man was the theoretical basis for the art of living, for achieving happiness." He believes that no psychotherapy goes very far unless the analyst recognizes "that his patient is sick because he has neglected his soul's demands." He concludes that "the analyst is not a theologian or a philosopher and does not claim competence in those fields, but as a physician of the soul he is concerned with the very same problems as philosophy and theology; the soul of man and its cure." [47]

Fromm is right. Given this conception of psychology and ethics, he is indeed faced with the same problems as philosophy and theology. And it will not do to ignore the problems on the ground that he is not a philosopher or theologian. He cannot at once admit he is dealing with philosophical subjects and refuse to treat them philosophically. I grant Fromm's point that the problem of the self is not exclusively a philosophical problem,[48] but it is that in part. Furthermore, the philosophical problem is the one which must be solved first. Fromm wants to make psychology the study of the soul, and he identifies the good with the realization of the self. He cannot have all this, and then simply ignore the fact that the terms soul and self, in the uses to which he puts them, raise hard philosophical questions. It is not enough to say, as Fromm in effect does, that modern man has lost his self somewhere in the smoke of his own civilization, and that we need only blow away the smoke to find again the true self, the self in its essence, the self intact and noble. There may be no self to find.

The loss of the self happened rather recently in philosophy. The Greeks never doubted that there was a self. Man possessed the unity of his rational nature, which philosophers could study and describe. Nor did the Christian philosophers ever doubt the unity of the self. For them it consisted in man's God-given soul. So long as philosophy rested content with the premise of the self as a simple substance existing permanently, so long could the other sciences be seen as tools for the attainment of selfhood. Then doubt entered philosophy. Inevitably, it spread from there to the special studies, so that what was once merely a crisis in philosophy has become a crisis in social science.

Doubt came to philosophy in 1739, the date of Hume's *Treatise*. Just as Berkeley had already dissolved the notion of substance in physics, so Hume dissolved it in psychology, and in the process denied psychology its premise. Hume argued that there was no impression of self, and therefore there could be no idea of self. When he looked most intimately into himself all he encountered were particular perceptions, never a general perception of himself. Some subtle doctors might be able to capture their selves, he sarcastically acknowledged, "but setting aside some metaphysicians of this kind, I may venture to affirm of the rest of mankind, that they are nothing but a bundle or collection of different perceptions, which succeed each other with an inconceivable rapidity, and are in a perpetual flux and movement." He expanded the thesis in a familiar metaphor:

> The mind is a kind of theatre, where several perceptions successively make their appearance; pass, re-pass, glide away, and mingle in an infinite variety of postures and situations. There is properly no *simplicity* in it at one

time, nor *identity* in different; whatever natural propen-
sion we may have to imagine that simplicity and identity. The comparison of the theatre must not mislead
us. They are the successive perceptions only, that con-
stitute the mind; nor have we the most distant notion
of the place, where these scenes are represented, or of
the materials, of which it is compos'd.[49]

Hume gave away the secret—there was no secret. Or,
rather, if there is a secret we shall never unlock it. We cannot know whether there is a simple substance called the self,
and thus we cannot postulate the self as any part of our
knowledge. The concept of the self as a substance, a notion
which for centuries had been the strongest offspring of the
metaphysical reason, was exposed by Hume as the bastard of
confused language and fevered imagination. Since Hume's
exposure, the self has never been restored to full philosophical legitimacy. At one stroke, he destroyed the last use
of the concept of substance in metaphysics, made it impossible for theology and psychology to gain knowledge of the
soul, and showed that the ancient epistemological distinction between subject and object was less than firm.

The echoes of Hume's assault drifted into Prussia and
awakened the lethargic Kant. He stayed awake long enough
to write the manifesto of the Copernican revolution in philosophy, which put the problem of the self on a radically
new footing. His argument was designed to show that we
can never arrive at a conception of the self as a substance
through the avenue of empirical observation and reasoning.
Therefore, we must conceive of the self not as an object of
experience but as a transcendental idea. Having done that,
we may take the concept as a regulative principle for the
ordering of empirical knowledge. Then we can build connections between phenomena *as if* the mind were a simple substance existing permanently and with personal identity. The

idea of the self, in short, is a conception of pure reason, not a concept whose nature and content can be determined by analysis of experience.[50]

Kant argued in effect that while we can know nothing about the self as an object of experience or reason, we need the concept of the self as an ordering or regulative principle of thought and experience. This is probably inadequate on the epistemological question. It is devastating on the moral question, for it reduces our feeling that we grow and develop, that we are centers of moral decision and responsible for our choices, to the level of a mere idea—that is, a mere fiction. The result of Kant's metaphysics was to make the self entirely metaphysical, a construct of reason and presupposition of thought alone, incapable of being shown to exist in or be understood by the experiences of men. The self no longer existed as an object of experience.

Now that the background is sketched in, the conclusions can be drawn in a moment. Fromm has failed to find that indestructible core called the self. His failure is due partly to bad metaphysics and partly to bad logic. Fromm rests his whole ethical and political philosophy upon the premise that something called the self exists and can be ascertained. The self is a substance with its own qualities, its own essence. On the basis of this dubious pre-Humean conception, he moves forward to build a theory of moral selfhood whose major article is that happiness means the realization of the inherent potentialities of the self. This whole Aristotelian notion of potentiality is as troublesome as the essentialist conception of the self. The notion of potentiality may be useful in some contexts, but it is very misleading in others. When it is used as a fundamental concept, as it is by Fromm, it leads to grievous confusion of thought. The notion is useful, in Russell's words, "provided it is so used that we can translate our statements into a form in which the concept is absent." [51] Thus, we can say "a block of marble is a potential statue" if we mean only that "if a certain type of person performs suitable acts upon this block of marble he can produce a statue from it." If we take the statement "a block of marble is a potential statue" to mean something like "this block of marble has an inherent urge to fulfill itself, which it can do only by becoming a statue" we are letting woolly language lead us into bad metaphysics. Fromm does exactly this. To say that the need for relatedness must be filled through love, and to mean by that statement what Fromm means by it, is to say in effect that the self has an inherent urge to become what it potentially is, and that it satisfies this urge through love. Such a formulation rests upon a pre-Humean conception of the self as a simple substance and upon an Aristotelian conception of potentiality as something inherent in matter.

Furthermore, if we take seriously the notion of inherent potentiality we are driven to a conclusion which makes the vocation of moral philosophy trivial. Men study ethics and build ethical philosophies because they wish to find some principles of guidance and judgment when values clash. The conflict may be between individuals or groups or it may take place within the self. The premise of ethical study is that the conflict, wherever it may take place, is between principles of equal reality and not between something that is real and something else that is only the distorted shadow of the real. When both are real and demanding, then the student of ethics summons reason and experience to adjudicate between them. When one is merely the shadow of the other, there is no place for reasoned ethical discourse. In a profound sense, Fromm, in spite of his explicit insistence on the objectivity of good and evil, defines the moral problem out of existence. This is a consequence of the logic of primary and secondary qualities. If you define the soul as a substance made up of certain primary potentialities which become actualized under appropriate conditions, and certain secondary potentialities which become actualized only when conditions thwart the actualization of the primary qualities, then the moral problem disappears. It becomes absorbed into sociology. We come again to the basic point. Fromm believes that a good society will make good men and that evil men are merely the unnatural reflections of evil social conditions. But now it appears that the argument is more than circular. It defines the ethical problem out of existence and makes the study of ethical choice an idle enterprise. This is ironic. Fromm starts from essentialist premises and arrives (unknowingly) at positivist conclusions.

A few pages ago I conceded Fromm's point that the problem of the self is not exclusively a philosophical problem. There is also an exceedingly important psychological problem of the self, in the sense that the empirical person must know who he is, must have an identity, a sense of I-ness. Fromm takes this need for identity to be one of man's basic needs, and he may well be right. The great difficulties in treating the psychological problem of the self are two. First, one may lose his self without knowing it. This was Kierkegaard's fear: "The greatest danger, that of losing one's own self, may pass off as quietly as if it were nothing; every other loss, that of an arm, a leg, five dollars, a wife, etc., is sure to be noticed." Secondly, one can go along for a long time with an illusory self, a self that is not one's authentic own but an echo of the voices of the others. This was the conclusion F. Scott Fitzgerald came to when he forced himself to account for the crack-up:

(1) That I had done very little thinking, save within the problems of my craft. For twenty years a certain

man had been my intellectual conscience. That was
Edmund Wilson.

(2) That another man represented my sense of the
"good life," though I saw him once in a decade, and
since then he might have been hung. . . . But in difficult situations I had tried to think what *he* would have
thought, how *he* would have acted.

(3) That a third contemporary had been an artistic
conscience to me. . . .

(4) That a fourth man had come to dictate my relations with other people when these relations were
successful: how to do, what to say. . . . This always
confused me and made me want to go out and get
drunk, but this man had seen the game, analyzed it and
beaten it, and his word was good enough for me.

(5) That my political conscience had scarcely existed for ten years save as an element of irony in my
stuff. When I became again concerned with the system
I should function under, it was a man much younger
than myself who brought it to me, with a mixture of
passion and fresh air.

So there was not an "I" any more—not a basis on
which I could organize my self-respect—save my limitless capacity for toil that it seemed I possessed no more.
It was strange to have no self—to be like a little boy left
alone in a big house, who knew that now he could do
anything he wanted to do, but found that there was
nothing that he wanted to do—[52]

In short, you can lose your identity without knowing it; and
you can think you have an identity without having one.

Fromm has formulated this problem clearly enough,
and he thinks he has found a solution to it. His solution is
that the person who achieves a productive fulfillment of the
five basic needs has by that achievement also achieved
authentic selfhood. The solution is not convincing: Fromm

has failed to come to terms with some of the central conceptions and conclusions of empirical social science. Just as philosophy lost the self, so has social science—but with the difference that now it is the psychological self that is lost. In order to see where the loss occurred and what problems it raises for Fromm's thought, I shall again make an excursion over the history of the question.

The excursion need not take long, for after Kant the course of thought on this subject was as nearly predictable as anything in intellectual history can be. Kant argued only that the idea of the self cannot be based on sensory experience or empirical examination, but is exclusively an idea of reason. He agreed, for example, that freedom of the will and immortality of the soul are the necessary bases of all moral action, but he did not attempt a proof for these two concepts: he simply put them down as necessary postulates for the exercise of the practical reason. But the question could not be left there, and what happened next was bound to happen, even though it ran against all Kant had hoped. While Kant wanted to show only that we cannot build our idea of the self from experience, men soon began to argue that *experience* denies any theory of the self as a simple substance having identity over time. In other words, while for Kant the problem centered around the nature of perception, in our time it appears in the sciences of psychology and sociology. Today the question is whether what we call the self is anything more than a social emergent, a product of social interaction. The question is whether the observed manifestations of the empirical Sweeney spring from some unity other than that of a mere organism which can be located in physical and social space and time. Is Sweeney merely a point or container where social forces converge to produce certain observable events; or does he have some essential self beyond and above a merely social self?

The problem is already apparent in Marx's social psychology, with its theme that the content of mind is a function of membership in a social class. Durkheim's *Suicide* of 1897 went far beyond Marx in the care and thoroughness with which it set forth the dependence of personality upon society. After Durkheim most of the additions were made by American writers: it was as though academic sociology had set out to document Tocqueville's observation that in America the individual's every thought is dominated by the social atmosphere. Sociology discovered the social individual, but sociologists never paused to reflect that they had discovered exactly what their methods were adapted to discover: if you seek social influences on the personality, you will find them. And no more. John Stuart Mill, that passionate individualist, was also aware of social influences, but he never supposed that you could reduce a man to them.

Cooley very nearly did. His notion of the "looking-glass self" leaves the self no privacy. The idea of the self has three parts: "the imagination of our appearance to the other person; the imagination of his judgment of that appearance, and some sort of self-feeling, such as pride or mortification." [53] What am I? I am what I think you think I am. Cooley's formulation supposes that when the others are absent the self disappears. The "I" is a creation of the "they."

Dewey, meanwhile, was doing for social philosophy what Baldwin and Cooley were doing for psychosociology. His *Human Nature and Conduct* of 1921 denied the presence of a separate psychic realm and asserted that there was no such thing as an original individual consciousness. Dewey's "individual" is only a bundle of energies which society either actualizes or immobilizes. The dynamic and creative principle is in society, not in the individual, and the individual can not be treated as a being with its own demands, demands whose nonfulfillment results in social explosion or personal disintegration. The individual is all but submerged in society, and the idea of the individual either disappears or leads a vague and confused existence. For Dewey, in short, human nature cannot be treated as something other than social conduct.

Mead set the capstone on the structure. In his thought, the self is entirely a social emergent. More than that, the distinguishing feature of selfhood—a once-noble term of moral philosophy—is the capacity of a person to take the roles of others, to see himself through their eyes. Without the others there is no self, for what we confusedly call the self is simply what we see in ourselves when we take the point of view of the others. This is Mead's germinal conception, repeated tirelessly throughout his book: "The individual experiences himself as such, not directly, but only indirectly, from the particular standpoints of other individual members of the same group, or from the generalized standpoint of the social group as a whole to which he belongs." [54]

That brings us back to Hume, but with a difference. While Hume stopped when he had dissolved the self into successive perceptions, Mead went beyond that and asserted that the source of those perceptions, which become stabilized into attitudes, some of which are ego-attitudes, is the "significant others" around one. For Mead, life is a play in which each of us takes roles defined by the others. But it is not quite accurate to say that each takes roles. He *is* his roles. The play is meaningless, and the actors are shadows of each other. What am I? I am—the roles defined by you. What am I? I am—"as you desire me." Pirandello's tortured search for the self turns out to be good sociology.

Mead pays almost no attention to the larger questions. How does the "I" arise and grow? How does it integrate and give a unique quality to the plurality of roles each of us assumes? The consequence of this silence, a silence shared by most modern social psychology and sociology, is an increasing stress on group norms as decisive in the molding of personality. So pronounced is this stress currently that its political and moral implications can no longer be overlooked.

The political implications of social determinism are conservative. The chain of propositions here seems unbreakable. The anchor point is the thesis that group norms are the decisive forces in the shaping of personality. It follows that stable group norms are needed in order to produce stable and secure personalities. Group norms can be stable only if they are bedded in a stable social framework. Hence, if the social framework undergoes rapid change, group norms too must change. The result is conflict among the norms. This conflict is internalized in individuals as role conflict, with the result that one is torn between competing self conceptions. This can ultimately lead to neurosis and chaos for the individual. If we want stable, secure, well-integrated personalities, we must have a stable, secure, unified social order.

Call this the theory of sociological conservatism. The program has been worked out by a number of writers, especially those who have followed in the steps of Durkheim, such as Mayo, Drucker, and Homans. These writers emphasize status as the bedrock of stable personality and stress the need for the continuity of institutions. Men can find a comfortable moral home only in the embrace of warm social institutions. In his hymn to the General Motors Corporation, for example, Peter Drucker pauses long enough to tell us that the next great problem to which the modern corporation must turn its benevolent genius is "the achievement of status and function" for the mass industrial citizenry.[55] Another theme in this literature is the fear of conflict within society. Conflict shatters security and threatens stability. A related theme is the stress on the value creating role of the leadership elements of the great institutions. The citizenry is a passive mass which is activated by and takes its direction from the creative elites of the great institutions.[56]

The moral implications are just as worrisome. We can approach them through the work of David Riesman, the writer who has done most to popularize the new perspective. Riesman is also useful to my purposes because he has taken so much from Fromm who, as the reader perhaps has forgotten by now, is the subject of this essay. Riesman has taken the middle from Fromm but has refused both Fromm's premises about the human condition and his whole critical position. Riesman's writings are characterized by a certain moral onanism. He carries the analysis of the modern situation right up to the decisive point, and then backs away. What is important about his work, however, is that it shows that even the sociologist can no longer refuse to recognize the problem of the loss of the self, if for no other reason than that his own self is now in as much danger as the others'.

Riesman's work is useful here because it exposes the tendencies outlined above in their most highly developed form. After Marx and Durkheim, James and Dewey, Cooley and Mead, no one will deny that social structure affects personality structure, that there is an observable relation between the type of society and the types of character structures in that society. Riesman has worked this commonplace into a neat three-part characterology which sets forth specific character types corresponding to specific social structures. In the society of high population growth potential and "primary" (Colin Clark's term) economy, the tradition-directed character prevails. The society of transitional population growth and "secondary" economy produces the inner-directed person as its typical character style. The society of incipient population decline and "tertiary" economy produces the other-directed character, which Riesman believes is becoming dominant in our time.[57]

The other-directed character has an insatiable need to be liked. This goes far beyond a prudent concern for one's reputation. Other-directed man shapes not only his external life and surface opinions in response to fashion and propriety, but his internal life as well. He makes *himself* over to fit the desires of his contemporaries and his peer groups. He retools his personality to keep up with the changing tastes of the personality market, a job to which he gives the same anxious care that Detroit gives to planning next year's model. For, like the Ford Corporation, he is engaged in consumer research, and the product he sells is himself. His personal disaster occurs when, even after anxious and intense consumer research, he makes himself into a commodity which the public just does not go for, thereby becoming a kind of Edsel of the personality market. He has no code at all except that which he picks up by keeping sensitively attuned to the signals sent out by the others around him. What *is* the other-directed man? He is—as he thinks the others desire him.

If Riesman is correct, what was once just a crisis in philosophy is now a crisis in the actual typical personality of our time. Riesman's other-directed men are quite without authentic selfhood. They are not the creators of their own values. Their souls are reflections of the stimuli around them, and there is no knowledge at all which makes us confident that the values they absorb from the others fit their own deepest needs and tendencies. If Riesman is right, the social environment does not merely influence personality, as we have always known it does, but actually constitutes it.

The problem that opened with Hume has now come full cycle. Under Hume's analysis, the concept of the self as simple substance dissolved into fleeting impressions, thereby creating a crisis in epistemology. By the time of Mead, the idea of the individual as the unit of society disappeared. In Riesman's popularization of the modern doctrine the individual himself has been absorbed into society: Mead's analytic constructs have become Riesman's men. The philosophers of the eighteenth century and the liberals of the nineteenth set out to free men from the ancient restraints which made it impossible for the individual to create himself. The conceptions of personality at the center of modern psychosociology indicate that there is no individual to liberate. So we must once more set out on the search for a theory of the self and a conception of moral selfhood which will be compatible with our vaunted commitment to human freedom. Only when we find that theory will we have a firm foundation for a critical political philosophy. For, if it is to be persuasive, a program of political reform in defense of the individual must base itself upon a conception of human nature which insists that man has certain inalienable claims upon society.

Fromm has undertaken the search for the indestructible human core, and he thinks he has found it in the five basic psychic needs. These needs are inherent in the human condition, he argues, and must be satisfied for men to thrive. Furthermore, they must be satisfied in certain ways if life is to be good. But there is the difficulty. All Fromm's categories of productive fulfillment are clearly cultural variables. The meanings of love, justice, creativeness, and the rest, vary from culture to culture. They are, in fact, products of culture. No amount of calling for love, for example, will alter the fact that the meanings of love are many and that what stands for "love" in one society may be entirely absent from or mean something very different in another. Given this intransigent fact, what can it mean to say that if man is to realize himself the need for relatedness must be satisfied through love, or the need for transcendence must be met through creativeness? When the Kwakiutl chieftains engage in their astonishing potlatches and destroy hoards of wealth in order to establish their place in the community and show their power to others, it looks to us, as it must surely look to Fromm, as though they are fulfilling the need for relatedness through hate and the need for transcendence through destructiveness. But the one thing we cannot deny is that they are fulfilling their needs and actualizing their potentialities—as these things are understood among the Kwakiutl.

At this point, it seems possible to summarize the foregoing pages in one proposition. Even if a self exists in the sense that Fromm has in mind, there is no proof that the five basic needs, as he has defined them, are part (let alone all) of it. On the contrary: Fromm's definitions of the needs and his criteria for measuring their fulfillment appear to be derivatives of a set of specific cultural norms.

So Fromm has failed to find that indestructible core of human nature and that essence of the self for which he has searched so diligently in all his books. The failure leaves his ethical and political philosophy on shaky foundations. Apart from that, however, the failure itself cannot be judged harshly for the difficulties of the search are enormous. In our time, perhaps only Freud has found a man with a core so hard that society cannot deny it. This he achieved through his theory of the instincts. The instincts can to a degree be bent by society, but they cannot be permanently reshaped and they cannot for long be denied. They make up the core of a human nature which constantly threatens society from below. For Freud, the very possibility of civilization is a problem, and the very existence of social cohesion is under a constant challenge. The *id* lurks below, ceaselessly awaiting the chance to fight for its original freedom. Culture demands instinctual renunciation, because it is built on sublimation, but the instincts are always prepared to burst their bonds and overthrow the whole confining structure. This view of human nature does give man a core which cannot be reduced to social conditioning, and Freud achieves this without recourse to the bad metaphysics of substance and potential. Freud's view could support a critical political and moral philosophy, even though he did little to spell it out.* Fromm's view of the self as having basic psychic needs which must be fulfilled in certain ways if the self is to realize itself neither gives man a solid core of qualities apart from culture nor provides a solid foundation for a critical moral and political philosophy.

This is the great misfortune of Fromm's work. Without wanting to, he has given human nature no real defense against society. He has, rather, turned man over to society (this is the necessary conclusion of his notion of the individual as a product of social evolution) and then pleaded that society ought to treat man decently. Erich Fromm cannot conceive of man outside history and culture, and by that failure of imagination he reduces man to history and culture.

* Philip Rieff has undertaken, with some success, the job of working out the moral and political implications of Freud's thought in his *Freud: The Mind of the Moralist* (New York: Viking, 1959). I should say here that in my comments on Freud as having supplied a theory of man which gives man a position against society I did not mean to imply that Freud's theory, unlike Fromm's, is without defects. Freud himself admitted that "the science of the instincts is the most incomplete part of the psychoanalytic theory." (Quoted from Rieff, p. 30.) And when Freud did turn his hand to this part of his theory, the product resembled mythology more than science.

The foregoing pages lead to one conclusion: Fromm's theory of ethics is not logically convincing. With justice the reader will protest that rarely have so many pages produced so few conclusions. That, however, is the way of the academic. While his labors are many and heavy and his harvest lamentably small, at least the fruit is well-ripened and plucking it takes but a moment. I hope my modest conclusion will be acceptable to all.

It would be a mistake, however, to think that when we have measured the logical strength of an intellectual work we have taken the full measure of the work itself. A system of thought is much more than an army of propositions drawn up in logical order and prepared to do battle. It is as well the expression of esthetic, moral, political, and religious convictions which the writer sometimes makes explicit, sometimes deliberately conceals, and sometimes does not know he holds. Furthermore, it is doubtful whether any man ever accepted or rejected a total intellectual system solely on grounds of logic. Hume knew very well that even after he had shown that we are not logically entitled to certain beliefs, we would still, and properly, go on believing them.

So I want to survey Fromm's thought from some of the perspectives beyond logic. In the chapters that follow, I shall state and criticize Fromm's ideas on three topics: (1) the theory of character and the model of the good man; (2) the reason why good men are so scarce; and (3) how good men can be made more plentiful.

CHAPTER II

Character and Goodness

Many voices berate and importune the one who goes in search of goodness and justice. One voice urges the pleasures of the senses while another affirms the ascetic ideal. A third voice insists that only the good will matters, while a fourth argues that acts must be judged by their consequences. Nor is this a distinctively modern malady, as we sometimes let ourselves think. Aristotle long ago lamented that the question of the just and the good "admits of so much divergence and variation of opinion that it is widely believed that morality is a convention and not part of the nature of things." [1] Distracted by so much querulous diversity, the seeker may give up the search and accept the relativist position: every man his own ethical philosopher. But in the end we know that cannot be so. Every man is not his own philosopher; he is the slave of the philosopher everyman.

Assume that the seeker has found his way among the voices to the haven of a firm conception of the good. He is still in danger. The light shifts, the context of action changes, and what was good suddenly seems evil. A virtuous action unaccountably produces harmful consequences. We praise courage; a man is destroyed by his own courageous act. We praise honesty; one's honesty brings the ruin of his friend. In the moral life, the hard problems arise not when good clashes with evil or virtue with vice but when good runs against good and virtue against virtue. Then goodness and justice appear under the aspect of radical ambiguity. Can we find no surer guide through this ambiguity than Aristotle, who can advise us only to shun excess, to take care for the context of action, and push nothing past its limits?

The source of this danger lies in taking particular virtues or vices as the subject matter of ethical study. The philosopher isolates, say, courage or honesty from their surroundings and takes them to his workroom. There he dissects them, hoping to lay bare their inner structure. Having done that, he has already committed the error that forecloses further understanding. A virtue or a vice taken by itself is ambiguous and loses its ambiguity only when it is seen in context. This context has two parts: the character structure of the actor, and the stage of action on which he plays his role.

The stage of action is as variable as life itself, so variable that no two situations are ever exactly the same. Hence the theorist can do little with this sector of the context of ethical study beyond keeping himself open to its heterogeneity and variability. He can at best think of typical contexts in which man must live. The theorist might, for example, treat of domestic virtue, virtue in the life of business, ethics in wartime and ethics in peacetime, virtue in public life, the ethics of friendship, and so forth. Such a classification must remain very rough, however, and the theorist must recognize that none of his arguments or examples can have universal application. He must be prepared to see each of his prescriptions modified by circumstance.

It is possible to say that a prescription can be at once universal and modified by circumstances. A number of old natural law theorists, such as Aquinas, as well as a number of modern writers, such as Stammler, with his search for a "natural law with a changing content," have said substantially this. That, however, is not a solution to the problem posed by the discontinuity between ethical situations, but only a way of stating it.

The theorist can do a good bit more with the sector of context which is made up of the character structure of the person of whom the virtue is predicated. Like events and situations, persons come in an infinite variety. Yet it is possible to talk about types of men in a language precise enough for ethics. Pythagoras divided those who came to the Olympic games into three types. Plato arranged the citizens of a state into three classes. These were early characterologies, that is, classifications of men on the basis of their salient talents, traits, and attitudes. Each category represented a certain way of looking at the world, a typical relationship to things and men, a style of life.

Recent developments in psychology make possible great advances toward the achievement of a subtle and scientific characterology. Such an achievement, quite obviously, holds great promise for the advancement of ethical philosophy. Depth psychology in general, and psychoanalysis in particular, have illuminated large and hitherto impenetrable areas of the psychology of ethics. Freud's explorations of the dynamic unconscious, and the analyses of such psychic processes as rationalization, sublimation, projection, and repression—these and similar advances make possible great strides in our understanding of ethical subjects and in the development of ethical philosophy.

It is evident that the promise of depth psychology for the development of positive ethical systems has not been fulfilled. On the whole, the application of psychoanalysis to ethics has meant a savage debunking of the latter. Psychoanalysis has been used to unmask ethical pretensions, to strip away the objectivity of ethical claims, to reduce ethical positions to rationalizations of instinctual demands. The application of psychoanalysis to ethics has been destructive rather than constructive. Perhaps this was inevitable, given the orientations of the early analytic movement. Or, it may be only a particular manifestation of the temper of our age, which is analytic and critical, rather than synthetic and constructive. Whatever the reasons, the fact itself is indisputable. Psychoanalysis has certainly contributed much toward a greater honesty in our attitudes toward ethics, but it has not contributed much toward the construction of sound and positive conceptions of the good life.

This suggests part of the interest and importance of Fromm's work. The chief strength of his approach to ethics is that it rests on a sensitive appreciation of the fact that any discussion of virtue or vice is ambiguous unless the discussion proceeds from the recognition that the meaning of a virtue or vice is a function of the character of the person of whom the virtue or vice is predicated. Fromm opens his study of ethics with a theory of character, for, as he puts it, "*the virtuous or the vicious character, rather than single virtues or vices, is the true subject matter of ethical inquiry.*" [2] Fromm's theory of character, and the conception of the good man which flows from it, represents one of the few attempts to apply psychoanalytic principles and concepts to the construction of a portrait of the good man and a conception of the good life.

The theory of character compels attention for another reason: its breadth. It represents a bold attempt to blend the dissimilar geniuses and insights of Marx and Freud. To this basic stock, just add a little Hippocrates for dramatic color, some Harry Stack Sullivan for that uniquely American tang, a dash of Rousseau for piquancy, and you have it. The mixture is remarkably successful. It is the finest part of Fromm's work, the one part of which it can be said without qualification that his eclecticism has issued in a fruitful synthesis. No single component of the theory is original with Fromm, but the ingredients are blended in such a way as to produce a new whole which is greater than the sum of the parts. The originality and strength of the theory come, I think, from the brilliant way Fromm makes one science mirror another. In this part of his work there is something more than a section of psychology, one of sociology, and another of economics—the usual result of interdisciplinary attempts in the social sciences. Rather, each science is reflected in the other and all are made to bear upon a single problem. Fromm achieves this integration of the several sciences through a closely knit fabric of definitions and conceptions which is at once descriptive and normative.

The Theory of Character

The theory of character starts with a definition of personality, which is "the totality of inherited and acquired psychic qualities which are characteristic of one individual and which make the individual unique." [3] In the main, inherited or constitutional qualities are synonymous with temperament, and acquired qualities are synonymous with character. Following Hippocrates, Fromm distinguishes four temperaments: choleric, sanguine, melancholic, and phlegmatic. Hippocrates connected each of these with a specific somatic source, and modern researches on temperament, such as those of Kretschmer and Sheldon, still retain this basic link between temperament and somatic processes. As a concept, temperament refers to the speed and intensity of one's typical reaction to experience. The choleric's reaction, for example, is "quick and strong." Temperament, since it is constitutional, is unchangeable. One does not choose or make his temperament, he inherits it. Hence "differences in temperament have no ethical significance." [4]

If we know a man's temperament we can say in general how he will react, but we cannot say what he will react to. To know that, we must know something about his character as well, for while temperament determines how one reacts, character determines both the kinds of persons, events, and situations he reacts to and the general content of his reaction.

Character, unlike temperament, is a social product. It is formed primarily by one's early experiences, though it can be changed to some extent by new insights and new experiences. It is the great problem of dynamic psychology to understand the processes by which character and culture interact. It is, similarly, the great problem of ethics to develop a critical characterology, for differences in character "are expressive of the degree to which an individual has succeeded in the art of living." [5]

Fromm's conception of character differs from both the behaviorist and the Freudian conceptions. Behaviorist psychology considers character traits as synonymous with behavior traits. Character is simply a pattern of behavior: a man's character *is* the cluster of behaviors typical of him. Freud, on the other hand, developed a penetrating theory of character as a system of strivings which underlie, but are not identical with, behavior. He appreciated the decisive point, which is that character traits underlie behavior and give behavior its real meaning. He also understood that the basic entity in character is not the single trait but the total character organization or orientation from which the single traits follow. Further, Freud recognized the conative and dynamic nature of character traits. He knew that a person's thoughts, feelings, and actions are in great measure determined by the structure of his passions and are not merely the results of rational responses to realistic situations: "man's fate is his character." Finally, with the insight of genius, Freud found that the seething energies which form the core of character inhabit a realm of psychic life which lies far below the rind of consciousness.

Fromm follows Freud on all these points—and disagrees on the fundamentals. In his view, Freud saw much that no man before him had seen, but he saw it all aslant. Freud, the greatest psychologist who ever lived, was just fundamentally wrong about human nature. His basic error, Fromm thinks, was to conceive of man as a closed system of biological forces rather than as a being who is fundamentally socially conditioned. This means that while Freud's clinical observations were strikingly keen and of great importance, his explanations and interpretations were profoundly wrong.

In contrast to Freud's biologism, Fromm sees man as essentially a social product. "Man's nature, his passions, and anxieties are a cultural product; as a matter of fact, man himself is the most important creation and achievement of the continuous human effort, the record of which we call history." [6] This difference in starting points has important consequences for psychology in general and for characterology in particular. Given the premise that man is primarily a social being, it follows that all psychology is at bottom social psychology. Here is Fromm's statement of the point.

Freud's essential principle is to look upon man as an entity, a closed system, endowed by nature with certain physiologically conditioned drives, and to interpret the development of his character as a reaction to satisfactions and frustrations of these drives; whereas, in our opinion, the fundamental approach to human personality is the understanding of man's relation to the world, to others, to nature, and to himself. We believe that man is *primarily* a social being, and not, as Freud assumes, primarily self-sufficient and only secondarily in need of others in order to satisfy his instinctual needs. In this sense, we believe that individual psychology is fundamentally social psychology or, in Sullivan's terms, the psychology of interpersonal relationships; the key problem of psychology is that of the particular kind of relatedness of the individual toward the world, not that of the satisfaction or frustration of single instinctual desires.[7]

For characterology, the difference means that the basis of character is to be found in the fundamental style of a person's relations with the world and not, as Freud thought, in various types of libido organization. Fromm offers two definitions of character, each of which emphasizes the differences between his own and Freud's conception. "Character . . . is the specific form in which human energy is shaped by the dynamic adaptation of human needs to the particular mode of existence of a given society." And: "Character can be defined as the *(relatively permanent) form in which human energy is canalized in the process of assimilation and socialization.*" [8]

"Assimilation" and "socialization" are technical words for Fromm. In the process of living, a person relates to the world in two ways: (1) by acquiring and using things; and (2) by relating to other people and himself. The former process Fromm calls assimilation, and the latter socialization. The two processes, patently, are closely related, and each has a number of forms. In anticipation of later discussion, it will be enough at this point simply to note that each process has five forms or orientations. The orientations in the process of assimilation are the receptive, the exploitative, the hoarding, the marketing, and the productive. The five styles of socialization are masochism, sadism, destructiveness, automaton conformism, and love. The orientations in both processes are respectively related as listed above: the person whose assimilative style is that of receptiveness will usually follow the masochistic way of socialization; the hoarding character is destructive; and so on.

The task of psychology, then, is to understand how the conditions of life make character and how character in turn molds history. Fromm's solutions to these problems are straightforward. To live, man must work and produce. It is through work that man is brought into the stream of society and assigned a certain place in relation to other men. Work is always concrete, a specific kind of work in a specific kind of economic system: one works as a slave in ancient Athens, a serf in feudal France, a salesman in modern America. Different kinds of work require and create different character types. Fromm holds with Marx that a man's character is a function of his position in the system of production and distribution: "the mode of life, as it is determined for the individual by the peculiarity of an economic system, becomes the primary factor in determining his whole character structure, because the imperative need for self-preservation forces him to accept the conditions under which he has to live." [9] In summary, Fromm's psychology, which is fundamentally social psychology, is specifically Marxian social psychology.

Fromm agrees with Freud that the early experiences are crucial in molding character, though he does not give them all the weight that Freud does. At first glance, this seems to run counter to Fromm's insistence that society, and especially its economic institutions, molds character. How can the child, who after all does not work and who has little contact with the life of society, be molded by it? The answer is, through the family, which transmits society to the child. "The character of the child is molded by the character of its parents in response to whom it develops. The parents and their methods of child training in turn are determined by the social structure of their culture. The average family is the 'psychic agency' of society. . . ." [10] Thus, the core of the child's character becomes similar to that which is common to the members of his class and culture. Fromm calls the complex of traits thus acquired the "social character," which he formally defines as "the core of a character structure common to most people of a given culture. . . ." The social character is *"the essential nucleus of the character structure of most members of a group which has developed as the result of the basic experiences and mode of life common to that group."* [11]

Around this common core cluster all the variations which make of each human being a unique individual. The variations arise from many sources: personality differences between parents; material and psychological differences between environments; genetic differences; and so forth. The relation between social and individual character may be thought of as a linear scale or continuum. On one end of the scale are people whose characters are composed almost entirely of social norms and conventions. At the other end are the extreme deviants, those who depart widely from the conventional patterns.[12]

At this point it is necessary to say again that Fromm's purposes are always both scientific and moral. His analyses of the social character and of the forces that make for individual variation are scientific, but his final concern is moral. Every society has a social character, but what matters is whether that social character is good or bad. Every individual deviates to some extent from the social character, but what matters ethically is not the amount of deviation but its direction. The deviant may be a creative genius or an ineffectual eccentric. Fromm's ultimate purpose is not merely to understand social and individual character but to make them good. He wants to build social conditions which will assure both that the social character will be good and that individual deviations from it will go in a productive direction.*

This part of the theory of character concludes with a treatment of the functions character performs for the individual and for society. One's character does for him what instinct does for the lower animals. It channels his energy and relieves him of the impossible burden of having to make a deliberate decision to cope with every situation. One need not think out his behavior in every situation: he acts "true to character." A person's character also conditions his perceptions, ideas, and values, thereby stabilizing the environment and making it appear consistent and reasonable. Character also provides the individual with motives for doing what his social position requires him to do and offers him psychological rewards for performing the role which society assigns him. As Fromm puts it, "the subjective function of character for the normal person is to *lead him to*

---

* One passage in the above should be modified. It is correct in principle to say that Fromm does not value individual differences from the social character merely because they are differences. But when the social character is radically bad, as it is in modern America, for example, then individual departures from it, even in a nonproductive direction, are valuable as such. This explains Fromm's admiration of the neurotic, for the neurotic is one who has not given in to the deadening demands of an evil social character. The neurotic knows he is sick and his differences from the mass make him feel the pain of his sickness. His pain provides the power which can move him toward a cure. But for the masses who share the sickness of a sick social character there is little hope. They do not feel the pain of sickness because they are like everyone else and hence do not even know they are sick.

*act according to what is necessary for him from a practical
standpoint and also to give him satisfaction from his activity
psychologically."* [13]

From the standpoint of the social order, character functions as a powerful cementing force. Through his incorporation of the social character, the individual "acquires
that character which makes him want to do what he has
to do. . . ." [14] ("Makes him want to do what he has to do"
in order for the social system to work, one should add, not
to be sane, or good.) The modern industrial system, for
example, requires that our best energies be given to work.
The industrial discipline to which we submit seems light
only because we are so thoroughly accustomed to it. If the
workers did not voluntarily accept their tasks the whole
system would either break down under its own frictions or
else would have to be held together by force. But modern
man does not have to be driven to work by external authorities. He has internalized a number of attitudes about the
value and duty of work which are far more effective in
controlling his work behavior than any authorities set over
him could ever be. These attitudes are part of the social
character, and each individual shares them to the extent that
he shares in the social character. From the standpoint of
the social order, then, *"the social character internalizes
external necessities and thus harnesses human energy for
the task of a given economic and social system."* [15]

Under normal conditions, the psychological forces
which are channeled through the social character cement
the social structure. But under abnormal conditions what
was once cement becomes dynamite. This happens when
changing economic conditions produce situations in which
the traditional character traits are no longer useful and may
be actual handicaps. Fromm made this notion of character
lag the key concept in his analysis of the rise of fascism in

Germany. He traced the process by which the traditional middle class virtues of frugality, industry, prudence, and obedience became irrelevant or of limited utility in the rising new industrial and business system, so that only a minority of the sons of the middle class could successfully use their character traits in their economic pursuits. The lag between economic and psychological evolution caused the psychological forces to become unfastened from the economic structure and made available for deployment in the political and military spheres. Only now, the old virtues, freed from all restrictions and energized by insecurity, frustration, and resentment, were transformed into the vicious energies which powered the German effort in World War II.

This completes the basic theory of the formation and function of character. On this foundation, Fromm builds a typology of character styles which will be presented in a moment. First, a few comments on the theory as developed to this point.

Fromm's theory of character formation is an excellent instrument of description and analysis. This part of his work represents one of the most successful of all attempts to bridge different levels of analysis and combine different styles of approach to social problems. Fromm achieves far more than a psychosocial parallelism. He shows that individual psychological experiences and social events do not just form two parallel cause and effect series. Rather, the series converge and interpenetrate, so that an understanding of individual problems and tensions requires an understanding of social problems and tensions, and vice versa. In this sense, *Escape from Freedom*, which was based upon the concept of character formation which has been briefly set forth here, is one of the finest examples in modern

social science of what C. Wright Mills calls "the sociological imagination." [16]

The second comment is in the nature of a question.
Is it as easy as Fromm thinks to assert that "differences in
temperament have no ethical significance"? Fromm is right
when he says that ideas, values, and actions have an emotional context and that they take their meaning from this
context. Part of the context is provided by temperament.
Hence it follows that love, say, will mean quite different
things to the choleric and the melancholic man. What is
even more troublesome is that it is doubtful whether spontaneity, which in Fromm's view is the mark of the full life,
can have any meaning at all to the phlegmatic man, who
by definition is . . . phlegmatic.

Temperamental differences can have another kind of
ethical significance, the nature and importance of which
are suggested by the close attention which such great political thinkers as Plato and Machiavelli gave to the question
of the *whole personality* of the ruler. The four temperaments differ in the ease, speed, and strength of their reactions to events. Assume a situation in which prompt and
vigorous action is required to stop an injustice, or forestall
a social catastrophe, or exploit a fleeting opportunity. To
have a phlegmatic man in charge of affairs in that situation
could be disastrous. He might be unmoved by the injustice
or unimpressed by the emergency until it was too late. This
is not a far-fetched example. Fromm at one point suggests
that German labor, despite its socialist and libertarian convictions, failed to act at the critical moment of Hitler's
advent to power because of the prevalence of authoritarian
character traits among the workers. Apart from other considerations, such as bureaucratic leadership and a conservative, rigid trade union organization, Fromm's analysis
does not persuade one that the phlegmatic temperament

of the German workers had nothing to do with the failure to act. Other examples could be provided, but one ought to be enough to show that temperamental differences can have moral significance.[17]

Turning to the scientific side of the theory, two comments should be made. The first again takes the form of a question. How strictly should one construe Fromm's formulation of the relations between the conditions of work and the formation of character? Read strictly, Fromm would seem to be saying that one's mode of work determines his character. To demonstrate that thesis would take far more, and far more systematic, knowledge concerning class differences than we now have. To be sure, there is a great amount of information available on differences of attitudes and opinions among the classes, but such differences are not the same as characterological differences. Also, nearly all the work that has been done on class-correlated characterological differences (*e.g.*, the work on the authoritarian personality) suffers from enough methodological weakness to make its interpretation a delicate and tricky matter. Furthermore, in a society such as the United States where social mobility is high, lines between the classes hazy, and the voice of the mass media so penetrating, really sharp characterological, or even opinion, differences among the classes are already hard to find and seem destined to diminish. Those who were once called the working classes have become the blue collar employees, and their collars get a little whiter each year. It is already hard to tell the classes apart in the daytime; and in the evening in suburbia they are practically indistinguishable.

If one construes Fromm's hypothesis strictly, he encounters hard problems of evidence. On the other hand, a loose or generous reading of the hypothesis would cause serious trouble in another part of his work. As will be pointed out later, Fromm's constitution for the sane society revolves around changes in men's relations to work and the instruments of production. Through changes in the organization of work he hopes to effect basic changes in the character of men. His scheme of social change, then, demands a strict construction of his hypothesis about the relations between character and work. This hypothesis seems to be one of the areas of Fromm's system which needs elaboration and clarification.

The final comment I shall make at this point concerns a certain inconsistency in Fromm's analysis of the relations between society and character and a certain vagueness about the source of the power which produces decisive social change. On the one hand, he offers the concept of character lag to account for tensions—even revolutionary tensions—in a social order: when economic development and social character are out of phase, the psychological forces which once cemented the social structure become transmuted into dynamite which can blow it apart. On the other hand, he gives us the concept of inherent psychic needs to account for tensions: when a society fails to afford productive satisfaction of the basic needs, men will react against that society and reform or overthrow it. These two explanations can lead in very different directions.

Escape from Freedom revolves around the concepts of social character and the character lag. Time and again the argument returns to the central thesis: economic changes resulted in an ever widening gap between economic reality and the social characters of the classes, with the result that the psychological forces were finally unfastened from the old social structure and made deployable for revolutionary adventures. Assume that instead of anchoring his analysis on the notions of social character and character lag, Fromm had used the concept of the basic needs. Then the fundamental thesis might have read somewhat like the following: as a consequence of certain economic and social conditions, the basic human need for transcendence was fulfilled destructively rather than creatively. Now, whatever else Fromm might say about fascism, he surely would not say it was progressive, in the sense that it was dedicated to the fuller productive satisfaction of the five basic psychic needs. Yet that is the conclusion toward which the concept of the basic needs would push him. The heart of that concept is Fromm's conviction that men strive for an ever higher and more productive fulfillment of the basic needs. Fromm asserts that history is progressive and irreversible. It might be possible for some persons still to believe, as many Communists did before the invasion of the Soviet Union, that the fascist era was a necessary step forward on the road to the final victory of humanism and the sane society, but I fear that another such step would undo us all.

The ambiguity in Fromm's thought concerning the source of the power which propels social change can be shown in another way. In *Escape from Freedom* he seems to argue that the energy which produces social change is generated by the tension between new economic conditions and an older social character structure. In *Man for Himself* and *The Sane Society* he maintains that the need for transcendence is what drives man to seek ever better solutions to the problems of his existence. The former thesis puts the source of change precisely where Marx put it—in the forces of production, not in a postulated need for transcendence. But if Fromm accepts this Marxist view, he unfortunately also loses its greatest benefit, which is the belief in the reality and inevitability of progress in history. There is a curious paradox here. Fromm's notion of the character lag, with its basically Marxist orientation, denies him the grand Marxist faith in the inevitable development toward ever higher forms of civilization. On the other hand, the notion of the five basic needs, with its thoroughly un-Marxist essentialist psychology, permits him to believe in the progressive character of social change. I leave this precisely where Fromm leaves it—in a woefully paradoxical condition.

When paradoxes are examined closely they have a way of dissolving into apparent paradoxes, or perhaps into mere tensions. So it is here; and this time I want to use the occasion to remind the reader of one of the general features of Fromm's work. The style of argument followed in the immediately foregoing paragraphs can be employed at point after point in Fromm's system because, as was indicated in the Prologue, the system itself contains a number of contradictory principles and concepts. The particular incompatibles here are social determinism versus an essentialist psychology. Others will appear in later pages.

Types of Men

The second half of the theory of character is the characterology. Fromm technically defines character as the "form in which human energy is canalized in the process of assimilation and socialization." The names he gives to the different types of character are those which describe the processes of assimilation, but it is important to remember that each character type includes orientations of both assimilation and socialization. To assure clarity on this point, I shall present in modified form a chart which Fromm uses to show how each character type is a blend of orientations in both spheres.

Two preliminary comments. First, the characterology is at once descriptive and normative. All the nonproductive orientations are ethically imperfect types. Each represents a specific thwarting and crippling of man's powers. The nonproductive orientations are analogous to Freud's neurotic character types. The productive orientation is the one which expresses the full unfolding of the human powers. Productive man is the good man, the counterpart of Freud's genital man.

The second comment is that Fromm's types are ideal constructions, not photographic copies of real men. Every real man is of course a mixture of several orientations, and he is assigned to one or another of the ideal types in accordance with the orientation that is dominant in the mixture.

Let us turn now to the characters themselves.[18]

Character Types [19]

ASSIMILATION	SOCIALIZATION
I. Nonproductive orientations	
A. Receptive (Accepting)	Masochistic ⎫
	⎬ Symbiosis
B. Exploitative (Taking)	Sadistic ⎭
C. Hoarding (Preserving)	Destructive ⎫
	⎬ Withdrawal
D. Marketing (Exchanging)	Automaton conformity ⎭
II. Productive orientation	
Working	Loving

The first of the nonproductive orientations is the receptive man. His distinguishing feature is a large and open mouth, for he is the ever expectant one, the eternal suckler, the one who locates the source of all good outside himself. Receptive man does not create, he consumes. He relies not on himself but on the "magic helper" for the satisfaction of his needs. By and large, he is an optimistic, friendly sort of chap, with little malice or suspicion toward his fellows.

He enjoys helping others and is loyal to his many friends, but in all his generous acts there is a taint; he really desires to secure the favor of the helped one in order to put him in his debt. For receptive man, loving means being loved. Left to himself, he is paralyzed, for he draws his sustenance from others. His anxiety is that his source of supply will be cut off.

Like receptive man, exploitative man also feels that the source of good is outside himself, but unlike receptive man, he does not look for gifts. He takes what he wants by force or guile. For him, everything and everyone is an object to be exploited, an object to be bitten off and ingested. Exploitative man is the man of the biting mouth and the clenched teeth. When he is fed up, when he has taken what he wants from the outside, he discards the rest. Exploitative man is suspicious, critical, envious. But like receptive man he is nothing without the others, for whatever he has he has stolen from them.

Next on display is the hoarder, the one whose arms are folded tightly across his chest, forming a forbidding barrier between himself and the world outside. Hoarding man relates to the world neither by receiving nor by grasping. He has little faith in anything outside and is concerned to save what is in himself. He is the miser. He hoards and saves. Spending and giving are uncongenial to him for he hates to let anything escape his grip. His psychic economy is one of scarcity. From his point of view, the whole world is determined to take from him the things that are properly and personally his, and he is just as determined to dig a moat which the others cannot cross to penetrate the fortress which is himself. His motto is "mine is mine and yours is yours." [20] For this man, loving means possessing, not sharing or creating. He admires order, strict justice, security, cleanliness.

Next is the marketing man, the man of the friendly

smile and the casual but correct attire. This one is for sale. He must give constant attention to the fashion of the moment in ideas, values, and tastes, for his own value is determined by how well he meets the demands of the personality market. Marketing man has no real self. His "self" is a sort of echo box, a hollow receptacle which collects and magnifies the things which others say about him. He learns about himself, as it were, only by rumor. If you catch this man in an unguarded moment you will see his smile twist into fear and worry, for of all men he is the most insecure. He knows how fickle the personality market is. Marketing man also judges others as commodities. For him, a man is worth what he brings on the market. Success is the sovereign criterion, and success means the approval of the others. This man is terribly afraid of being "peculiar," out of fashion. His relations with his fellows, while friendly and fair, are always superficial. He manipulates and is manipulated. The superficiality of his relationships has led him to put a desperate faith in finding a real union in romantic love, but "it is an illusion to expect that the loneliness of man rooted in the marketing orientation can be cured by individual love." [21] Marketing man lives on the edge of despair, and he fills the emptiness of his life by trivial busyness and movement. Meanwhile, as he waits for the Big Opportunity, he looks more and more like Willy Loman.

This completes the somber collection of the nonproductives. Fromm adds that one or another of the types predominates in a given historical period in accordance with the economic structure and social relations of the era. Thus the receptive orientation is typically found in societies where the authority of one group over another is firmly established. Since the subordinate groups cannot shape affairs and direct their own destinies, they look up to the masters as the providers, as those from whom all blessings flow. The exploitative character, with its motto "I take what I want," goes back to piratical and feudal origins and reached its highest development in the imperialistic and rapacious capitalism of the nineteenth century. In those days, the great exploiters roamed the earth in search of power and profit. Supporting them were the hoarders, the methodical, industrious, sanctimonious middle classes, to whom property was security and thrift the highest virtue. Marketing man is distinctly the man of our day, the authentic product of the mass market society. He is accompanied by growing numbers of receptive types, who have come to expect society to gratify their every felt need and wish.

The characterology does not stop with description and criticism but accepts the perilous task of construction. "In discussing the *productive character* I venture beyond critical analysis and inquire into the nature of the fully developed character that is the aim of human development and simultaneously the ideal of humanistic ethics." [22] Coming from a man of our day, that is a bold proposal; a proposal, we cannot help but feel, that only an innocent could make. Our age is not kind to visionaries and projectors. And when he deals with productive man Fromm explicitly adopts the vocation of the visionary, for productive man has yet to be born. He lives only in Fromm's imagination.

The fact is, Fromm stands almost alone among today's writers in this effort to paint in detail the portrait of the good man. To my knowledge, Freud is the only other recent writer who has built both a penetrating theory of character and an image of the good man. His clinical descriptions of the pregenital character types are thorough and brilliant, and this judgment stands even if one agrees with Fromm that his theoretical concepts are in need of revision. Freud's portrait of the genital character, however, is unfortunately vague and shadowy, lacking the precision of his portraits of the pregenital types. In technical terms, the genital man is one in whom oral and anal libido have been subordinated to genital sexuality, the aim of which is sexual union with a person of the opposite sex. It is not easy to say much more about him. At most, genital man might be described as the man who has come to terms with himself and who recognizes that the inner life must always be a life of conflict. This conflict, however, can be tempered by self-knowledge and curbed by reason. It can be lived with. Genital man can spare enough energies from the inner battle to function capably in the public sphere. Freed from extravagant hopes and false fears, genital man knows that something of value can still be found in this life. While rather vague, this is surely not an unheroic ethic.*

In an important way, productive man is the equivalent of genital man. If we think of Freud's term symbolically rather than literally, genital man is the one who produces new life through union with another person. Productive man also produces through union. The great difference be-

---

* Philip Rieff's recent exploration of Freud's thought leaves me uncertain of the accuracy of my sketch of genital man. In his last chapter, Rieff outlines that new character type known as psychological man, who is replacing political man, religious man, and economic man as the character ideal of Western civilization. I am unclear whether Rieff's intention here is to expound Freud or to describe the impact of Freud on the modern mind. In either case, psychological man does not look much like my brief description of genital man. Psychological man is the trained egotist, the connoisseur of the inner life. He lives beyond reason and conscience. He has given up the public sphere. He has relinquished all hope of salvation for himself and others, in this world as well as the next. He accepts the hospital as the permanent home of man. Rieff's final sentences seem to suggest that this sickness is health. "Aware at last that he is chronically ill, psychological man may nevertheless end the ancient quest of his predecessors for a healing doctrine. His experience with the latest one, Freud's, may finally teach him that every cure must expose him to new illness." Philip Rieff, *Freud: The Mind of the Moralist* (New York: Viking, 1959), p. 357. Carved above the portals of that gigantic hospital which shelters all Rieff's psychological men is this emblem: "Abandon hope, all ye who enter here."

tween the two is that productive man persists in Christian man's praise of faith, hope, and love. So productive man is not a new type on the earth, but the realization of a very old type. He speaks in modern accents, however, and this makes a difference.

"Productiveness" is the term that counts here, and to avert misunderstanding, I shall repeat one of Fromm's fullest definitions of it.

> Productiveness is man's ability to use his powers and to realize the potentialities inherent in him. If we say *he* must use *his* powers we imply that he must be free and not dependent on someone who controls his powers. We imply, furthermore, that he is guided by reason, since he can make use of his powers only if he knows what they are, how to use them, and what to use them for. Productiveness means that he experiences himself as the embodiment of his powers and as the "actor"; that he feels himself one with his powers and at the same time that they are not masked and alienated from him.[23]

Productive man can be known by his works, for he is the doer, the builder, the creator. The artist is "the most convincing representative of productiveness," [24] but do not be discouraged if you cannot paint great pictures or compose great symphonies. To do those things requires gifts which few have, while to be productive requires only a set of attitudes which all may have. Fromm saves us all by saying that productive man's noblest product is himself. He lives to live, that is, to actualize his potentialities: *"by far the most important object of productiveness is man himself."* [25]

Productive man's guide on the journey of self-realization is his conscience. A word must be underscored: *his* conscience. Fromm believes there is a true or humanistic and a false or authoritarian conscience. "The authoritarian conscience is the voice of an internalized external authority, the parents, the state, or whoever the authorities in a culture happen to be." [26] This is the equivalent of the superego, and Fromm agrees with Freud that it is a hard master. It governs by fear of punishment and hope for reward. Guilt is its harsh sanction and approval its dubious reward. Its most cruel and subtle weapon is repression, by which the victim unknowingly turns his fears and desires back upon himself, until they consume his finest powers and leave him pale and drawn. He grows deaf to his own inner voice, so cut off from the truth about himself that his whole life becomes a sterile hypocrisy. Worst of all, the authoritarian conscience conquers its victims while they are still too young to resist. For his unavoidable transgressions the child receives not mild correction and loving forgiveness but a conditional pardon, which makes his guilt and his need for forgiveness all the stronger. Thus the will is paralyzed and the powers sapped. The prisoner of the authoritarian conscience serves a life sentence, confined by his own desire to gain the pardon of the authorities. It may happen that the commands of the authoritarian conscience are also "good." Then, of course, the subject will move toward the good. But what matters is that the authoritarian conscience imposes its commands in the interests of the authority rather than those of the subject, so that any similarity between the dictates of the authoritarian conscience and the true good is purely accidental.*

* It is strictly correct to say that in Fromm's view any similarity between the dictates of the authoritarian conscience and the true good is purely accidental. But the tenor of his work suggests that lean accuracy is not enough here. In a very real sense, Fromm goes beyond the view that might and right may accidentally correspond, to the view that might is always wrong. The dictates of authority are wrong even when they may be good for the subject, because the authority always has his own interests foremost in mind. The interests of the subject are secondary. This violates the canon that no man should be treated as a means. It also violates Fromm's canon that

Fromm believes that "this is only one form of conscience or, possibly, a preliminary stage in the development
of conscience." [27] Another and truer conscience also calls to
each of us, if we will but listen for it. "Humanistic conscience
is the reaction of our total personality to its proper functioning or dysfunctioning. . . . Conscience judges our functioning as human beings; it is (as the root of the word *con-
scientia* indicates) *knowledge within oneself*, knowledge of
our respective success or failure in the art of living." [28] So
emphatic is Fromm's advocacy of this notion that I must
quote extensively from his fullest formulation of it.

> Actions, thoughts, and feelings which are conducive to
> the proper functioning and unfolding of our total
> personality produce a feeling of inner approval, of
> "rightness," characteristic of the humanistic "good"
> conscience. . . . *Conscience is thus a re-action of our-
> selves to ourselves.* It is the voice of our true selves which
> summons us back to ourselves, to live productively, to
> develop fully and harmoniously—that is, *to become
> what we potentially are.* It is the guardian of our in-
> tegrity. . . . If love can be defined as the affirmation
> of the potentialities and the care for, and the respect of,
> the uniqueness of the loved person, humanistic con-
> science can be justly called the voice of *our loving care
> for ourselves.*[29]

Productive man breaks out of the circle of loneliness
through love, which is the only way one can unite with
others and still retain his and their uniqueness. Love is a

---

we ought to love and care for others as for ourselves. In addition, submission
to authority is also always wrong, because any act of submission means a
crippling of one's human powers. Fromm's view on this comes close to saying that might is always wrong, that there can be no right in an authoritarian-
inegalitarian relationship between two men. Where there is a superior-
inferior relationship there is evil.

feeling made up of care, responsibility, respect, and knowledge. Love for self comes first, for without that no man can love another, but self-love by no means excludes love of others. "On the contrary, an attitude of love toward themselves will be found in all those who are capable of loving others." [30] In Fromm's view, the injunction "love thy neighbor as thyself" is no stern command against selfishness. It is, rather, the only real meaning of love and the attainment of any man who has affirmed his own life. "Love of one person implies love of man as such." [31] A mere *égoïsme à deux*, or a primary love for one's family, say, is not authentic love but its caricature. Whoever loves, loves all mankind.

Like all other men, productive man has faith. He has religion too. Productive man's faith is a "certainty of conviction based on one's experience of thought and feeling, not assent to propositions on credit of the proposer." [32] His religion, by whatever name he calls it, is in content humanistic; that is, it is a religion which furthers his powers and develops his capacities. Insofar as his creed is theistic, God is not a symbol of power over man but a symbol of man's own finest powers. Insofar as his religion is productive and humanistic, it will have the following articles, which, Fromm says, express the core of ideas and attitudes common to all the great spiritual teachers from Lao-tse to— Fromm?

> Man must strive to recognize the truth and can be fully human only to the extent to which he succeeds in this task. He must be independent and free. . . . He must relate himself to his fellow men lovingly. If he has no love, he is an empty shell even if his were all power, wealth, and intelligence. Man must know the difference between good and evil, he must learn to listen to the voice of his conscience and to be able to follow it.[33]

That is the message of humanistic religion, the message at the heart of the inspirations of the great spiritual teachers. All religions are at bottom one, and poor mankind would never have lost sight of this truth had not subtle metaphysicians, vested authorities, and the superficial differences of time and place conspired to conceal it. Again Fromm speaks in the authentic accents of Rousseau. "As soon as the nations took to making God speak, every one made him speak in his own fashion, and made him say what he himself wanted. Had they listened only to what God says in the heart of man, there would have been but one religion upon earth." [34]

Productive Man Re-examined

So rare are portraits of the good man in our time that each deserves a careful examination. For this reason, and not because of its inherent excellence or its superiority over the portraits of the nonproductive types, I shall look with some care at Fromm's model of the productive man.

He is a smiling figure, and the smile tells us at once that here is a man who has affirmed life. He is able to think for himself and he can enjoy the sensuous pleasures without guilt and anxiety. He enjoys and respects his fellows and does not regard their lives as instruments to the advancement of his own. All these amiable traits make him quite pleasant and attractive. He is no hero, certainly, but he does seem a sane and competent fellow; and if he never does anything heroic, neither will he do much that is vicious. He is decent, responsible, and generous, the sort of chap who would fit comfortably into any fairly liberal circle. There is that troublesome little thing about becoming like God, to be sure, but one feels confident that productive man would never commit any of the more desperate sins of pride, just as he would never lose his head in any passion or for any cause. He is not angular and tense, given to extreme actions. On the contrary, he is well-rounded, buoyant, sympathetic, at peace with himself and his brothers.

That is one's first impression. A second look brings a disturbing discovery: the face of productive man is empty. It lacks character.

What passions, what conquests and defeats, what joys and sorrows have etched their lines on his face? What does productive man live for? Fromm answers that he lives for himself, he lives for living. It is not easy to understand what that statement means. Does it mean that productive man is at bottom the sensualist? In a certain sense, yes. Productive man is a sort of prudent sensualist. He wants to experience as much as he can—within certain limits of safety. He has no taste for extreme experiences as such, and there is no danger that he will consume himself in any Verlainean explorations of the bizarre and the grotesque. Although open and sensitive to experience, like a delicate hi-fi, he is not quite preoccupied with the gadget of the self. He knows instinctively that when one conceives of the self primarily as a marvelous receiving instrument, he inevitably experiments with ways of increasing the current to the set, thinking in that way to heighten its fidelity. He may get only noise. I suspect that is what Itchy Dave, that new anti-hero of the Beat, got when he "turned on":

> Sometimes it is a heightened sense of self that is sought [through the use of marijuana]. . . . As Itchy Dave Gelden expresses it, "It's like this, man, we need more awareness of the I. It's like, before I light up I'm drug with the ten thousand things . . . you can't concentrate," but when you light up you can "follow the song of yourself. You're listening and you're hearing the song and you're swinging along with it." ". . . I never really

heard the music till I started listening with pot," is something you hear often in beat circles. "It's like switching from an old-fashioned phonograph to hi-fi." [35]

Itchy Dave is not totally unlike productive man, in this as in other ways. Both live for living; or, at least, both seem unwilling or unable to formulate a meaning for life beyond the living of it. Both also seek to open the self to a whole range of deliciously novel experiences. Both share the ethic of spontaneity and productiveness, and give not a damn for the world's judgment of their products. Both are resolutely dedicated to developing the potentialities of their selves. With Rousseau, both could say "I may not be better than any other man, but at least I am different."

The foregoing sentences, I know, have serious connotations. Is productive man really a Beatnik in disguise? Is Fromm really the philosopher of the Beat, when all along he has seemed to be saying something else? About the first question, one can say at least that, while productive man might not quite be a Beatnik, he would certainly be at home among them. About the second question, I can say that my own modest researches among the Beatniks convince me that Fromm is read and admired by them, though he certainly is not their foremost hero.

But this is a theme which could lead us far afield. At the moment, I am concerned to make only one point about the injunction "live for living." To say that productive man lives for living is to say something that is wrong on its face. Truly productive men do not live for living. They live for ends, for purposes outside themselves. This man lives for his work, that one for his family, and the one over there for his god. The greatest, the freest, the most creative men live in obedience to some unfulfilled, perhaps only vaguely understood, purpose. A life without some purpose larger than its own cultivation is a life without direction and meaning, for a man realizes himself through working toward his ends. To make "live for living" the categorical imperative is to counsel man to emptiness. It is to counsel him either to a vulgar Epicureanism or to a kind of moral dilettantism.

The previous sentence is not quite correct. It needs a qualifying phrase. The imperative "live for living" is an invitation "to a vulgar Epicureanism or to a kind of moral dilettantism" *under the modern conditions of economic abundance and the prevalence of the marketing orientation.* This phrase suggests both that "live for living" may mean different things under different social circumstances, and that it may have a broader import which has not yet been examined. The first needs no argument or illustration: moral imperatives are colored by their social contexts. The second needs a fuller discussion, which can be best opened by examining the imperative under the light of another of Fromm's favorite concepts, the concept of "life as an art." This formula, which at first glance seems only an evocative phrase, even if not a new one, has an importance in Fromm's thought which is more than rhetorical.

The attitude toward life which is implicit in the notion of life as an art is one which a moralist can maintain only by denying his own vocation, for it is an attitude which assumes that the canons of one field, esthetics, can be applied in another field, ethics. This is an assumption which no moral philosopher can grant—unless the intention of his teaching is moral anarchy. Ethics and esthetics are different subjects, each with its own canons. When the canons of either field are promiscuously applied in the other, grievous confusion must result. When the perspectives of esthetics are substituted for those of ethics in the judgment of the quality of human life, the necessary result is something that verges on moral anarchism. It is easy to see how that happens.

The ways of art—both its methods and its ends—are diverse and numerous, perhaps infinite. The artist is a creator, and the stuff of which he creates his world of art comes only in part from the external world. The rest comes from the secret depths of his own being. From these materials he fashions a world which is governed by its own laws, which he also creates. What is lawful in his artistic world may not be lawful in the real world, and vice versa; just as what is true in his artistic world need be true only there, and not in the real world. This means that esthetic criticism must start from the premise that the only question which may legitimately be asked of a work of art is, did the artist succeed in doing what he set out to do? The success or failure of a work of art can properly be measured only by the standard of how well the artist used the means he chose for his task and how closely he came to the end he set for himself. The question of whether the end chosen is a good or a bad one is beyond the province of esthetics. Since the artist is God in his own world, he enjoys an enormous latitude in the choice of ends and means, a latitude far greater than that permitted to the moralist. The point that matters here can be summarized in the following form: the chief canon of esthetic criticism is that there is no such thing as *the* good work of art; the chief canon of moral criticism is that there is such a thing as *the* good life.

Now, to see life as an art is to see it within an esthetic framework. This is an attitude toward life which has relinquished every hope that life might have a purpose fixed in the nature of things, an end and meaning outside itself toward which it ought to be directed, and by which it may be judged. When life is seen within this esthetic frame-work, each individual is permitted complete freedom in his choice of means and ends. The only question that may properly be asked is how well did the individual do what he set out to do. The question of whether the end chosen was good or bad is foreign to the esthetic perspective. There can be many ends—in principle, as many ends as there are individuals—but from the point of view of life as an art there is no such thing as *the* end, no *summum bonum*. There are only good lives and bad ones; and the question of whether a particular person's life was a good or a bad one can be answered only by the data and the criteria *internal to that life*. In short, to conceive of life as an art is to accept a latitudinarianism in the choice of the means and ends of living which is indistinguishable from moral anarchism.

This, I think, is the necessary tendency of Fromm's esthetic orientation toward moral questions. I am quite aware that this is not apparent on the surface of his thought; and the reason it is not is clear enough: he has not thought through the implications of the esthetic position. In fact, he has concealed these implications under a superficially attractive picture of the good man who would emerge from such an orientation toward life. Here Fromm does what almost all the writers who have adopted this idea of life as an art have done. The few writers who have seriously at-tempted this theme have been restrained by their own train-ing and their inherited decency to create and treat in their art only decorous and decent men—men like themselves. (Henry James is an excellent example of this.) Such writers rarely treat of the "terrible ones." But this is a limitation imposed by the artist's temperament and training, not by the concept of life as an art. From the esthetic point of view, there are no good or bad men in a moral sense. There are only good or bad men in an artistic sense. Artistically, Hamlet is no greater and no better than Macbeth; Iago is as good as Othello. And, if life is an art, then Caligula was as good as Aurelius, Savonarola as good as St. Francis, Hitler as good as Roosevelt, for all these men worked consummately with the means at their disposal and all in a large degree realized their capacities and achieved the ends they had set for themselves.

It is only at this point that some of the larger implications of Fromm's well-known idea of "positive freedom" become apparent. In *Escape from Freedom*, he developed the distinction between negative and positive freedom, or freedom from and freedom to. Modern man has won the former, Fromm argued, but the victory has turned to ashes because he has not won the latter. Negative freedom has left men isolated, anxious, powerless, eager to escape into new submissions. Salvation lies in adding positive freedom to negative freedom. "To know how to free oneself is nothing," Gide wrote in *L'Immoraliste*, "the arduous thing is to know what to do with one's freedom." "What to do with one's freedom"—that is the precise question which the moral and political philosopher, or any man whose vocation is the cure of souls, must be able to answer. When Fromm says that positive freedom means "the realization of [the] individual self; that is, the expression of [one's] intellectual, emotional and sensuous potentialities," [36] he provides no substantive answer to the question of freedom for what. He supplies only the form and not the content of an answer. In a very real sense, Fromm is a moralist without a conception of the moral life.

Fromm worships Eros; and for the followers of Eros the meaning of life is sensation—fuller, closer, warmer feeling—not for the sake of some end, but for the sake of the sensation of living itself. This is a view of life as a voluptu-

ous Strauss waltz, or a kind of Balinese love play, an un-
dulating surge and counter-surge of emotions and energies
which never break outward in one direction, but remain in
a ravishing equilibrium: stimulation without climax. In its
slightly tarnished innocence, this idea, it seems to me, is
deeply expressive of a specifically American sentimentality
about man and life. No other of Fromm's ideas shows more
clearly the triumph of America over the Marxist and Freudian elements of his thought. We cannot be sure what
answer the modern age will finally give to the question of
freedom for what—beyond the freedom to enjoy more of
the pleasures of consumption—but we can be sure that when
the answer comes it must contain more than a hollow "live
for living."

The imperative "live for living," furthermore, is incompatible with one of the finest of Fromm's own conceptions, the conception of a "negative psychology," a psychology which aims not to force the secret of man by a full
and positive knowledge of man's soul, but to remove the
distortions and illusions which keep each of us from knowing himself and others. The internalized voices of the others,
the cares and habits of the daily round, and all the forgotten
pains and sorrows build layer upon layer of sedimentary
materials over the bedrock of the psychic life. The authentic
self, the I which underlies the countless things one does
and means and says each day, can in time become entirely
buried. Each day we see men who are totally guided by
what they think they ought to be, and we know that such
men are nothing more than the demands of others. A man's
greatest despair, as Kierkegaard said, is "choosing to be
another than himself." So the most serious search of one's
life is the search for the self he really is. The important
point, however, is that this search is done negatively; it is a
work of stripping away the things that one is not. In this

process one comes closer to knowing who he is, but he does so by finding out who he is not. That is a very different matter from Fromm's positive formulation of the productive man's creation of himself.

The task of stripping away the sedimentary layers is the first and the hardest duty of the man who would find himself. In this work he begins to discover what he is not. He also begins to realize that he is much more than he had known, and he begins to accept that "much more" as belonging to him. He begins to explore hitherto unknown reaches of his psyche, and he learns to respect its infinite depths. Such a man knows that the command to realize his potentiality is foolish, for he is a being of infinite potentialities, only some of which he can realize, often at the pain of thwarting others. In a brief essay, Carl Rogers, who appears to share Fromm's basic perspectives on the nature of man and the method of approaching him, has given a good account of the kind of person one becomes as a result of this process.[37] The person becomes more open to experience, both of himself and of the world around him. At the same time he becomes more realistic and discriminating. He can tolerate ambiguity and variety because he has developed an internal locus of evaluation which rests upon a trust in his own organism as a suitable instrument for choosing the best behavior in changing situations. Purified of distortions and illusions, the person knows he is a process rather than a product, and he accepts this, rather than the achievement of some fixed and final state, as the necessary condition of man. In short, a self begins to come to life. But what matters is that the process of birth is primarily negative, a matter not of trying to create oneself but of trying to rid oneself of what he is not.

I hope I shall not be misunderstood on this. In the

previous chapter I tried to show that there are severe defects in Fromm's essentialist psychology. In particular, I argued that his explanation of evil and destructiveness as the results of thwarted primary urges toward love and creativeness is not convincing. On this topic, Fromm's thought expresses, albeit in a different vocabulary, something like the frustration-aggression hypothesis of early stimulus-response psychology, and suffers from about the same defects. Another way to put this point would be to say that Fromm has no real appreciation of the concept of sublimation; or, at least, the idea plays no important part in his thought. In the immediately foregoing passages I argued that the injunction "live for living" and the conception of productive man producing himself are also unconvincing. But nothing in the previous chapter and the foregoing passages should be taken as a denial of something that everyday observation confirms: there are men who have a powerful drive toward a certain goal, or who have a compelling urge to test some capacity of their nature. Such capacities must be realized, or at least tested, or else life is indeed diminished. In this sense, there are life-demands which are peculiar to one's nature and which must be expressed: as Milton put it, there are talents which it is "death to hide." If such talents are thwarted, the personality may be arrested and life may go bitter and dry. Destructiveness may result. On the other hand, the person who is blocked in one sector of his life may divert the blocked energies into magnificent creativity in another sector. Or, the one who has seen his powers crippled may develop a loving sympathy for the other crippled ones around him and may strive to ease their pains and smooth their paths. There are, I think, no general rules here, certainly none so general as Fromm's "destructiveness is the outcome of unlived life." Nor are there any so general as to give us confidence that his "live for living" provides a useful ethical guide for the living of a life. That is as far as the foregoing passages are meant to go.

What has been said thus far suffers from a certain distortion, which must now be corrected. My critique of productive man is based not on the man Fromm has in mind but on the man who would naturally emerge from the moral premises he lays down. Fromm's emphasis on life as its own end is to be explained by his hatred of authoritarianism, which posits an end outside of and imposed on man. The motive power here is repulsion from, not attraction toward. What drives Fromm to the position that life is its own end is not so much the attractive power of the "live for living" idea, as the repulsive power of the authoritarian idea. But in backing away from authoritarianism, with its imposed and alien ends, Fromm stumbles into a formulation which leaves man no ends at all. I have argued that the implications of this conception are shabby, but I have not argued that he accepts them, only that they are inherent in his own premises. This means that Fromm can be criticized for failing to find a good solution to the question of what ends a man should live for, but he can not be criticized for consciously recommending a shabby solution.

The conception of productive man as his own chief product would be less troublesome if one were more confident of the existence and the nature of what Fromm calls the humanistic conscience. Fromm seems to agree with Rousseau that "there is . . . at the bottom of our hearts an innate principle of justice and virtue, by which, in spite of our maxims, we judge our own actions or those of others to be good or evil; and it is this principle that I call conscience." [38] Fromm speaks of this innate principle almost as though it were a faculty or sense in the meaning of

Jefferson: "This sense is as much a part of [man's] nature, as the sense of hearing, seeing, feeling; it is the true foundation of morality. . . . The moral sense, or conscience, is as much a part of man as his leg or arm. It is given to all human beings in a stronger or weaker degree, as force of members is given them in a greater or less degree. It may be strengthened by exercise, as may any particular limb of the body." [39]

This makes Fromm's usage understandable, if not acceptable. In this sense, the creation of oneself is a sort of psychic exercise. The athlete of the productive life trains himself to understand the voices from within and to follow their directions. Creation of oneself is, strictly, a process of discovery. One brings to life what is already there: it is analogous to the Platonic *anamnesis*. This usage is consistent with Fromm's essentialist conception of the self and his teleological metaphysic. Unfortunately, the conception of the moral sense is a postulate of reason and not an idea of experience. It is an attempt to "explain" certain phenomena by positing an underlying psychic force or agency which brings them into being and gives them meaning.

Perhaps Fromm does not mean to postulate a moral faculty in Jefferson's sense. What then might he mean? If by the distinction between the authoritarian and the humanistic conscience he means only to distinguish between ethical norms which are good for man and those which are not, then we must permit him to stipulate meanings as he wishes, although the stipulation may not strike us as a particularly useful one. But Fromm also says that the content of norms in the authoritarian and humanistic consciences may be the same, with the difference being that in the first case one obeys the norms out of fear of an external authority while in the second case he obeys out of respect for himself. At this point meanings again become clouded, for it is doubtful whether Fromm can show a consistent ethical superiority in actions undertaken in response to some moral code absorbed in the process of socialization. Furthermore, it is probably impossible to tell just when an individual obeys himself and just when he only seems to obey himself, while actually obeying an internalized command of his group or authority. For Fromm, with his tension between essential human nature and social determinism, this is probably an insoluble problem. At least, it is for him a far harder problem than it ever could be either for a thoroughgoing individualist like Freud or for a thoroughgoing social determinist like Dewey. To use the language of social science, Fromm does not seem to take into account the work that has been done in reference group theory. To use an older language, he fails to come to grips with Pascal's maxim that "custom is our nature."

It is clear, also, that Fromm wants to make something more than a subjective or nominal distinction between the authoritarian and the humanistic consciences. He believes that movement toward the humanistic conscience is inherent in the moral evolution of the race. The authoritarian stage may have been a necessary step toward the creation of the humanistic conscience, but what matters is that moral evolution progresses inevitably toward the full flowering of the humanistic conscience. Fromm even suggests that, after a certain point, we can leap intermediate stages and go directly to the highest stage:

> Julian Huxley has pointed out that acquisition of an authoritarian conscience was a stage in the process of human evolution necessary before rationality and freedom had developed to an extent which made humanistic conscience possible; others have stated this same idea with regard to the development of the child. While Huxley is right in his historical analysis, I do not be-

lieve that with regard to the child, in a nonauthoritarian society, the authoritarian conscience has to exist as a precondition for the formation of humanistic conscience; but only the future development of mankind can prove or disprove the validity of this assumption.[40]

Athens and Sparta existed side by side, until they finally set out to destroy each other. The two cities still symbolize opposing conceptions of the good life. But the two cities were coeval. How can we talk about moral evolution here? The citizens of Athens certainly had as much freedom, gave as much admiration to reason, and were as magnificently productive as any citizenry before or since. Which way has moral evolution been running? Finally, Plato, who had some appreciation of the moral life, thought that authoritarian Sparta was morally superior to humanistic Athens, while his student Aristotle was, on balance, inclined toward the opposite view. Why should two philosophers hold opposed views on a question which, according to Fromm, has the same logical status as an empirical question?

Before leaving this conception of the innate humanistic conscience, one further point, which is probably already obvious, ought to be made explicit. Here I shall only state the point and defer fuller discussion of it to a later section.

Few writers on ethical subjects have let us believe that the way of righteousness is easy. It may well be the highest immorality to say that morality is easy. "All noble things are as difficult as they are rare," wrote Spinoza, and his melancholy reflection epitomizes a dominant theme in ethical thought. Man is weak and lacking in knowledge. He is driven to evil by forces he cannot master and exposed to temptations which he lacks the will to resist. Man must prepare for the good life as for a battle. He must train, develop discipline, study the wiles of the enemy who is both within and without. He must make himself hard so he might endure in the endless and relentless fight against evil. The evil is always within one, waiting to lead him into error and wrongdoing, and he must constantly wage war against himself. He must recognize that authority—laws, judges, punishments—is absolutely necessary in this struggle, and he must learn the virtue of obedience. He will lose more battles than he will win; therefore, both to help him and to protect others, society needs codes and sanctions, punishments and repressions.

Fromm rejects this whole orientation. He denies the need for external as well as for internal authority in the moral life. He repudiates the judge and the hangman. For him, a society makes its members virtuous not by punishing evil but by creating the conditions of good. Since both the meaning and the conditions of the good are known, this is no impossible task. The fight against evil can lead to no victory, for there is no enemy. Rather, if there is an enemy, it is the very idea that evil inheres in human nature, the idea that men must take precautions to see that it is confined there and not freed to attack other men or society itself. As Fromm puts it:

> Virtue is proportional to the degree of productiveness a person has achieved. If society is concerned with making people virtuous, it must be concerned with making them productive and hence with creating the conditions for the development of productiveness. The first and foremost of these conditions is that the unfolding and growth of every person is the aim of all social and political activities. . . .
>
> Every increase in joy a culture can provide for will do more for the ethical education of its members than

all the warnings of punishment or preachings of virtue could do.[41]

Here only one thing need be said about this. Fromm's vision of a society actively engaged in creating the conditions of the good life and in providing "increases of joy" echoes a theme which runs as far back as Plato's *Republic* and Aristotle's *Politics*. This implies a very "positive" view of the state, a view which assigns the state an enormous range of functions and responsibilities. This is no mere welfare state view; and it goes far beyond anything like T. H. Green's conception of the role of the state as the hinderer of hindrances to the good life. But along with broad functions and heavy responsibilities goes great power. And that opens a theme which will require more attention when we come to Fromm's vision of the good society. Here it is enough to suggest that Fromm's generous conception of human nature and his notion of the humanistic conscience lead him—though he will not admit it—toward the perilous conclusion of the omnicompetent state. If the state is to create the conditions of the good life it must acquire enormous powers, at least during the transitional period between the old order and the new. In political life, such transitional periods have a way of becoming permanent.

This hint of the omnicompetent state would arouse little concern were the Frommian state frankly impossibilistic or hopelessly Utopian. But it is not. In Fromm as well as in others, Eros strains toward satisfaction and will have it. The familistic state is always a possibility, for men are always cold. The ideal of the all-embracing state has always been a feature of erotic thought. In this part of his work, Fromm continues the tradition of Rousseau and Comte.

For the moment, let us return to productive man.

There are two further observations to make about him. The first concerns his style of religion, the second his style of love.

The notable feature of Fromm's view of religion is its thoroughgoing pragmatism, a word I shall use here exactly as James did in his famous essay in definition.[42] James wrote that the term meant both a method of settling philosophical disputes and a certain theory of truth. As a method, it means the attempt "to interpret each notion by tracing its . . . practical consequences. What difference would it practically make to any one if this notion rather than that notion were true?" It means an *"attitude of looking away from first things, principles, 'categories,' supposed necessities; and of looking towards last things, fruits, consequences, facts."* As a theory of truth it means *"that ideas . . . become true just in so far as they help us to get into satisfactory relation with other parts of our experience. . . .* Any idea upon which we can ride, so to speak; any idea that will carry us prosperously from any one part of our experience to any other part, linking things satisfactorily, working securely, simplifying, saving labor; is true for just so much, true in so far forth, true *instrumentally."* In this view, the true and the good are not distinct categories. Rather, truth is a species of good. *"The true is the name of whatever proves itself to be good in the way of belief. . . ."* As James promised—the promise must seem a dire threat to devout religionists—pragmatism thus understood "may be a happy harmonizer of empiricist ways of thinking with the more religious demands of human beings."

Productive man turns out to be James's happy harmonizer. Productive man has a religion, of course, just as all other men have, but his main concern is not with the truth of his religion but with its utility. Nor is he interested in the question of the existence of God; that hypothesis he, like Laplace, no longer needs. For productive man, God is a symbol "whose significance is essentially historical." [43] Thus Fromm offers a definition of religion which carefully excludes a theistic component. Religion is *"any system of thought and action shared by a group which gives the individual a frame of orientation and an object of devotion."* [44] It is evident that this definition would embrace, say, a political ideology as easily as it would the doctrines and institutions ordinarily included in the term religion.

What matters to productive man is not whether his religion is true in some objective sense but whether it is useful. Does it liberate your powers and help you grow? If it does, then it is true and good in exactly the sense James had in mind. Pascal asked what do you stand to gain or lose by accepting or rejecting the hypothesis of God. Fromm asks what do you stand to gain or lose by choosing one meaning of the God symbol rather than another. It is clear that religion can do without all the paraphernalia of theology, authority, and organization that traditional religions have always had. In Fromm's view, religion and the church are not just in tension; they are incompatible.[45] It will come as no surprise to learn that the religious tendency Fromm admires most is mysticism, in which the seeker crashes through all barriers to a personal union with God, becomes indeed one with God.* It is not easy to see how

* Here too Fromm joins James, though this time the harmony is psychological, not logical. In the *Varieties of Religious Experience*, James almost totally ignored anything that has to do with churches and organized religion. He conceived of religious experience as a heightened or intensified psychic state, verging on the pathological. He treated of conversion experiences, religious visions, mystical union, inspired prophetic utterance, morbid gloom, and the like—as though the religion experienced among men and in an enduring congregation were somehow not "real" religion. Real religion means enthusiasm or special grace. Fromm also comes very close to this conception of the religious life.

Fromm can square his admiration for mysticism with his distaste for symbiotic relatedness and his admiration of individuality; the mystical union, after all, is the complete absorption, the total disappearance of the one in the One. It is even harder to determine what he might mean when he says that mysticism is the "highest development of rationality in religious thinking." [46] Whatever else one might say about mysticism, he should not confuse it with a rational enterprise. "By love, He may be gotten and holden," wrote the author of *The Cloud of Unknowing*, "but by thought of understanding never." [47]

These eccentricities in Fromm's thought are not central to my purpose, so I shall not pursue them. My purpose was to show Fromm's pragmatic view of religion. It may seem curious that Fromm, who believes in the objectivity of ethical norms, should hold such a view of religion, but here I only point out that he does. The picture becomes clearer when one merely says that when Fromm talks about religion he is really not talking about religion at all but about ethics. He has reduced religion to ethics; or, if that expression seems pejorative, he has incorporated religion into ethics. Let us turn to Fromm's real religion, which is love.

Love is a risky and compromising subject, for when a man writes about love he necessarily writes about his own loves. And when we know a man's loves we have caught a glimpse into the secret center of his being. Everything you say about a man's conception of love you say *de hominem* and *ad hominem*. I feel uncomfortable about this, for it comes too close to confession on the one side and prying on the other. Hence I shall restrict myself to the most general comments on the broadest features of Fromm's conception of love.

Start with the central conception, which is Fromm's idea of the universality of love: "Love of one person implies love of man as such." [48] The implications of this can be summarized in the formula "all are capable of love and all who love, love all." Then add a formulation which is manifestly inconsistent with the first one and the problem is set: erotic love "is by its very nature exclusive and not universal. . . ." [49] These two conceptions can never come together, unless we force a word entirely out of shape. Is love universal or is it exclusive? The answer to this question decides all the others.

Fromm will not tolerate exclusiveness: the magic circle of love must be opened. So in the end he denies the essential exclusiveness of erotic love and fuses it with universal love. "Erotic love is exclusive, but it loves in the other person all of mankind, all that is alive. It is exclusive only in the sense that I can fuse myself fully and intensely with one person only. Erotic love excludes the love for others only in the sense of erotic fusion, full commitment in all aspects of life—but not in the sense of deep brotherly love." [50]

What has happened is clear: this is another of those places in his work where Fromm juggles opposites. He will not choose between two diametrically opposed conceptions. He refuses the choice and asserts that the two conceptions are "basically" one. The necessity of this refusal is apparent in all aspects of his thought, as are its consequences. At bottom we are dealing with aristocratic and democratic orientations toward life, and Fromm is a democrat. He will not abide exclusiveness and privilege. He would make all men equal. This is the theme of what I shall say about Fromm on love.

How else can we account for the paleness, the lack of color and vigor, of Fromm's treatment of erotic love?

Fromm understands the fundamental point in any discussion of love, which is that love is the most total act of a human soul, but he will not go on to accept the obvious corollary, which is that the nature of a man's soul will determine the character of his love. A man's love is as he is. If he is shallow, his love will not be otherwise. If he is coarse, or inconstant, or noble, so will his love be. A man's way of love expresses his total constitution—his vital energy, his perceptiveness, his intelligence, his ability to communicate. Hence love has degrees of psychic pressure, depth, and temperature, and these variations reflect the powers of the being who loves. It is misleading to conceive of love as a capacity which all may possess in the same degree. Love is a talent, and just as some men have a great talent for poetry, others have a great talent for love. There are aristocrats of love just as there are aristocrats of painting, music, politics. Whether the love be erotic, religious, or brotherly, an extraordinary love reflects an extraordinary person. By making love the birthright of all, Fromm necessarily denatures it. That, I think, accounts for the paleness of his treatment of love.

Fromm makes love synonymous with sympathetic relations among men. This of course is one of the characteristics of our day, which has agreed to make love mean affection, loyalty, care, and concern, as it usually does, for example, in the state of matrimony. This strips love of the aura of mystery and enchantment which has always surrounded it. Again, it must be insisted that the enchanted circle does not protect only profane love, where the idea is captured in the motifs of the magic potion, the philter, and the secret formula, but is just as powerful in sacred love. In the Bible, love is the ultimate mystery, the mystery of mysteries, impervious to reason and analysis. The simple words "For God so loved the world, that he gave his only begotten Son . . ." [51] are as "reasonable" on the hundredth as on the first reading: they yield nothing to reason.

Fromm's rational and democratic conception of love rests on a confusion. He confuses love with its consequences. Many things, such as the care, responsibility, respect, and knowledge which Fromm speaks of, grow from love, but they are not love itself. They are its products. They presuppose love because they arise from it. To take them for love itself is to take accidents for essence. Or, if I may adapt a metaphor from Kierkegaard, "the tree is known by its fruits," each tree by its own fruits. We do not say that the tree is the fruit, however, but only that we can learn something about the nature of the tree by its fruit. The inward secret life of the tree is unknown to us. We know only that the life of the tree becomes partially manifest in the fruit. So too with love, which may also be partially known by its fruits, but which is not one and the same with them. The essence of love is mysterious, graspable by only a few rare spirits. Most men never truly love another nor are they ever truly loved by another on this earth. We can accept that sadness or we can with Fromm try to conceal it by equating sympathy with love.

What is worse, sympathy may falter. Fromm's democratic conception of love grows from his desire to establish solidarity among all men. He thinks that love is the only force capable of forging that bond. But I doubt whether this sympathy-love of Fromm's is adequate to its assignment. Human feelings are inconstant, and a bond forged of them alone becomes brittle or soft with changes in the psychic temperature. It is for this reason that I must disagree with Fromm's formulation of brotherly love. He claims to express the Biblical conception:

> The most fundamental kind of love . . . is *brotherly
> love*. By this I mean the sense of responsibility, care,
> respect, knowledge of any other human being, the wish
> to further his life. This is the kind of love the Bible
> speaks of when it says: love thy neighbor as thyself.
> Brotherly love is love for all human beings. . . . If I
> have developed the capacity for love, then I cannot help
> loving my brothers.[52]

The Bible, however, does not "speak of" love in quite
this way. All Fromm has left out of the Biblical expression
is its foundation and its middle term, that is, God. In the
Biblical conception, God's love is both the ground of all
love and the middle term in the love between man and man.
From God's love and back to it all lesser loves flow. Christianity teaches that all human love, no matter how intense
or pure, is still but the reflection of the eternal love, still but
the shadow of God's love. Indeed, the Christian teaching
starts with a terrible secret question: do men really love
themselves and their neighbors, or is it that they desire to
be loved? In answer to the question, neighbor-love is made,
not the first, but the second commandment, because men
are capable of loving their neighbor, or even of desiring that
their neighbor be loved, only when they themselves are
assured of the love of God. That is the pain of trying un-
aided to love one's neighbor, for the demands of human
love cannot be satisfied by men alone at all.

> As the peaceful lake is grounded deep in the hidden
> spring which no eye can see, so a man's love is grounded
> even deeper in the love of God. If there were at bottom
> no wellspring, if God were not love, then there would
> be no quiet lake or human love. As the quiet lake is
> grounded darkly in the deep spring, so is human love
> mysteriously grounded in God's love.[53]

Fromm has left out something else; two words which are decisive to the rest, the words: "Thou shalt." It is critical here that we remember the precise context in which Christ gathered up the Old Testament witness to a God of love. One of the Pharisees, thinking to tempt and confound him, asked Christ this question: "Master, which is the great commandment in the law?"

> Jesus said unto him, Thou shalt love the Lord thy God with all thy heart, and with all thy soul, and with all thy mind.
>   This is the first and great commandment.
>   And the second is like unto it, Thou shalt love thy neighbor as thyself.
>   On these two commandments hang all the law and the prophets.[54]

The whole context is one of law, duty, obligation. Man is *commanded* to love. Furthermore, he is commanded to love God and the neighbor unequally. The "first and great" commandment is, not to love God as the neighbor, but "with all thy heart, and with all thy soul, and with all thy mind." One need only love the neighbor as himself. The Christian teaching recognizes degrees of love, and the highest degree is owed to God. To love man as much as God is for the Christian not the delicious vision of a poet, but blasphemy. Central to the conception is the idea that man is indebted to God for the limitless love God gives man. Hence man must strive to repay the debt through love. The Biblical conception further requires the presence of a God who loves and judges and punishes as a father loves and judges and punishes.

There is in the Christian command no pretense that it is easy to love our neighbor and no easy assertion that he who loves, loves all mankind. We know from all experience that such an assertion is just not true. Human love is partial, selective, erratic. We believe, I think rightly, that our love is a valuable thing, not to be thrown about indiscriminately and given to all men regardless of merit. We believe we act unjustly toward those few who deserve or have won our love if we put all others on a level with them. We believe that if we broadcast our love there will be but a meager portion for each. We feel, perhaps rightly, that some men have a stronger claim to our hatred than to our love. The Biblical formula recognizes all these hard objections, and then— commands. The command is on its face anything but rea- sonable and just. It is in the highest degree unreasonable and unjust. This is the brotherly love of the Bible, but it plainly is not the brotherly love of Erich Fromm. In the end one has to say that Freud, for whom the whole business of religion was a fraud, understood the spirit of the Biblical command in a way that Fromm, with his easy and generous religion of man, has not. Freud's reflections on the "Thou shalt love thy neighbor as thyself" are those which any ethical man (in Kierkegaard's sense) must make.

> We will adopt a naive attitude towards it, as if we were meeting it for the first time. Thereupon we find our- selves unable to suppress a feeling of astonishment, as at something unnatural. Why should we do this? What good is it to us? Above all, how can we do such a thing? How could it possibly be done? . . . What is the point of an injunction promulgated with such solemnity, if reason does not recommend it to us?
>
> When I look more closely I find still further diffi- culties. Not merely is this stranger on the whole not worthy of love, but, to be honest, I must confess he has more claim to my hostility. . . . If it will do him any good, he has no hesitation in injuring me. . . .
>
> I imagine now I hear a voice gravely adjuring me:

"Just because thy neighbour is not worthy of thy love,
is probably full of enmity towards thee, thou shouldst
love him as thyself." I then perceive the case to be like
that of *Credo quia absurdum*.[55] *

Freud's soliloquy suggests that a certain form of genetic
argument can be brought against Fromm's thesis that "love
for one person implies love for man as such." I hesitate to
approach such exalted subjects as love with such mean
devices as genetic argument, but here, for whatever it may
be worth, is the argument.

Fromm would have to agree that for love to grow the
lover must first have knowledge of the existence of the beloved. Hence to love mankind requires knowledge of the
existence and nature of mankind. What is the source of
knowledge of "mankind"? Unless Fromm is prepared to
show (and of course he is not) that such knowledge is innate,
he must admit that it comes through experience. But if
knowledge of mankind is not innate, neither is love for it.
Both love and knowledge of mankind must derive from
experience. Here it is sufficient to say that only under certain
conditions and only in certain contexts does knowledge of
mankind lead to love for it. Suppose that the only men outside the small circle of family and kin one has ever had
close knowledge of are the foreign soldiers who burned
his crops and ravished his women. How will that victim be
led to love all mankind, regardless of how loving and productive his small group relationships may be? †

* There is a tantalizing hint of stealth in Freud's argument. Is the case
really "absurd"? The absurdity would seem to be that precisely because
enmity of the neighbor is like the enmity of the self toward itself, there is
no way to feel toward the neighbor which does not reflect self-orientations.
That "voice gravely adjuring" sounds like the voice of the analyst—Freud
speaking to Freud?

† This argument can be used to clarify another tendency of Fromm's
thought. Fromm could reply to my genetic argument along the following
lines. He might say, with Hobbes, that one can read mankind in himself:

The Biblical conception of brotherly love can make the sense of human solidarity vital and compelling in a way that no purely secular and ethical conception can. Furthermore, is it really true that the only way we can achieve care, concern, and respect for our fellows, and ultimate affirmation of their right to live and grow, is through love? It is entirely possible to find delight, just simple delight, in taking people as they are, in enjoying their infinite and motley variety, and not asking any man to be other than he is. But this does not mean loving them. It means only taking pleasure in them. Love, I think, must remain secret and mysterious, the talent and the privilege of the few. It must also remain exclusive, except in that specific Biblical sense, which includes some elements which Fromm will not accept.

To me it seems that Fromm loves love. With Augustine, he cries from the depths: "Out of a deep-seated want, I wanted, in love with loving." What is loved matters little: all men are at once equally deserving and capable. This is dangerous counsel today, when the mass media have cosmeticized sensualism and sold it for love. It is dangerous

---

knowledge of self is knowledge of man. Access to such knowledge comes through listening to the voice of the humanistic conscience. Unfortunately, most men never gain such knowledge, because they live in sick societies, societies which block access to the humanistic conscience and stifle or pervert the satisfaction of the basic psychic needs. This would be a sound reply to the genetic argument. But it proves too much. Fromm cannot say that *every* man can accurately read mankind in himself. Rather, only *productive* men can do so, for all other types of men are as alienated and cut off from the truth about themselves as they are alienated and cut off from true knowledge about other men. Hence only productive men have knowledge of and love for mankind. But where shall we find productive men? Only in sane societies; you cannot have productive men without having sane social conditions. But that comes back to the basic point of my genetic argument: you cannot expect a man to love mankind unless his social experience of mankind has been an experience of productive men living in sane societies. Here again Fromm is attempting to juggle incompatibles, this time social determinism versus essential human nature.

counsel for a people who, as Fromm himself has so incisively shown, are coming to regard all pleasures as their due and to think of their every desire as a command which the world ought to gratify. Fromm has called us the ever expectant ones, the eternal sucklers, the ones who have only to utter a need to have that need become a command upon the universe. An age of the sucklers is exactly the one to confuse desire with love and to fall in love with love. In such an age, it is precisely the duty of one who is concerned with the quality of life to insist on the exclusiveness of love and the importance of its object.

Look at the choice here, and the opportunity Fromm has lost. He takes issue with Freud for "seeing in love exclusively the expression—or a sublimation—of the sexual instinct, rather than recognizing that the sexual desire is one manifestation of the need for love and union." [56] The criticism of Freud may or may not be sound; that does not matter here. What does matter is that while he specifically criticizes Freud's reduction of love to sexuality, Fromm himself commits an error that is remarkably like the error of Freud's pan-sexualism. Fromm fails to see that the exact difference between the sexual instinct and love is that the former is undiscriminating and universal while the latter is discriminating and particular. The sexual instinct craves satisfaction: any object will do. The amorous sentiment is entirely different. Its essence is choice: only this unique object will do. Love is a choice not on all human beings but on this particular human being. It is true, as Fromm has shown, that love completely affirms its object and defends its right to exist. But it affirms *its* object. Love is the affirmation of a certain type of humanity, a beautiful humanity with a noble future. It sees that humanity and that future already existing in the one other being who is the object of love. That is the whole point: love is not an affirmation of all mankind; it is the affirmation of a certain good and beautiful mankind which exists now in one person, the beloved.

Hence the essential feature of love is choice, decision, discrimination. It is false to think that the one who loves affirms mankind as such, respects all men equally, and takes everybody into his care and concern. Indeed, I think it is quite the other way round. It is true that the one who loves sees the world through rose glasses. His smile falls graciously on those around him, and seems warm and generous for all mankind. But look at that smile more closely. Does it really fall on the beholders with love, or is there in it a note of benevolent superiority, perhaps even a hint of amused arrogance? Does the smile really embrace the beholders, or does it seem to hint that the smiling one looks down on the smaller ones from a supreme height they cannot reach? Perhaps the smile expresses the joy of a man who is above the world, immune to its cares and desperations. The lover smiles on men not because he loves and affirms them but because he really has no intercourse with them. When the lover smiles on those around him his smile does not mean he has affirmed them, but that he has fundamentally overlooked them. His smile is really a projection onto others of his own well-being, not a genuine concern for theirs. Why, this smile of the lover expresses not universal love, but Byronic disdain, for surely there is no higher disdain than failure to see the defects, the pains, and the limitations of others. The lover disdains the whole world. If you doubt this, if you think the lover's generous smile affirms you, then try to keep him from his beloved. Try to detain him or send him somewhere else. Try merely to interest him in your affairs. He will thrust you aside—forcefully, without remorse. I want to emphasize that this is true of love as a passion, not only of erotic love. Try detaining the mystic or the man who conceives himself to be in a state of grace. He will push you aside as firmly as the erotic lover.

So I think Fromm's democratic conception of love is wrong both in itself and because of its possible consequences in our age. His great error is to confuse the products of love (care, respect, etc.) with love itself. He makes this error because he refuses to see that love is a talent which only a few possess in the highest degree. He also fails to see that the lover affirms not the whole of mankind as it now is but a future beautiful mankind. "Love is a desire for generation and birth in beauty." That is how Plato defined the divine madness; and in his formulation lies the heart of love's mysterious creativity. Love is a desire that is consummated only in the birth of beauty.

In denying the mystery of love, Fromm tries to make love rational. That is the import of the emphasis he puts on knowledge as one of the dimensions of love. And yet, though the emphasis is there, its meaning is not entirely clear. In Fromm's analysis, knowledge apparently has two main relations with love. The first is that we cannot know another person unless we love him. That, I think, is the meaning of the following passage:

> To respect a person is not possible without *knowing* him; care and responsibility would be blind if they were not guided by knowledge. Knowledge would be empty if it were not motivated by concern. There are many layers of knowledge; the knowledge which is an aspect of love is one which does not stay at the periphery, but penetrates to the core. It is possible only when I can transcend the concern for myself and see the other person in his own terms.[57]

The first infinitive clause is untrue. My Webster defines respect as "to consider worthy of esteem; hence, to refrain from obtruding upon, as a person's privacy." As synonyms it offers "honor," "revere," "venerate." In this sense, one respects many people he knows little or nothing about. I respect Erich Fromm though I know him not at all. The second sentence is dubious. I can know a good bit about people without having much concern for them. It is even possible that the more I learn about a man, the less concern I will have for him. Finally, it is hard to say whether the passage as a whole means (1) knowledge is impossible without love; (2) love is impossible without knowledge; (3) both; or (4) neither. I have taken it to mean that we cannot have full knowledge of another without love for him.

The second relation Fromm posits between knowledge and love is that love is the only way to gain full knowledge of another *without violating him*. There is a "specifically human desire," Fromm asserts, to know the secret of man, to fathom the inmost recesses of the human soul. There are two ways to know the secret. The first is to gain power over a man and force him to submit to your probes and experiments. The other path is through love, not thought about love, but the act of love. "The only way of full knowledge lies in the *act* of love: this act transcends thought, it transcends words." [58] "However," he continues, "knowledge in thought, that is psychological knowledge, is a necessary condition for full knowledge in the act of love." Thus objective knowledge about a person is the first step on the ladder to loving union with him, just as thought about God is the first step toward mystical union with Him. This leads Fromm to the bold conclusion that just "as the logical consequence of theology is mysticism, so the ultimate consequence of psychology is love." [59]

Here Fromm has found the right words for a discourse on love. And notice how emphatically those words convey the themes of exclusiveness, mystery, incommunicability.

Fromm's guiding analogy here is with mysticism, which is the perfect sacred counterpart of profane love. Now, the way of the mystic has always been lonely and secretive, and whatever discoveries he makes he cannot communicate. The mystic's knowledge, unlike the knowledge usually called scientific or rational, is essentially private and inward. "The mystic may say—is indeed bound to say—with St. Bernard, 'My secret to myself.' Try how he will, his stammering and awe-struck reports can hardly be understood but by those who are already in the way." [60] So it is with the lover.

But Fromm will not accept the full implications of his own analogy, which, to say it again, is the correct analogy. The "logical consequence" of theology is not mysticism at all. The mystic and the theologian go separate ways, and each has always mistrusted the other. Theology fears mysticism for mysticism has no need of theology and usually feels hampered by it. Nor does this mutual animosity have anything to do with the old and complex question of the relationship between reason and faith: it is a matter of different kinds of reason and different kinds of faith.

This suggests similar ideas with regard to profane love. Fromm says the "ultimate consequence of psychology [that is, scientific knowledge of human nature] is love." The folk adage says "love is blind." It seems to me that the adage comes closer than Fromm to understanding the relations between knowledge and love. It is not true that love requires "objective knowledge" of the beloved. Like the mystic, the lover has no need of that and most likely will be impatient with it. Love never asked for facts nor consulted learning. The lover, as Stendhal's notion of crystallization makes clear, in a very real sense invents, that is, creates the beloved. Again we run up against the ineluctably exclusive and aristocratic meaning of love.

Fromm regards love as producing an enrichment of the

mental life. The lover knows more deeply, sees more clearly, senses more vitally than the one who does not love. In one sense that is true and in another it is false. The lover is one who has concentrated his whole being on one object. All the rest is shut out or perceived only in relation to the object of love. Hence the poets describe love as a mania, a madness, an intense concentration of energy upon one object. The lover feels his life to be richer than before, his psychic and emotional faculties keener, but this feeling of enrichment is partly a function of the fact that his whole being has become fixed on one center. His life is richer because it is narrower. Thus what from the point of view of the lover seems an enrichment of the psychic life is from the point of view of the outside observer an impoverishment of it.

I am arguing, in summary, that Fromm's universalistic conception of love overlooks essential dimensions of the meaning of love. Rather, Fromm does not actually overlook those other dimensions; he just will not give them full importance in his thought. This is a consequence of his wholly admirable desire to vindicate the brotherhood of man. But I have also argued that love, excepting the Biblical and specifically theistic expression of it, is not suited to that end. Human love is essentially exclusive and attempts to universalize it run two risks; the risk of diluting it, and the risk of confusing it with its consequences. I have argued further that to praise love in the style of Fromm is in our day to run the risk of adding to a debased conception of love as the right to be accepted as one is and the right to have one's sensual wants gratified. We must all in this age of national parochialisms long for the day when mankind realizes its larger solidarity. But I think we must work for that community with the methods that, in Thoreau's phrase, raise the individual to a higher power. That means we should respect greatness, learn to delight in the variety and uniqueness of men, and above all strive toward a tact and a respect in our relations with our fellows that will make it possible for each to work toward his own destiny without violating the private destiny and the inner universe of another. Tact, respect, pride in achievement, delight in variety, admiration of excellence—these, and not sympathy and sincerity disguised as love, are the basic constituents of that larger and nobler community of human excellence toward which our age can aspire.

Our age has silently but massively resolved against the conceptions of love which dazzled the Western imagination and seared the Western heart for centuries. We have ended both the epic of Christian love and the dream of romantic love which succeeded it. We have chosen sympathy-love over the stern imperatives of Christian love, and we have chosen sentimental love over the agony of romantic love. In these respects, Fromm's work is an appropriate epilogue to the story of Western love. In Fromm's pages, Christian love appears only as a bland residue of sympathy and benevolence left over after all the stringent elements of duty, debt, and sacrifice have been distilled out. Romantic love, too, has lost its perfume, its mystery, and its terror in his work, and remains only as a wispy haze of sentiment for the brotherhood of all mankind. In the Western story of romantic love, individualism found its supreme expression. And as the individual grew more and more spiritually autonomous, and hence, as Fromm himself has shown, more and more lonely, he came to worship Eros as the only god capable of breaking through the individualistic isolation. The romantic lover sought in the beloved not merely a beloved, but salvation. But this charged love with unmanageable spiritual demands, so that in the end romantic love had to be an agony, a shipwreck of the soul. Fromm has lifted this burden from love and assured us that we can all be happy in the benign aura of fellow-feeling. In Fromm's pages on love, we can see on display some of the deepest resolutions of the modern mind—its conviction that the visible world it comprehends is the only real world there is, its wish to risk only small stakes in the game of life, its faith in the reality of happiness.

Pleasure and Happiness

With that ringing word happiness I come to my last series of remarks on productive man. In the following pages I shall discuss Fromm's thought on those two central terms in ethical discourse, pleasure and happiness. I shall be particularly concerned to examine his attempt to solve the problem of subjectivity in a hedonistic ethic by recourse to the sovereign notion of productiveness.*

Authoritarian ethics, Fromm begins, has the virtue of simplicity: it solves all problems by making authority's dictates the standard of good and evil and by making obedience synonymous with virtue. Humanistic ethics, which rejects the authoritarian solution, has one great difficulty: "in making man the sole judge of values it would seem that pleasure or pain becomes the final arbiter of good and evil." The humanistic solution thus understood is obviously no solution at all, for it is radically subjectivistic and can lead to grotesque and self-destructive results. Are we left then with a choice between two grossly bad alternatives?

Fromm thinks not. He thinks that "this alternative between submission to authority and response to pleasure as

* Fromm's treatment appears in *Man for Himself*, pp. 172–197. Since I shall state his case largely in his own words, it would be tedious to footnote each quotation. Unless otherwise noted, all quotations in this section will be found in the aforementioned pages.

guiding principles is fallacious." It is fallacious because it fails to recognize that "pleasure, satisfaction, happiness, and joy . . . are different and partly contradictory phenomena." With the aid of psychoanalytic methods and findings, we are finally in a position to solve the ancient problem of humanistic ethics, the problem of the qualitative analysis of pleasure, in a way that overcomes subjectivism and results in an objectively based ethics. Thus Fromm undertakes an analysis which will show that "happiness and joy although, in a sense, *subjective* experiences, are the outcome of interactions with, and depend on, *objective conditions* and must not be confused with the merely subjective pleasure experience. These objective conditions can be summarized comprehensively as productiveness."

For the better appreciation of the new wisdom, Fromm turns first to some older writers on pleasure and happiness. He starts with Aristippus and ends with Spencer, bowing along the way to Epicurus, Plato, Aristotle, and Spinoza. His treatments of these writers are so brief as to be valueless in themselves (Aristippus gets a short paragraph, Epicurus, Plato, Aristotle, and Spinoza get medium paragraphs, and Spencer a full page), so it will do to summarize Fromm's findings before moving on to the new science.

> The concepts of Plato, Aristotle, Spinoza, and Spencer have in common the ideas (1) that the subjective experience of pleasure is in itself not a sufficient criterion of *value*; (2) that happiness is conjunctive with the good; (3) that an objective criterion for the evaluation of pleasure can be found.

All these theorists were handicapped by the fact that they wrote before psychoanalysis had been invented. They built on coarse data, data not refined by subtle techniques of observation and study. Aided by such techniques, Fromm attempts to push the discussion of pleasure as a norm for living beyond its traditional scope.

At the outset, psychoanalysis joins the opponents of hedonistic ethics in the view that "the subjective experience of satisfaction is in itself deceptive and not a valid criterion of value." As examples, Fromm mentions the psychoanalytic insight into sadistic and masochistic strivings. Although satisfaction of such strivings is accompanied by pleasure, psychoanalysis can show that both the strivings and the pleasure are "objectively harmful" to the total personality. He also mentions the psychoanalytic discovery of the ambiguous dynamics of repression. The discovery that pain and pleasure, unhappiness and happiness can be unconscious as well as conscious leads to an important principle, the principle that "happiness and unhappiness are expressions of the state of the entire organism, of the total personality. Happiness is conjunctive with an increase in vitality, intensity of feeling and thinking, and productiveness; unhappiness is conjunctive with the decrease of these capacities and functions." This principle is important because it permits Fromm to say that a man can be unhappy despite his belief that he is happy. It is not enough to have the "illusion of happiness." There must be real happiness, which is a product of certain definable objective conditions. Fromm would take as nothing an affirmative verbal response to the question "are you happy?" He would insist that a valid answer to that question must come from an analysis of the person's total personality and social situation.

At this point Fromm turns to the analysis of the qualitative differences among the various kinds of pleasure. This analysis is "the key to the problem of the relation between pleasure and ethical values." The argument can be best developed by presenting a number of definitions.

Satisfaction. Fromm defines this as the subjective

feeling of pleasure which accompanies the relief of physiological tensions, such as hunger, thirst, the need for sexual
release, and the like. Satisfaction can be very intense, and
it is the easiest, the most common, and for many men the
only kind of pleasure attainable. Desires for this kind of
pleasure are rhythmic and satiable; that is, such desires appear only when a physiological need is unfulfilled, and they
disappear when the need has been met. Such pleasures are
perfectly normal. Many writers, Freud among them, have
made the mistake of thinking that satisfaction is the essence
of all kinds of pleasure.

Irrational pleasure. This type of pleasure also comes
from relief of tension, but from irrational psychic tension
rather than from physiologically based tension. This kind
of tension often manifests itself in physiological forms, but
the origin remains psychic. Thus, the need for drinking is
often not due to thirst but to some psychic dysfunctioning.
An insecure person who has an intense need to prove his
worth to himself may try to do it by "making" others sexu-
ally. He may rationalize his desire as due to the virile
demands of his body, but it is really due to his need to
justify himself or to dominate others. It is in the very nature
of such irrational psychic tensions that they cannot be
"satisfied." They spring from a basic deficiency within oneself; hence they are insatiable. Such pleasures are an indication of pathological desires and basic unhappiness.

Gratification. This is the pleasure which accompanies
the accomplishment of any task one has set out to do—
making a sale, building a boat, writing a book. Achieving
a desired goal is gratifying, even if the goal is not a productive one, because the achievement gives proof of one's
powers and shows his ability to cope with the world.

Pleasure. Fromm reserves this word for the one type
of good feeling which is based not on effort, but on relaxa-

tion. It accompanies effortless but pleasant activity. It means rest and relaxation, easeful activity.

Happiness and joy. Both satisfaction and irrational pleasure are part of a "system of scarcity." They are types of pleasure which result from fulfillment of some lack, and the lack itself is the basis of the pleasure. Satisfaction is the pleasure which accompanies fulfillment of a physiological lack. Irrational pleasure comes from the temporary mitigation of a psychic lack, a lack which is always "rooted in the fundamental lack of productiveness."

Beyond the realm of scarcity rises a nobler realm, the realm of abundance. In this higher realm, not satisfaction and irrational pleasure but happiness and joy prevail. This is "the realm of productiveness, of inner activity." This realm comes into existence only to the extent that the province of scarcity is diminished, so that men need not consume their best energies in the struggle for subsistence. "The evolution of the human race is characterized by the expansion of the realm of abundance. . . . All specifically *human* achievements of man spring from abundance."

The pleasures of the realm of scarcity are pleasures of satisfaction. Those of the realm of abundance are pleasures of joy. The distinction between the two realms is to be found in all spheres of life—work, love, eating, sex, and the rest. To clarify his point, Fromm offers a number of examples. One will suffice here. "Hunger is a phenomenon of scarcity; its satisfaction, a necessity. Appetite is a phenomenon of abundance; its satisfaction not a necessity but an expression of freedom and productiveness. The pleasure accompanying it may be called joy." He goes on to say that joy and happiness are the same in quality and differ only in usage: "joy refers to a single act while happiness may be said to be a continuous or integrated experience of joy. . . ." The sequence closes with a definition of happiness, which is "the indication that man has found the answer to the problem of human existence: the productive realization of his potentialities. . . ." Happiness is thus the feeling of pleasure which accompanies productive living. As such, it is *"the criterion . . . of virtue in the meaning it has in humanistic ethics."*

Let Fromm state the conclusions of the analysis.

> We are now in a position to formulate our view on the ethical relevance of pleasure. Satisfaction as relief from physiologically conditioned tension is neither good nor bad; as far as ethical evaluation is concerned it is ethically neutral, as are gratification and pleasure. Irrational pleasure and happiness (joy) are experiences of ethical significance. Irrational pleasure is the indication of greed, of the failure to solve the problem of human existence. Happiness (joy), on the contrary, is proof of partial or total success in the "art of living." Happiness is man's greatest achievement; it is the response of his total personality to a productive orientation toward himself and the world outside.[61]

This theory of the "ethical relevance of pleasure" presents a distressingly large number of complex questions, so the first task is to limit the scope of the discussion. First of all, since the theory is only a special application of Fromm's general theory of good and evil, it is not necessary to retrace the arguments of the first chapter. That already removes most of the basic questions from the present discussion. Secondly, I shall limit the discussion by directing most of my remarks to the relations between the theory of the ethical relevance of pleasure and the concept of productiveness. My argument will move toward one conclusion: in the end, productive man is without anything that can be meaningfully called moral obligation, either to himself or to his fellows.

At the outset, it should be said that Fromm's distinctions among the types of pleasure make a real contribution to ethical discourse. They make possible an accuracy of expression which is often lacking and always valuable in ethical study. It seems to me too that the distinctions represent real differences in the realm of experience. Fromm has made a contribution to the understanding of pleasure as well as to the language of ethics.

Useful as the distinctions may be, however, they are not watertight. This is especially clear in his treatment of "satisfaction" and "irrational pleasure." It is impossible to tell just where physiologically based needs leave off and psychologically based needs begin. Take even the simplest case, the need for food or sleep. Even here no purely scientific measurement will quite do the job. And when we come to sex, the intermixture of the psychological and the physiological is so intimate that no filter, no matter how fine, can separate the two components and measure their respective weights with much accuracy. This ambiguity seriously weakens Fromm's contention that "satisfaction . . . is neither good nor bad . . . [but] ethically neutral. . . ."

Fromm's dismissal of satisfaction-pleasure as ethically neutral permits him to avoid two of the central problems of moral philosophy: (1) by what methods should satisfaction-pleasure be pursued and achieved; and (2) given a condition where supplies (food, for example) are scarcer than the demand for them, by what principle should the available goods be distributed among needy claimants. As soon as one poses such questions, he is compelled to realize that satisfaction-pleasures are not ethically irrelevant at all; rather, they go to the heart of moral and political philosophy, for it is precisely in this area that the hard problems arise, the problems men have to face in this world. Consider the tortuously complex ethical and moral questions raised

by the legal and customary regulation of property ownership, say, or of sexual behavior. Here, where men must live
and work and concern themselves with distributive justice
and social well-being, Fromm coolly tells us that ethical
philosophy can offer no counsel.

This is one aspect of the thoroughly utopian (in the
bad sense, meaning artificial, unrealistic) character of
Fromm's treatment of these matters. Another is his distinction between the realm of scarcity and the realm of abundance, and his assignment of happiness exclusively to the
latter. This is a cruelly utopian distinction, for it informs
those who endure shortages that happiness can be theirs
only after scarcity is abolished by abundance. Meanwhile,
the life that must be lived in the realm of scarcity—and
that of course is the life of most of us—is just "ethically
neutral." It is hard to think of a doctrine with harsher consequences than this one. Taken seriously, it would put an
end to the moral ties among men, abolish all ideas of social
justice, and return us to a kind of Hobbesian state of nature.
We are dealing here with a secular chiliasm; and chiliasm
has always meant rejection of this world.

"All specifically human achievements of man spring
from abundance." When one reads that memorable
Frommian sentence for the first time, he is warmed by its
generosity. It is radiant with love for mankind, humble
with respect for the grandeur of the human enterprise,
powerful in its affirmation of the nobility of man. We feel
that all the author's instincts are with the right and human
cause. Successive rereadings do not destroy that impression,
but they do evoke others less pleasant. The sentence rests
on a special use of the adjective human which is all the
more ruthless precisely because of its face nobility and
generosity. The sentence epitomizes the unintentional
cruelty and the terrible blindness of the utopian.

Men have done an infinite number of things. Is Chartres cathedral a more specifically human achievement than the Kremlin? The one may in some sense be specifically French and the other specifically Russian, but surely both are generally human. What does it mean to talk about specifically human achievements? Presumably, it means that some (small) portion of the actions of men is human while another (much larger) portion is, perhaps, nonhuman or inhuman or subhuman. This distinction would define the works and lives of most men out of the human realm. Somehow, this seems less "humanistic" than the ancient "nothing human is foreign to me."

What does it mean to say that all specifically human achievements "spring from abundance"? This really seems to suggest that men behave in a "specifically human" way only after they have fulfilled their drives for gratification, satisfaction, and pleasure. This is incomprehensible. What of the prodigious works of pride? Are they not human? And if they are, in what meaningful sense can we say that they spring from abundance? What of the achievements of sacrifice? Do they not suggest that men are often willing to forego abundance? What of the enormous achievements that have been made in the face of extreme scarcity, or perhaps at the cost of abundance? Taken seriously, Fromm's notion would simply deny that most of history is "human" history.

It seems that Fromm has accepted the very modern idea that men begin to act like good men only after they have gained something called security—a strangely materialistic idea for one who calls himself a humanist. Furthermore, where could one find the evidence that would support the thesis of a direct and positive correlation between degree of abundance and degree of happiness or virtue? Many teachers have thought the opposite was the case: It

is easier for a camel to go through the eye of a needle than
for a rich man to enter the kingdom of God. Fromm himself has charged that our riches have corrupted us. My only
point is that we just do not know much about these matters; certainly not enough to support Fromm's thesis that
abundance is the necessary foundation of happiness. We
do know one thing for sure, and it is a thing which brings
into question Fromm's whole distinction between the
realms of scarcity and abundance: scarcity and abundance
are both social definitions, which vary widely from place
to place. What is scarcity at one time or for one people
may seem abundance at another time or for another people.
In such matters, we must be content with relatives and cannot hope for absolutes.

From these particular considerations I now move to
two more general matters which will, hopefully, lead to the
promised conclusion that productive man really has nothing
that can properly be called a moral or ethical code.

The first of these matters is what may be described as
the static quality of Fromm's treatment of the "ethical
relevance of pleasure." The point can be developed by com-
paring Fromm with a man he doubtless does not admire,
Thomas Hobbes. I shall try to show that although the two
start from just about the same point, Fromm never moves
much beyond it, while Hobbes, of course, does reach conclusions, baleful though they be.

The details of Hobbes's general psychology need not
be inquired into here. What is most relevant is his principle that the human organism inherently, instinctively,
strives to maintain and to increase its vitality. This rule governs all behavior, and from it may be built a whole psychology and a theory of value. Every stimulus, every condition in the environment, affects vitality either favorably or
unfavorably. If the stimulus enhances vitality, man moves

toward it; that is, he tries to gain and preserve the favorable condition. If the effect is unfavorable, the organism retreats or tries to modify the deleterious condition. Movement toward an object Hobbes calls desire; movement away, aversion. Whatever a man desires he calls good, and whatever he hates he calls evil. Hence there is nothing good or evil as such, for each man calls that which he desires good. There is also no final end, or *summum bonum*, but only a succession of ends which a man from time to time desires. Success in achieving one's ends Hobbes calls felicity, and since there is no final end felicity is always a condition of movement or activity, not of calm or rest. One is always striving after felicity. He never attains it once and for all. In the pursuit of felicity, certain habits of mind are useful and others are detrimental. The former Hobbes calls virtues; the latter he calls defects. The means or abilities a man uses to attain felicity Hobbes comprehensively calls powers. Hence the struggle for felicity is virtually identical with the struggle for power. Men perpetually strive to increase their power, for that is the only way to assure success in the pursuit of felicity:

> I put for a general inclination of all mankind, a perpetual and restless desire of power after power, that ceaseth only in death. And the cause of this, is not always that a man hopes for a more intensive delight, than he has already attained to; or that he cannot be content with a more moderate power: but because he cannot assure the power and means to live well, which he hath present, without the acquisition of more.[62]

Hobbes's bleak description of the state of nature follows ineluctably from this account of human motivation. That description need not detain us. What matters is that Hobbes recognized that in such a state there is neither right nor wrong, justice nor injustice. The only rule of life is "that to be every man's that he can get; and for so long, as he can keep it." Hobbes recognized too that such a state is a state of fearful insecurity. Men must use their reason to build a civil order that can overcome the anarchy of nature. To build a civil order means that men must establish rules and conventions, and they must erect a sovereign who can see that the rules are obeyed.

The similarity between Hobbes's and Fromm's fundamental psychological premises is remarkable. Fromm shares Hobbes's principle that the human organism acts to increase its vitality. He also shares the idea that to live and to develop one's powers are one and the same. His definition of virtue is almost exactly that of Hobbes: virtue is that which increases man's powers. But there the similarity ends. Fromm will not unfold the implications of these dynamic premises. He will not face up to the social consequences of a psychology which defines man as the creature driven to preserve and fulfill himself, the creature who must always increase his powers to achieve his ends. Instead, Fromm concludes—and the conclusion is entirely out of harmony with his premises—with a static conception of happiness that applies only in the realm of abundance. He simply dismisses all problems raised by the search for satisfactions (felicity) in the realm of scarcity. Above all, Fromm seems unable to understand that the so-called ethic of productive man is no ethic at all. He fails to grasp Hobbes's insight that morality consists of a conventional body of rules which men have collectively agreed to obey so that the interests of each can be secured. This brings me to my last point.

The point can be opened by developing the answers to two questions. (1) What is the specific nature or content of value in Fromm's ethical system? (2) Is the source of value in Fromm's ethical theory internal or external to the individual?

In answer to the first question, it is obvious that Fromm's ethic is not hedonistic, whether pure or modified. He rejects the naive hedonism of Aristippus as well as the more prudent and sophisticated hedonism of Epicurus. Fromm's position is closer to that of Spinoza. Like Spinoza, he regards happiness (joys) as both the reward of and the evidence for the productive, that is, the good life. Productiveness is its own end and the only end. Happiness accompanies it; happiness is the feeling-state which is produced by productiveness. Since this is so, happiness is also the evidence or indicator of productiveness. Happiness is not an end in itself; rather, it is "proof of partial or total success in the 'art of living.' " [63] In sum, Fromm's ideal is an ideal of health or hygiene. Physical and psychological fitness, vibrant growth and expansiveness—these are the *summum bonum*, the highest end and good. Happiness is merely their reward and indicator.

The answer to the second question is unequivocal. Time and again Fromm has said that the individual is the sole source of value. The consequences of this simple affirmation are profound. In a basic sense, "ought" loses all its traditional meaning, for it no longer refers to anything outside of the individual. "Ought" implies a source and locus separate from the actor. It has no meaning when it is self-contained. In Fromm's ethics, to say someone ought to do something is like saying God ought to do something—an idea which, given the notion of God, is absurd. From the point of view of ethics, there is no metaphysical difference between an ethics of pure pleasure-seeking and one of health, self-realization, self-denial, or anything else, *so long as these refer to nothing outside of the individual.* If nothing outside of me is a source of value for me, I can be obliged to no man, nor he to me. We are each alone and sovereign; we are to each other as man is to man in the state of nature.

Let me offer an example. A number of American soldiers taken prisoner in Korea were confined in a small hut in North Korea under extremely harsh conditions. Inside the hut, there were filth, malnutrition, cold, crowding, despair. Life was reduced to the struggle for survival. Outside the hut, the temperature was far below freezing, and the ground was covered with snow. One of the prisoners was stricken by a noisome and debilitating diarrhea. He needed attention and care which the group could not provide him without danger and sacrifice to itself. One of the soldiers whose bunk was next to that of the sick man, fearing for his own health and no longer able to endure the stench, threw the invalid out of the hut, where he died. The soldier who committed the act might have reflected as follows. This man is the sole source of value for himself, just as I am for me. His "ought" does not extend to me, nor mine to him. And there is no source of "oughts" outside of and above us both. I conclude that I owe him no help. There is no moral reason why I should care if he dies. Now, of course, Fromm argues that I *will* care, if I am a productive man; and if I do not care I am by definition unproductive, that is, sick. Given Fromm's meaning of productiveness, this is probably true. But note what has happened here. There is still no *moral* obligation to help this man, my injured neighbor. Any inclination I may feel to help him is merely an *accidental* manifestation, a by-product of my productiveness. Furthermore, I would repeat, though it is not necessary to my thesis here, that I tried to show some pages back that the brotherly care and concern which Fromm thinks would move me does not even necessarily result from productiveness. More broadly, I suggested that mere sympathy and pity for the pains of one's fellows will not provide the roots of secure mutual aid. As La Rochefoucauld's chill maxim has it, "we all have strength enough to endure the troubles of others."

Thus it turns out that all this talk of pleasure, irrational pleasure, satisfaction, and the rest, is really not very important. The important thing about Fromm's ethics is not his choice of productiveness (happiness, joys, health) over pleasure but his choice of the individual as the sole source of value. It is now possible to see in a fuller light the meaning of a statement quoted earlier, the statement that "this alternative between submission to authority and response to pleasure as guiding principles is fallacious." [64] There *is* a course between authoritarian and hedonistic ethics, and Fromm has found it in his ethic of health.* But the course is just not very significant. Fromm took the decisive step when he centered value in the individual. After that, definite and severe consequences follow, no matter what the content of value may be.

This is the ultimate expression of Fromm's utopianism, and the measure of the failure of his ethical theory. By banishing all moral authority external to the individual, he banishes all inter-individual morality. This, in effect, is to banish all morality whatever. Fromm has simply failed to come to grips with that hardest of all problems for a theorist who, like Hobbes or Locke, starts from individualistic premises—the problem of forging moral links among individuals. Hobbes and Locke attempted the problem. So far as I can see, Fromm has not. He refuses to introduce into his theory of ethics any element of convention, of art, of rules of conduct which men rationally make and agree to follow. There is a distressing paradox here: Fromm, who

* Actually, there are many such courses, but they are not germane to this discussion.

explicitly vaunts reason, implicitly discards it as an element in the moral life and encourages us to return to nature.

Not all the way back to nature, however. Fromm will not do that, even though the price of not doing so is to leave the major problem without a solution. It must be emphasized that the root of the problem here is Fromm's individualism. Starting from such premises, he must either go forward and confront the problems which Hobbes and Locke confronted, or he must go back and accept one of the two solutions to this problem of forming bonds between men which Erotic thought has developed. The first of these solutions is to maintain the passionate connections among men by assuring that the desire for closeness never reaches absolute fulfillment, thereby binding the members of the community together in a tense network of constant yearning and unfulfilled desire. (The previous remarks on the Balinese love-play quality of Fromm's ethic are relevant here.) The high effectiveness of this solution is suggested by the findings of Shils and Janowitz in their work on cohesion in the *Wehrmacht*.[65] Fromm cannot accept this solution because for him love (desire, yearning) must come to completion. The second Erotic solution is to stamp out individuality altogether, to build a community which has no notion of difference, of distinctness, of separateness. In such a community, no member can calculate the utility and the advantage of action for himself alone, distinguished from the group. The purest forms of this type of community appeared in the ancient world, before the notion of individuality had developed. The Band of Thebes is an excellent example; the army of Sparta another. Compare either of these with the squabbling, selfish, unruly, and yet in some way more admirable pack which Xenophon described in the *Anabasis*, and the contrast will be clear. Fromm, of course, cannot accept this solution because it abolishes the individual. Rejecting both of these primitive and "incestuous" solutions, and failing to come to grips with the problem of a rational morality, Fromm is left with no solution at all.

Having dissolved morality in productiveness, the only social adhesive he has left is the natural tendency of productive individuals to love and care for each other. Seen in this light, the necessity of his theory of love to his whole system becomes apparent. Perhaps too it is now clear why I spent so much time discussing the aristocratic element in love and the element of command in Christian love. That was my way of preparing the conclusion that Fromm's theory of love, which is basic to his whole system, is wrong. We do not look for allies when we love; rather, we set ourselves apart. I would repeat here that even if Fromm is right on the nature of love, even if productive individuals will care for one another, this care is a non-moral phenomenon. Fromm indeed banishes all morality in the grand hope that, given abundance, men can get along harmoniously by their good will and natural generosity. That is the ultimate meaning of the "morality" of productiveness. In the meantime, as we endure in the realm of scarcity, any talk of values is merely empty, or perhaps deceptive. One is compelled to Auden's lines:

> All the ideals in the world won't feed us
> Although they give our crimes a certain air.[66]

With this, I leave productive man and move to the next question, which is, why are productive men so scarce?

CHAPTER III

Alienation

The question which ended the previous chapter can be answered in a few words: productive men are scarce because modern society is sick. This answer raises two further questions, which this chapter will explore. The first one, which will be treated very briefly, is, in what sense can a society be sick? The second is, what, in Fromm's view, is the specific sickness of modern society?

Can Society Be Sick?

In what sense can a society be called sick? What are the symptoms of social disease and social health? How can a social sickness be diagnosed? This decisive question is the first one that any doctor of social reform ought to explore, carefully and at length. It is remarkable how few have done so. Plato did, and so did Aristotle, Machiavelli, Hobbes, Marx, and Durkheim. This completes the list of names of the first rank, and one needs only a glance to see how various the answers are. Plato, for example, thought social sickness meant a derangement in the proper relations of the classes, while Marx thought it lay in the very existence of classes. Hobbes saw social sickness as a lack of shared meanings among men, a lack which could be remedied only by the creation of an absolute rule maker. Durkheim, on the other hand, thought social sickness was expressed in the very growth of the state power. When such wise doctors disagree, not much can be expected from a novice. I shall try only to show how Fromm approaches the problem and to indicate some of the difficulties of his approach.

At the outset, it should be noted that the problem is an important one in Fromm's thought. His use of such terms as social pathology, sick society, and sane society is not metaphorical. He means such expressions literally, and he means them scientifically. Basic to his thought is the idea that a society as well as an individual can be in various degrees and states of sickness or well-being. Further, thanks to modern social science, it is possible to determine objectively the state of health of a society. Once the diagnosis is made, remedial measures can be scientifically prescribed.[1]

Fromm believes there are universal and objective criteria of mental health. He further believes that we know what these criteria are. It follows that mental well-being is measured not by the degree to which one is "adjusted" to his society, but by the degree to which he fulfills the objective criteria. In formal terms we can say that the mentally healthy person is one who has achieved a productive fulfillment of the five basic psychic needs. In more substantive terms, Fromm defines mental health as follows:

> Mental health is characterized by the ability to love and to create, by the emergence from incestuous ties to clan and soil, by a sense of identity based on one's experience of self as the subject and agent of one's powers, by the grasp of reality inside and outside of ourselves, that is, by the development of objectivity and reason.[2]

To the degree that one meets these criteria, he is healthy. Whether or not he will be healthy, however, is a matter largely out of his hands. It is determined by the society in which he lives. A healthy society makes healthy men and an unhealthy society makes unhealthy men. A healthy society can be defined as one which provides the conditions for the productive fulfillment of the basic needs.

> A healthy society furthers man's capacity to love his fellow men, to work creatively, to develop his reason and objectivity, to have a sense of self which is based on the experience of his own productive powers. An unhealthy society is one which creates mutual hostility, distrust, which transforms man into an instrument of use and exploitation for others, which deprives him of a sense of self, except inasmuch as he submits to others or becomes an automaton.[3]

A large gap appears in the system at this point. Fromm nowhere explains how one should conduct a diagnosis of society. Of course, a certain amount of direction is implicit in his analysis. You could presumably tell whether and how society is sick by looking at a sample of individuals in it. To know how society was making men sick you would probably look first at the conditions of work and then at the family, since the former largely determines the social character, and the latter transmits it to the new generations. Beyond that, Fromm says little about the art of social diagnosis.

Finally, the cure of social pathology follows the same procedures as the cure of individual pathology. As Fromm puts it at the beginning of his discussion of "roads to sanity":

> If this chapter is to discuss . . . methods of cure, we had better . . . ask ourselves what we know about the

nature of cure in cases of individual mental diseases. The cure of social pathology must follow the same principle, since it is the pathology of so many human beings, and not of an entity beyond or apart from individuals.[4]

The conditions for the cure of individual and social pathology, then, are the same. These conditions are: (1) a development must have occurred which conflicts with the requirements of human nature; (2) this development causes suffering, conscious or unconscious; (3) the sick person or society must be made aware of this suffering, and of the repressed or shut out or thwarted sectors of the psyche; (4) awareness of suffering becomes fully effective only if the sufferer goes on to alter the realistic situation and the norms and values which produced the pathological tendencies in the first place. With this, the cure is complete.*

All this seems clear enough; but it is not without difficulties. Two appear right away. First, Fromm's description of the characteristics of the healthy society is very loose and general. He employs terms whose meanings must be specified more carefully than they have been before we

* The fourth point again indicates the gulf between Freud and Fromm. For Fromm, cure is complete only when the sufferer has altered the realistic situation which produced the sickness. And, since Fromm stresses the relevance of *current* (as opposed to early childhood) situations in the production of neurosis, it follows that current realities are the ones which must be changed. This is an emphatically *political* conception, one which calls for large changes in the social order. In his conception of a cure, Fromm sheds the mantle of the doctor of the soul and takes up the sword of the reformer. The healer of the Freudian persuasion, on the other hand, includes no such political element in his formulation of the conditions of cure. He does not say "change reality"; he says "recognize reality." Furthermore, he stresses the realities of early life over current realities. Fromm wants to tell people how to live. The Freudian wants to help people understand what reality is, so that they themselves may learn to choose a path through it. I know this overstates the case, because the Freudian also recognizes that current realities must sometimes be changed for treatment to be meaningful, but it does usefully point up the differences in time orientations and the relative politicalness of the two schools.

can be confident that we know what he has in mind. The second difficulty is closely related. Loose and ambiguous though it is, Fromm's description of the healthy society makes it clear that no actual society has ever been very healthy. We are confronted with something like the Platonic problem. There may be a model of the perfect society laid down somewhere in the objective law of nature, but since no actual society has ever very closely approximated this model, how shall we gain knowledge of the perfect society? Such knowledge, clearly, must come from methods which are designed to study something other than historical or actual social systems.

Fromm's reply to this question, presumably, would take the form of saying that we can recognize the sane society by inspecting its members: if they are good, it is good. Put another way, the good society is the good man writ large. Under most circumstances, this expression need be taken only as a convenient shorthand statement of a social-individual parallelism; but in this case, it can be used to open an interesting difficulty in Fromm's conception of social health and sickness.

The formula ". . . social pathology . . . is the pathology of so many human beings, and not of an entity beyond or apart from individuals," rejects the decisive idea that society or the social system is in some sense an entity or unit subject to its own laws and different from the individuals who compose it. Fromm recognizes only one kind of body, as it were, and that is the body of the individual human being. It follows that, if he is to be consistent, all he can mean by social pathology is something like "individual pathology in the plural." When he speaks of a sick society he can mean only that so many members of a group are sick that it is convenient to call the group sick. To speak of a sick society in this sense is like speaking of a nation of shopkeepers, say, or a nation in arms. It refers to a condition which exists widely among the members of a collectivity. A good example of this is Fromm's idea of the socially patterned defect, which is a defect that is widely shared among the members of a group. A socially patterned defect is, in this special sense, a social neurosis.

This is not a conception of social pathology at all, in any sense other than a statistical one. By denying the existence of an "entity beyond or apart from individuals," Fromm is left with nothing but individuals. Only individuals can be sick, for they are the only entities there are. If this analysis is correct, it makes no sense to talk about diagnosing the pathology of a society, for the idea of pathology assumes the existence of some entity which can be sick, and Fromm denies that society is such an entity. Nor can he talk meaningfully and consistently about the social causation of individual pathology, for the idea of causation requires both a causal entity and a condition which is caused. In denying the existence of society as an entity, Fromm is left with no causal entity.

Here we reach a logical dead end. Starting from a radically nominalistic conception, a conception which sees society as nothing but a convenient name for a number of individuals, it is impossible for Fromm to answer the question: How does society produce neurosis in individuals? What makes men neurotic? Fromm can answer only that men make themselves neurotic, or that *some* men make *others* neurotic. But does this not run in the face of his thesis that there is in all men an inherent "primary" urge toward self-realization and health? Does this not suggest that in some men the secondary urges are stronger than the primary ones?

No writer can long endure such frustration. He must escape it, even at the cost of inconsistency. That is the price Fromm pays. Fromm assuredly does have a conception of society or the social system as an entity which is in some sense real and apart from the individuals who compose it. While he never offers a formal statement of this conception, the conception itself appears on page after page of his work. Consider the following passage, in which the terms "society," "social structures," and "social system" are patently used in a realistic rather than a nominalistic sense:

> Each society is structuralized and operates in certain ways which are necessitated by a number of objective conditions. These conditions include methods of production and distribution which in turn depend on raw materials, industrial techniques, climate, size of population, and political and geographical factors, cultural traditions and influences to which society is exposed. There is no "society" in general, but only specific social structures which operate in different and ascertainable ways. Although these social structures do change . . . they are relatively fixed at any given historical period, and society can exist only by operating within the framework of its particular structure. The members of the society and/or the various classes or status groups within it have to behave in such a way as to be able to function in the sense required by the social system.[5]

What should one do when he catches a writer with his consistency down? A gentleman would proceed as though the misfortune had not occurred. A critic, however, must take the opportunity to see what the exposure reveals about the writer's thought.

So powerful is the realistic theme in Fromm's writing that one's instinct is to dismiss the nominalistic expression as just an accidental aberration. Fromm's whole work, after all, is an attempt to chart the relations between character and social structure, and such work presumes the real existence of society as something other than a number of individuals. A closer look, however, shows that each of Fromm's two usages of "society" serves a special function in his thought.

The nominalistic usage, the essence of which is the denial of reality and value to society as such, provides the foundation for Fromm's program of radical change. In this view, society is a collection of individuals acting in concert —nothing more, nothing less. Since each individual has an inherent urge toward self-realization, neither a single person nor a collection of them will long persist in ways of behavior contrary to human nature. When men feel that something is wrong with their behavior, they will try to change it. All that is required is the concentration of natural intelligence and the will to self-realization upon the present ways of behavior. This nominalistic conception, in brief, denies all value to tradition, to vested interests, to established institutions, customs, and beliefs and sees only the present. It also denies the need for any special science of society. That is to say, it excuses Fromm from examining the hard questions of the relations between social structure and character from the point of view of the possibility of social change. And it excuses him from doing so precisely at the point where he is trying to convince men of both the possibility and the desirability of vast social change. It relieves his advocacy of the burden of answering such questions as the following: Can society be sick while individuals are well; that is, is social sickness a manifestation of something other than the sickness of individual members of the society? Can individuals be sick without impairing the functioning of society? Just how, and why, does social malfunction cause individual malfunction? These matters would have to be examined in any real diagnosis of social sickness, and they cannot be examined without calling on a real "science of society." Fromm avoids this through his nominalistic usage. All that is needed is knowledge of the laws of human nature, which can then be used to order the relations among men after the model of human nature. The nominalistic conception, in short, at once provides that radical denial of the value of the established order and nourishes that faith in human perfectibility without which the revolutionary would lack confidence. Fromm's nominalism is the fulcrum of his radicalism.

The realistic usage, whose essence is the belief in the independent existence and value of society as such, serves the same end, but in a very different way. Fromm employs this conception in two large divisions of his thought, first in his analysis of the origins and development of the modern crisis, and again in his construction of utopia. Between history and utopia lies the excluded middle of the revolutionary present, when he always reverts to the nominalistic conception. By employing the realist conception in historical analysis, Fromm is able to identify certain concrete structures, such as "capitalism," "Calvinism," "private property," "the market," and talk about their "essential properties," their "real character," and their vicious influence on human life. He is able to identify the forces that chain man and corrupt his finest powers. Men are thus given real powers and structures to contend against, real institutions to blame for felt unhappiness.

The realist conception is useful in the construction of utopia because it enables Fromm to fall back on his premise that a "real" society really does mold character, and that if men would only build certain institutions, along the lines he suggests, they would have established the conditions for the good life.

In summary, Fromm's talk of the "sick society" and

the diagnosis of social pathology is to be understood not as the language of social science but as the rhetoric of social reform. So strong is the magic of science in our day that even the reformer must make his case in its terms. I have argued before that this appeal to science clutters Fromm's case and confuses his arguments. Fromm has a great subject—humanity as it ought to be—and he has a solid core of "data" from which to start—humanity as it actually has been in a few of its noblest representatives—but confusion enters when he superfluously tries to dignify his subject and universalize his data by the appeal to science. An important theme and a keen sense of the data relevant to one's theme are essential to all good work. Beyond that, only insight and passion and intelligence can make a good work great. Like many generous men before him, Fromm is outraged by the moral and esthetic niggardliness of his world. He hungers for righteousness and yearns for love. He would build a spacious social mansion fit for the noble human soul. He refuses to see why he must live among men who are wretched and crippled, unable to love and be loved. These are enough strengths for a moralist. Science does not add to their power.

Diagnosis of the Modern Condition

Fromm brings three assets to the task of understanding the modern condition. The first is his appreciation of the problem of the present as a problem of history, his recognition that present conditions can be fully understood only in the light of their origins and developments. The second is his possession of a generous measure of the sociological imagination, the ability to detect the social causes of personal troubles. The third is his possession of a body of convictions, even a dogma—if that word is understood as something other than a term of abuse—about the relations between character and social structure. Fused into one compound, these three elements form the substance of his method of diagnosis. His Marxist convictions lead him to focus on economic institutions as the chief personality-molding force. His historical orientation and his sociological imagination lead him to analyze changes in economic institutions and social character through time. Fromm's theme is the impact of the changing nature of capitalism on the character of man.

> The problem, then, of the socio-economic conditions in modern industrial society which create the personality of modern Western man and are responsible for the disturbances in his mental health requires an understanding of those elements specific to the capitalistic mode of production, of an "acquisitive society" in an industrial age.[6]

Although I am most interested in the modern period, at least the outlines of the historical analysis ought to be presented.*

Capitalism, Fromm begins, has been the dominant economic system of the West since the seventeenth century. During all this time, and despite all changes, capitalism has had four common and enduring features: (1) the existence of politically and legally free men; (2) the fact that free men sell their labor to the owners of capital on the labor market; (3) the existence of the commodity market as the mechanism by which prices and the distribution of

---

* Fromm presents his fullest history of capitalist development in *The Sane Society*, pp. 83–103. My account draws heavily on those pages. Of course, much of his writing is concerned with one or another aspect of this problem. The whole of *Escape from Freedom* may be read as a treatment of the social psychology of capitalism.

the social product are regulated; and (4) the principle that each acts to seek his own profit, and that by this competitive self-seeking the interests of all are advanced.

Fromm then divides the history of capitalism into three periods, each with its distinctive features.

The early period, covering the seventeenth and eighteenth centuries, had two distinctive features. The tools and techniques of production were still quite primitive. A residue of medieval ethical ideas restrained economic practices and kept the competitive ethic within some limits.

In the nineteenth century the system triumphed, and man lost. This was the century of capitalism rampant, of capitalism coming close to a realization of the wildest utopian scheme that men had ever entertained.[7] The most characteristic element of nineteenth-century capitalism was the ruthless exploitation of the workers. Man had lost his central place in society and had become just another commodity. The principle of the use of man by man prevailed across the whole social order, and capital, the dead past, ruled labor, the living present. The market was freed of all restrictions and its laws determined the price of everything. The competitive ethic supplanted all others and was perceived to have a redemptive power. Technique grew apace. The goal of production was not use but profit. Owing to the supreme authority of the market and the ethic of profit and competition, all genuine human solidarity and reciprocity broke down. Income lost all relation to the amount and social value of work. Finally, on the institutional level, nineteenth-century capitalism was still private capitalism, not yet the capitalism of huge corporations which nobody really owns.

Along with these institutional and ideological features went a certain social character, which Fromm describes as the hoarding orientation. The core of this character type was its love of saving and its pride in property and in mastery over things. Around this nucleus other traits clustered: competitiveness, individualism, aggressiveness, and exploitativeness. Characterologically, then, this was a period of repression and exploitation.

On his way to the twentieth century, Fromm pauses to observe that the reform movements of the nineteenth all started from these symptoms. The socialists wanted to end the exploitation of man by man. The liberals worked to liberate man from the irrational authorities who dominated him. Concentrating on sexuality, the forbidden land of the nineteenth-century bourgeois mind, Freud brought a heavy attack against the ethic of repression. Then Fromm notes what numerous observers before him had noted: to a remarkable degree, the programs of nineteenth-century reformers—socialists, liberals, and psychoanalysts alike—have been realized. In addition, our century has enjoyed an almost undreamed-of material prosperity. According to the lights of the nineteenth century, then, the life of the twentieth ought to be beautiful. Such is not the case. "In fact, it seems that in spite of material prosperity, political and sexual freedom, the world in the middle of the twentieth century is mentally sicker than it was in the nineteenth century." [8] Like Tantalus, we grasp for the cooling drink and the delicious grape, only to see them slip away. This is the condition that Fromm would diagnose and cure. Not for a moment does he seriously consider the thought that the condition of Tantalus might be the condition of man. Fromm does not forsake the eighteenth century.

Fromm turns next to the economic and social features which characterize the new capitalism. In a ruthlessly summary form, which loses much of the depth and power of Fromm's analysis, these are: the technological revolution, which is already well into the stage of automation; high concentration of capital and the separation of ownership and control (Fromm follows the classical analysis of Berle and Means); the declining number of independent, self-employed entrepreneurs, and the consequent rise in the number of employees of the great corporations; the practical disappearance of the old middle class, with a consequent increase in the rise of a new employed middle class, whose members increasingly manipulate not things but people (Fromm follows C. Wright Mills here); and, finally, the "miracle of production," which has made increasing consumption the vital principle of the economy, and which has brought in its train a whole new industry designed to manufacture the desire to consume.

Bridging the gap between socioeconomic structure and character structure, Fromm asks:

> What kind of men, then, does our society need? What is the "social character" suited to twentieth-century Capitalism?
>
> It needs men who co-operate smoothly in large groups; who want to consume more and more, and whose tastes are standardized and can be easily influenced and anticipated.
>
> It needs men who feel free and independent, not subject to any authority, or principle, or conscience—yet willing to be commanded, to do what is expected, to fit into the social machine without friction.[9]

Alienation: Hegel, Marx, Fromm

Fromm's description of the social character of the capitalist era is at once precise and impressionistic, subtle yet comprehensive. Nothing important is excluded, yet the description escapes superficiality because the whole canvas is bound together by one theme. Despairing of the possibility of a useful condensation of Fromm's pages, I shall move directly to that theme. The sickness of modern man is the sickness of alienation:

> By alienation is meant a mode of experience in which the person experiences himself as an alien. He has become . . . estranged from himself. He does not experience himself as the center of his world, as the creator of his own acts—but his acts and their consequences have become his masters, whom he obeys, or whom he may even worship. The alienated person is out of touch with himself as he is out of touch with any other person. He, like the others, is experienced as things are experienced; with the senses and with common sense, but at the same time without being related to oneself and to the world outside productively.*

Alienation has reached plague proportions in modern society. It pervades man's self-perceptions and his relations with his fellows. It contaminates the spheres of work and consumption and poisons man's relationships to politics, the state, and the social structures and forces which shape his

---

* *The Sane Society*, p. 120. This diagnosis goes beyond that offered in Fromm's first book, the broad theme of which was that "European and American history since the end of the Middle Ages is the history of the full emergence of the individual. It is a process which . . . only now seems to have come to a climax. . . . But while in many respects the individual has grown, has developed mentally and emotionally, and participates in cultural achievements in a degree unheard of before, the lag between 'freedom from' and 'freedom to' has grown too. The result of this disproportion between freedom *from* any tie and the lack of possibilities for the positive realization of freedom and individuality has led . . . to a panicky flight from freedom into new ties or at least into complete indifference." (*Escape from Freedom*, p. 37.) *Escape from Freedom* was written under the shadow of Hitlerism. Fromm was trying to analyze the anguish that led a nation to flee freedom and embrace fascism. In *The Sane Society*, he tries to explain the "complete indifference" to freedom which he finds in the United States today—and especially to explain that indifference to the moral powers and the moral demands of the self which is the essence of alienation.

destiny. Nor has religious life remained pure; it is as tainted by alienation as all the relationships of secular life. In all sectors of existence, "*man does not experience himself as the active bearer of his own powers and richness, but as an impoverished 'thing,' dependent on powers outside of himself, unto whom he has projected his living substance.*" [10]

In some of its meanings, the idea of alienation is as old as literary history. The outsider existed before Colin Wilson made a hero of him, and there were strangers before Camus' Meursault. Homer had written of the "tribeless, lawless, hearthless one," the one outside the fellowship, doomed to work his way through the desolate regions beyond the friendly fires of clan and kin. The motif of the eternal wanderer begins in the dawn of Jewish tradition and weaves in and out of the whole subsequent history of Western religion. Abram is the prototype and universal symbol of alienated man. Separated from his family, his nation, and his national religion, he wanders without a home in soil, society, or faith. He is the nomad, unable to love and belong. Unable to love, he subjects himself to a transcendent power and substitutes law for communion, subordination for love. Estranged from himself, Abram projects all that is good in him unto a strange absolute being, which is no longer *his* absolute being. In return for this, he gains a new identity, which is symbolized by the change of his name to Abraham. All this was long before the modern Existentialist teaching that alienation is rooted in the human condition.

What is distinctive about our era, however, is that alienation is increasingly coming to be one of the words that men use to describe the temper of the age. "Homelessness has become a world fate," Heidegger wrote, and his words state the theme of a swelling current of modern writing. In poetry and the novel, theology and philosophy, and even in sociology, the theme of alienation is used to describe the

inquietude of our age. So Fromm's work must be seen as
one current of a much larger stream of tendency. It is a
current whose sources are in Hegel and Marx. In order to
understand Fromm, it will be useful to look first at the concept of alienation in these two writers.

A "few words" about Hegel are nearly worthless. That
original, profound, and grandiose cathedral called Hegelian-
ism cannot be divided into parts for, as its architect wrote
on the cornerstone, the part has meaning only in the whole.
The discussion of alienation which appears in a brief section of the *Phenomenology of Mind* (1807) is just an explicit statement of a theme which weaves in and out of the
book and which cannot be understood without understanding the *Phenomenology* as a whole. Now, the *Phenomenology* fairly heaves with gravid abstractions. Whatever is
there to be delivered, be it a passing remark on current
affairs, a sermon, an account of a philosophical dispute,
a grand vision, or just a fact of history, must struggle for
light and air through a wheeze and murk of language that
chokes all but the fleetest and strongest. It takes a long time
and a firm will to work through Hegel's pages; and you can
never be sure until the very end that the product was worth
the labor. Too often one gets the feeling that H. G. Wells
reported after he had read Henry James: James's huge sentences with their small rewards reminded him of a hippo-
potamus struggling to pick up a peanut from the corner of
its cage. Furthermore, the whole work of Hegel is held together by a conception of philosophy and logic which must
seem the grossest obscurantism to a mind at home in the
atmosphere of positivism and pragmatism. A genuine com-
prehension of the *Phenomenology* is beyond me, but in
the faith that Hegel was a great philosopher and not, as
Bertrand Russell would have it, a pompous fool hiding his
confusions and trivia under verbiage, I shall attempt a few

remarks in the hope that they will set the background for a discussion of Marx's idea of alienation.

Hegel's philosophic vision is usually regarded as an optimistic one, and, in the large, that is a correct judgment. He achieved a triumph over all change and seeming irrationality in his vision of history as objectified reason. But the optimistic vision itself sprang from a profound pessimism. Hegel was bitterly aware of the separation of himself and his age from both antiquity and Christianity. He wrote at a time long after the sun of the Greek spirit had set, and he sensed that the Christian faith had been shattered beyond all possibility of resurrection. The present was a period of change and purposelessness, which men met with mixed frivolity and ennui. The future was shrouded, and men looked toward it with foreboding. In the introduction to the *Phenomenology*, written on the eve of the battle of Jena, when he was thirty-seven, Hegel described his epoch as "a birth-time, and a period of transition. The spirit of the age has broken with the world as it has hitherto existed, and with the old ways of thinking, and is in the mind to let them all sink into the depths of the past and to set about its own transformation." [11] In such an age, the consciousness of man is fragmented, and the soul is a scene of conflict and division. So Hegel's largest question was, how can the consciousness of man become total, unified, at rest? His guiding purpose was to restore meaning and unity to a shattered world, and the *Phenomenology*, the *Philosophy of History*, and the *Logic* are his metaphysical account of how the process takes place. The three books trace the dialectical progression through which the Spirit realizes itself in history.

Hegel can be understood on alienation if the basic idea of the *Phenomenology* is kept in view. This is the idea that mind is not a simple substance distinct from and existing independently of the outside world. Rather, it is a complex entity which develops from the animal stage of mere sense-awareness through a progression of stages in each of which more and more of its potentialities are unfolded, until it finally arrives at a stage of complete self-consciousness. This ultimate stage loses none of the earlier stages, but absorbs each of them and fashions them all into a new and larger synthesis. Trusting the reader to keep this fundamental notion in mind, I am going to risk an excursion over Hegel's description of the main stages which consciousness goes through on its journey to the ultimate stage of perfect freedom and self-consciousness, which Hegel usually called Reason, or Realization. After that, I shall return to the broader aspects of his conception.

The section in which Hegel sets forth the stages of self-consciousness is entitled "Freedom of Self-consciousness: Stoicism, Scepticism, and the Unhappy Consciousness." The historical background of the mental chaos and dissolution of Stoicism and Scepticism is found in the political and social chaos and dissolution of the Roman Empire. Since consciousness could not find fixed and stable objects outside itself, self-consciousness could not find a permanent subject in itself. Chaos and division prevail in all realms of life, internal as well as external, with the result that man becomes the slave and victim of his own formless subjective and objective life. The first stage through which the mind gropes in an attempt to end this slavery is that of the Stoic consciousness. The Stoic asserts freedom by holding aloof from the entanglements of real existence. Self-consciousness closes its gates against the stream of life and escapes into the freedom of pure thought. This freedom in thought, however, is not real freedom, not living freedom, but merely the notion of freedom, for it lacks the concrete content of life. The Stoic achieves freedom through refusing to play the game of life.

This is only a transitory stage in the development of mind toward real freedom. Hegel insists on an advance from freedom in thought to "living freedom." The next step in this progress is taken in the Sceptical form of consciousness. At this stage, man does play the game of life, but with no solid conviction that either the self or the world exists in real and stable form. The Sceptical consciousness regards the self and the world as delusions, with the result that it is unable to form a conception of either, and finally breaks down through its own contradictions. The recognition of these contradictions prepares the way for the next stage, that of the Unhappy Consciousness. Before turning to that, however, Hegel's decisive statements on the contradictions in the Sceptical consciousness ought to be quoted at some length, both because they convey the flavor of his style, and because they are the most difficult passages in the whole analysis of alienation:

> Sceptical self-consciousness thus discovers, in the flux and alteration of all that would stand secure in its presence, its own freedom, as given by and received from its own self. . . . This certainty does not arise as a result out of something extraneous and foreign which stowed away inside itself its whole complex development; a result which would thus leave behind the process by which it came to be. Rather consciousness itself is thoroughgoing dialectical restlessness, this mêlée of presentations derived from sense and thought, whose differences collapse into oneness, and whose identity is similarly again resolved and dissolved—for this identity is itself determinateness as contrasted with non-identity. This consciousness, however, as a matter of fact, instead of being

a self-same consciousness, is here neither more nor less than an absolutely fortuitous imbroglio, the giddy whirl of a perpetually self-creating disorder. This is what it takes itself to be; for itself maintains and produces this self-impelling confusion. Hence it even confesses the fact; it owns to being an entirely fortuitous *individual* consciousness. . . . But while it passes in this manner for an individual, isolated, contingent, in fact animal life, and a lost self-consciousness, it also, on the contrary, again turns itself into universal self-sameness; for it is the negativity of all singleness and all difference. . . . This form of consciousness is, therefore, the aimless fickleness and instability of going to and fro . . . from one extreme of self-same self-consciousness, to the other of contingent, confused and confusing consciousness.[12]

These hierophantic sentences work remarkable effects on the mind. After the first few astonished readings, the mind balks and yearns for safety and release. At this point, the words of James Frederick Ferrier, a leading English student of Hegel, offer comfort. In his *The Institutes of Metaphysics* (1854), Ferrier confessed that, although he had read "most of Hegel's works again and again," he was still "able to understand only a few short passages here and there." These few he "greatly admired for the depth of their insight, the breadth of their wisdom, and the loftiness of their tone." But for the rest, Hegel remained "as unpenetrable almost throughout as a mountain of adamant." Give the passage a half-dozen more readings, and a new effect appears. You become quite convinced that if you could but penetrate to the center of the mountain of adamant, you would find there the key to the mystery of the universe. That is the dangerous stage; and one should postpone his interpretation of Hegel until it has safely passed.

(Most of his commentators, it seems to me, have not heeded this warning.) Then, it is safe to go back and see whether there might actually be some meaning to be delivered from the passage. In the faith that there is, I offer the following plain version.

The Sceptical consciousness, Hegel seems to be saying, appears to be individual and isolated. This seeming self-certainty is deceptive, however, for the Sceptical consciousness cannot establish a basis for itself which is impervious to doubt. It also, therefore, cannot distinguish itself from anything else in the universe. Thus it is the very opposite of true individuality, which must be able to distinguish itself from everything else.

One might note here that Hegel is right. The Sceptic must try to prove that the real world exists by the evidence of his consciousness. But in doubting the real world he also must doubt his consciousness, which is part of the real world. Furthermore, he cannot understand the world except as a part of himself, because whatever he proves can only be a construct of his own mind. It follows that if he succeeds in proving to his own satisfaction the existence of the real world, he can no longer distinguish himself from this "proved" world, which is only an outgrowth of himself. This seems to be Hegel's argument in the quoted paragraph. The argument is an excellent special application of his general fundamental principle, the thesis that an absolute idea is needed for ultimate knowledge.

Let me now move backward from the conclusion of Hegel's argument to his description of the life of the Sceptical consciousness. The Sceptical consciousness arises through the interplay of thoughts and impressions, which the mind resolves into a sense of its own identity. But since the Sceptical consciousness sees itself as a mere collection of impressions and sensations (Hume's argument on the self was well known to Hegel), it must ceaselessly dissolve this identity into its constituents. Thus an enduring self-conception is impossible, and all the Sceptic can achieve in the mental life is the "giddy whirl of a perpetually self-creating disorder." This means simply that the knowledge of self which the Sceptic has at any given moment is merely a conception which will change with each succeeding impression. There is no stable self which may come to be known, for in the very act of knowing the self, the self is altered.

The remaining stages in the development of the spirit can be described more briefly. Hegel sets the historical background for the "Unhappy Consciousness" in the life of the Middle Ages. The craving of the mind for certainty and stability amidst change and uncertainty was recognized by the Church, which tried to build a permanent connection between the insecurity of this world and the perfection of an Immutable Reality beyond the material realm. The methods by which the Church attempted to forge the bond only reflect the great contrast and distance between the two realms. Moving desperately and uncertainly between these two realms, repeatedly falling short of the perfection which it had placed above it in the heavens, the free mind is tortured. This inner process Hegel calls the "Unhappy Consciousness," unhappy because the spirit craves but never gains complete consciousness of self and complete union between itself and its objects.

This gives way to the stage of reason, which comes when the mind realizes that it had closed itself to the real world and tried to realize itself in the world beyond. The stage of reason is reached when man enters into the world in full consciousness that it is not an alien world but his own. The subject admits the distinction between itself and its objects but yet asserts that the distinction is not a real distinction but one within itself. The contradiction between subject and object is resolved. In this stage, man realizes that the world and the soul are alike rational and real. He then can observe the external world, mental phenomena, and the nervous organism as a unity, as the common meeting ground of body and mind, object and subject. Having completed its long journey toward self-realization, the soul is now unified and complete, at rest in the knowledge that the rational is the real and the real is the rational.

Having followed Hegel's account of the journey of the spirit toward self-realization, I shall now return to the broader questions and try to delineate the largest outlines of his analysis. It should be clear from all the above that for Hegel the mind is process, activity. Activity of course produces objects, and the mind best becomes aware of itself by reflecting on the objects its own activity has brought into being. In the beginning, the mind sees only opposition and distinction between itself and its objects. It sees them as alien. But there can be no mental development at all without opposition, without a sense of the distinction between the mind and the non-mind. Thus Hegel writes of the "labor of the negative"; and this use of "labor" is not just a metaphor, for the mind learns about itself not by looking within itself but by going out into the world which its own work has produced and reflecting on the objects of its labor. Throughout the *Phenomenology* Hegel offers concrete examples to show how man's consciousness of himself is improved by work and by reflection on the products of his work—architecture, painting, music, philosophy, religion. The mind develops only by working for its living, as it were, by putting itself into objects and then reflecting on and drawing meaning from those objects.

This "going outside itself" Hegel calls *Entäusserung*, alienation. Without it, life is merely animal. Civilization cannot exist and develop without opposition and division. And this division exists in the minds of men, for, on the one side, there is mind as externalized in its works; while, on the other, there is mind that confronts its works and senses that they are foreign. Hegel discusses certain historical epochs when this opposition between the mind and its works is acute, when the world is seen as totally alien. He mentions, for example, the position of the early Christians in the Imperial period. This perception of the gap between the spirit of man and the world produces felt turmoil and unhappy divisions in the minds of men, and this unhappy state of mind Hegel calls *Entfremdung*, estrangement. Full freedom is reached only when man transcends these divisions and absorbs them into a higher synthesis. In summary, the major theme of the *Phenomenology* is the progress of the human spirit from unreflective living through opposition, labor, alienation and estrangement to ultimate self-consciousness.

Hegel, then, had set the problem of alienation on a metaphysical and ideal-historical foundation. Marx borrowed Hegel's term and translated it from the language of metaphysics into the language of sociology and economics. Thus translated, it became one of the central categories of his critique of the capitalist era. It is in this form that the idea has come down to Fromm.*

* Marx's major statements on alienation were made in his earlier writings, especially in the *Economic and Philosophical Manuscripts* (1844); *The Holy Family* (1845); and *The German Ideology* (1846). Some of these have not yet fully appeared in English, but substantial extracts may be found in T. B. Bottomore and Maximilien Rubel, *Karl Marx: Selected Writings in Sociology and Social Philosophy* (London: Watts & Co., 1956). Few statements on alienation appear in Marx's later, more mature writings, although the problem receives some attention in the first volume of *Capital*. This has led some interpreters to conclude that the concept of alienation was just a part of Marx's Hegelian baggage, of no decisive importance in his real

Marx took from Hegel the germinal idea that man creates himself in history through the practical activity of living and working in society. "The outstanding thing in Hegel's *Phenomenology* . . . is thus first that Hegel conceives the self-genesis of man as a process . . . ; that he grasps the essence of *labour* and comprehends objective man as the outcome of man's *own labour*." [13] But Marx thought Hegel's idealism had led him into a radical misunderstanding of the nature of the process of self-creation through labor. Hegel had pictured the historical process as the movement of abstract categories, the activity of pure spirit, of which individuals were merely the masks and mouthpieces. Marx insisted that the historical process through which man created himself must be seen as a process of real work, real labor, not the labor of the abstract spirit. In conceiving labor as the work of the pure spirit, Hegel had in fact conceived labor in an alienated form. This criticism, of course, is less than fair to Hegel, who had a clear and full conception of the relationships between actual work and consciousness.

The broad connection between Hegel's conception of alienation and Marx's conception of it will be clear if it is remembered that what Marx did was to write a huge analogue to Hegel, but in the language of sociology and economics rather than in the language of metaphysics. Note, for example, how closely Marx's philosophy of history follows the form of Hegel's account in the *Phenomenology*.

---

thought. It has led others to distinguish between the earlier "humanistic" and the later "scientific" Marx. I think that neither of these quite hits the mark, though the second comes closer than the first. Alienation receded from Marx's work as he gave more and more time to technical questions of historical, philosophical, and especially economic analysis. But Marxism was from the beginning a cry of protest against the degradation of man under capitalism. And from this point of view, the idea of alienation stands at the center of all Marx's work.

Hegel's theme was the mind's progress from unreflecting existence through opposition and alienation to ultimate freedom. In Marx's philosophy of history, man moves from primitive communism through class conflict to the ultimate freedom and harmony of the new communism, in which men finally take full, rational control of their own destinies. Nothing has changed but the language. Similarly, Marx's account of the condition of the proletariat in capitalist society is analogous to Hegel's description of the divided and estranged mind. Just as Hegel described the estranged mind which is lost in the world of objects which it has itself created, so Marx explains how under capitalism men are crippled and bewildered by a social world which, though they have created it, appears to them as alien and menacing. Marx's work is a point-by-point translation of Hegel's metaphysical categories into economic categories. Only at the very end of his analysis does he depart from Hegel. He either did not understand, or else willfully rejected, Hegel's notion of synthesis—though, of course, he used the word itself. In the whole of Marx's thought there is no real idea of synthesis, but only of the conquest of one extreme (capitalists-proletarians) by the other. That, however, is not of direct concern here.

The historical link between Hegel's idealistic conception of the problem of alienation and Marx's socioeconomic conception of it was provided by the materialism of Feuerbach. In *Das Wesen des Christentums* (1841), Feuerbach set out to interpret religion by the concepts of projection and alienation. He presented religion as the essence of man projected outside himself and personified in god-figures: the capacities ascribed to the gods were really man's own capacities in an alienated form. Marx started from this position and put the question more generally. He wanted to know under what conditions men projected their own powers onto forces or entities outside themselves and then permitted themselves to be ruled by these alien forces which they themselves had manufactured. How did man's own powers and capacities become transformed into self-subsistent entities alien to him and in control of his actions? This problem of alienation, now conceived as a sociological or socioeconomic problem, dominates all his writings.

The foundation of Marx's critical position is an essentialist view of human nature, which, regrettably, he never worked out systematically. Accompanying this is an almost Aristotelian, or at least a teleological, conception of freedom. To Marx, the free man was the man who each day realized the potentialities of his being through works which gave his inner capacities the form of concrete embodiments. The great evil of alienation is that it constrains liberty. Alienation is a form of slavery, an especially vicious form, because it is one which man unknowingly makes and imposes on himself. Each of man's activities and products ought to be so many steps along the road to self-realization; that is, they ought to be at once the manifestations and the foundations of man's freedom. Instead, they have become alien forces standing outside man and hostile to him. Instead of enriching man, they deplete him. Instead of liberating man, they enslave him.

Marx never offered an explicit account of the genesis and growth of alienation, but it is reasonably clear that he thought its origins lay in the division of labor: "the division of labour offers us the first example of how, as long as man remains in natural society, that is, as long as a cleavage exists between the particular and the common interest, as long therefore as activity is not voluntarily, but naturally, divided, man's own act becomes an alien power opposed to him, which enslaves him instead of being controlled by him." [14] Occasional references to the idea also appear in his history of the changing forms of private property. More frequent references appear throughout his discussions of political economy as an ideology. These passages, however, do not substantially alter the general conclusion that he never offered an explicit and systematic account of the development of alienation.

At first glance, this omission seems to be a fault. A closer view shows that what appears as a fault is really a necessity of Marx's whole analysis of capitalism and his whole concept of alienation. Alienation is nothing but capitalism seen from one angle of vision, capitalism seen from the point of view of its evil impact on man. Hence, when Marx wrote the history and analyzed the dynamics of capitalism, he did the same for alienation, because alienation was not an incidental feature of capitalism but capitalism itself, capitalism in its social-psychological aspect. From this it follows that alienation advances as capitalism advances and disappears when capitalism disappears. It is a superficial view, albeit one shared as often by his ostensible friends as by his enemies, which sees Marx's work as primarily a technical or scientific analysis of the capitalist system of production and exchange, and his appeal to revolution as a kind of demand for fair shares and equal treatment. Marx's scientific work was but an aid to, as his call for revolution was but an appeal for, the realization of his moral vision of man restored, man liberated from the alienations of capitalist society and in command of his own destiny.

This is not the place to say anything at all about the whole Marxist system. I just remind the reader that the concept of alienation is embedded in a complete intellectual structure. Let me assume a familiarity with that structure, and especially with those parts of it which deal with the materialist conception of history, the relations between existence and consciousness, and the origins, development, and nature of capitalism. Let me assume that one has followed Marx through his description of the institutions and the ideology of mature capitalism and is now prepared to follow his account of the meaning of work and the character of human relationships in such a society. Here the concept of alienation enters.

It is possible to distinguish four main forms of alienation in Marx's treatment: (1) alienation of the worker from the process of work; (2) alienation of the worker from the product of work; (3) alienation of each from himself; and (4) alienation of each from his fellows. For the purposes of exposition, the first two forms can be gathered under the category of "alienated labor," and the second two can be abbreviated as "alienated human relations."

Alienated labor. Here Marx attempts to show the impact of capitalist labor on the psychodynamics of individuals and classes. Under the conditions of capitalism, the process of work has become external to the worker, not a part of his nature. Consequently, the worker experiences work not as fulfillment but as impoverishment. Work gives him not a feeling of well-being and accomplishment but a feeling of physical and moral debasement. He feels at home with himself only during his hours of leisure; while at work he is homeless. Work is not voluntary but forced labor. "His labour is therefore not voluntary, but coerced; it is *forced labour.* It is therefore not the satisfaction of a need; it is merely a *means* to satisfy needs external to it." [15] The alien character of work appears clearly, Marx said, in the fact that as soon as there is no compulsion to work, men avoid it like the plague.

Out of this world of alienated labor grows another world, a world of objects. Though created by human energy, this realm of objects acquires an independent power hostile

to man. Marx's decisive statement deserves extensive quotation.

> The more the worker expends himself in work, the more
> powerful becomes the world of objects which he creates
> in face of himself, and the poorer he himself becomes in
> his inner life. . . . It is just the same as in religion. The
> more of himself man attributes to God, the less he has
> left in himself. The worker puts his life into the object,
> and his life then belongs no longer to him but to the
> object. . . . What is embodied in the product of his
> labour is no longer his. . . . The *emptying* of the
> worker into his product means not only that his labour
> becomes an object, takes on its own existence, but that
> it exists outside him, independently, and alien to him,
> and that it stands opposed to him as an autonomous
> power. The life which he has given to the object sets
> itself against him as an alien and hostile force.[16]

In trying to describe man's relation to this world of
commodities, Marx again had recourse to the religious
analogy. The productions of the human mind become rei-
fied and projected into a realm beyond the human. In the
mist-shrouded regions of the religious life, the phantoms of
man's brain take on concrete shape and appear as independent beings with their own indwelling spirit and their
own powers and laws. These phantoms then enter into relations both with one another and with the fearful race of
men. So it is with the world of commodities. The productions of the human hand also seem to take on independent
existence and develop laws and powers of their own. What
is really nothing but the product of definite and specific
social relations between men assumes in the eyes of men
the fantastic form of a relation between things which have
objective characteristics. This phenomenon Marx calls by

the evocative name of the fetishism of commodities. The core of the idea is contained in the following extract:

> . . . the mutual relations of the producers, within which the social character of their labour affirms itself, take the form of a social relation between the products.
>
> The mystery of the commodity form, therefore, consists in the fact that in it the social character of men's labour appears to them as an objective characteristic, a social natural quality of the labour product itself, and that consequently the relation of the producers to the sum total of their own labour is presented to them as a social relation, existing not between themselves, but between the products of their labour. Through this transference the products of labour become commodities, social things whose qualities are at the same time perceptible and imperceptible by the senses.[17]

Alienated human relations. Marx returns repeatedly to his central theme: capitalism as human tragedy. It has shattered all genuine community and reduced social life to a commercial enterprise. Capitalist society is nothing but a series of bi- and multi-lateral exchanges, a tawdry business of buying and selling, in which every man is at once a salesman and a commodity. In this vast marketplace, men respond to themselves and each other not as vital, free, precious human beings but as objects, lifeless articles to be bought and sold and used, and discarded when no longer useful. Man is no longer in direct contact either with himself or with his fellows. His "human" relations are now controlled by an alien intermediary. This alien intermediary is money; and again Marx's description of its character and power cannot be excelled.

> The nature of money is . . . that [in it] the *mediating activity* of *human* social action by which man's prod-

ucts reciprocally complete each other, is *alienated* and becomes the characteristic of *a material thing*, money, which is external to man. When man exteriorizes this mediating activity he is active only as an exiled and dehumanized being; the *relation* between things, and human activity with them, becomes the activity of a being outside and above man. Through this *alien intermediary*—whereas man himself should be the intermediary between men—man sees his will, his activity and his relation to others as a power which is independent of him and of them. His slavery therefore attains its peak. That this *intermediary* becomes a *real god* is clear, since the intermediary is the *real power* over that which he mediates to men. His cult becomes an end in itself. The objects, separated from this intermediary, have lost their value. . . . This *intermediary* is thus the exiled, alienated *essence* of private property . . . just as it is the . . . *alienated* social activity of man. All the qualities involved in the production of this activity, which really belong to man, are attributed to the intermediary.*

Alienation affects the capitalists as well as the workers, though in different ways. The owning class is satisfied with its situation, recognizes self-alienation as the source of its own power, and retains at least the semblance of a human existence. The proletarian class, on the other hand, recognizes that it is condemned to an inhuman existence. Caught

* Bottomore and Rubel, *op. cit.*, pp. 171–172. Compare this with a passage where Aristotle describes money as a requisite to community, precisely because it mediates between man and man, and man and commodities: ". . . all goods must have a price set on them; for then there will always be exchange, and if so, association of man with man. Money, then, acting as a measure, makes goods commensurate and equates them; for neither would there have been association if there were not exchange, nor exchange if there were not equality, nor equality if there were not commensurability." (*The Basic Works of Aristotle*, Richard McKeon (ed.), New York: Random House, 1941, pp. 1011–1012 (*Ethics*, Bk. V, Chap. 5, 1133^b).

in the contradiction between their "humanity" and their inhuman situation, the proletarians are forced to revolt against the degradation which alienation imposes on them. From the political point of view, therefore, "the property owners are the *conservative* and the proletarians the *destructive* party." [18] Since alienation is endemic to capitalist society, it will disappear only with the victory of the "destructive party." Marx never showed very clearly how socialism would end alienation, but if we take strictly his thesis that *all* forms of human servitude stem from the relation of the worker to the privately owned instruments of production, it follows that alienation will end when the emancipation of society from private property is complete. If, however, we also take seriously his hint that the genesis of alienation is the division of labor as such, it is hard to see how socialism alone can do much to cure the disease of alienation, unless the socialists are willing to forego the advantages of the division of labor and return to a more primitive economic order.

This exposition will have served its purpose if it has elucidated the core meaning of Marx's concept of alienation. The question now is: What does Fromm do with these ideas? What changes does he work on Marx's formulation?

From one point of view, the answer is that he has not basically altered the ideas of Marx. He has kept intact the core of Marx's concept, which, in Fromm's formulation, is the idea that "*man does not experience himself as the active bearer of his own powers and richness, but as an impoverished 'thing,' dependent on powers outside of himself, unto whom he has projected his living substance.*" [19] This core identity also can be seen in many of Fromm's specific applications. He retains Marx's four types of alienation, follows Marx in his treatment of commodity fetishism and the worship of money, analyzes the impact of the market on man just about as Marx did, and accepts the broad outlines of Marx's discussion of work. In all these areas, Fromm has added little beyond some modern illustrations and citations.

While Fromm has kept the core constant, he has considerably expanded the idea at its margins. This expansion takes two forms. First, he has broadened the idea to cover a greater range of phenomena. Secondly, he has given the idea more psychological depth. Put slightly differently, Fromm has brought Marx's notion up to date by applying it to modern phenomena and by giving it firmer psychological underpinnings. In this expansion lies Fromm's contribution. In it also lies his peril, for in his hands, alienation becomes so protean a term that it loses some of the precision, and therefore the analytic utility, of Marx's formulation.

On balance, I think Fromm has gained more than he has lost. If this is so, the gain derives from a specific feature of this analysis: his perspective is that of mass society, not class society. He liberates alienation from the confinements of class analysis and discusses it under the conditions of massness. This liberation at once makes Fromm's analysis more relevant to modern conditions and permits him to escape some of Marx's shortcomings. Fromm, for example, does not romanticize and glorify the proletariat. Similarly, when he comes to offer a cure for alienation, he avoids Marx's narrow class solution and offers a more broadly social and moral remedy.

These points will appear more clearly in later discussion. At the moment, I want to turn to a few of Fromm's applications of the idea of alienation. What follows is not intended to be a full exposition of his usage of the concept, for such an account would be as long as his critique of capitalist society. My purpose is to convey a reasonably full

sense of Fromm's broadened and deepened idea of alienation.

Fromm starts by saying that alienation is at bottom
the same thing as idolatry. Idolatrous man spends his capacities on building an idol and then worships this idol as
though it were an independent being and not merely the
lifeless creature of his own hand. What the idol gains, man
loses. In contrast to this, Fromm argues, the central principle of Old Testament monotheism is the idea that God
is indefinable and infinite. Since man is made in God's
likeness, man too is the bearer of infinite qualities. Hence
in worshiping God man escapes the error of hypostatizing
one partial quality of himself into the whole, and then submitting to it. Unfortunately, Fromm complains, Protestant
Christianity itself regressed to a form of idolatry, for in the
theology of Luther and Calvin man was commanded to
yield his own finest powers to God and then trust to grace
that these powers will be returned to him.*

In our time, the major organized religions have escaped
active idolatry only by emptying religion of spiritual content. Religion is just another of the commodities on display
in our sumptuous show windows. Some of us buy it, while
some do not; on the whole, it is probably better if one has
it, but it is certainly not one of the things we simply could
not do without. It is a good prestige item in most circles,
and for a great many of us it is a pleasant leisure time activity; but neither of these should be confused with the real
religious meaning of the Jewish-Christian ideal, which is the
search for salvation and the quest for answers to the deep-

---

* I forego comment on this, for an adequate comment would have to be
very extensive. Although psychologically sound, Fromm's analysis is disas-
trously wrong from the religious and historical points of view. After all, Old
Testament monotheism assumes the real existence of a transcendent being:
God is not merely the symbol of man's powers.

est problems of our existence. "Our culture is perhaps the first completely secularized culture in human history. . . . The majority of us . . . take it for granted that God exists. The rest . . . take it for granted that God does not exist. . . . In fact, whether a man in our culture believes in God or not makes hardly any difference either from a psychological or from a truly religious standpoint. In both instances he does not care—either about God or about the answer to the problem of his own existence." [20] God has been promoted. He is the man upstairs, the benevolent general director of the corporation who will watch out for you as long as you do your part. As some wit has put it, when a man of today tells you he knows God, you can be pretty sure he is only name-dropping.

Turning to the state, Fromm finds the same phenomena of idolatry-alienation. Masses of men have abdicated their own powers and bestowed them on a political leader or on the state. "In Fascism and Stalinism the absolutely alienated individual worships at the altar of an idol. . . ." [21] Other masses simply have no or little interest in and no real knowledge of public and political matters. Fromm thinks this is the situation in most of the Western republics. In those countries, everyone has the right to express his will, but what does this right mean if individuals have no real will of their own, if their will is merely an echo of the chorus around them, or a product of the machinery of opinion formation? In Fromm's view, our politics has become just another commodity, to be merchandized like automobiles or soap. The only difference is, not as many people care as much about politics as they do about automobiles. Fromm accepts Schumpeter's judgment that the typical citizen has little sense of reality and no effective volition toward the great issues of politics. These factors in turn account for the monumental ignorance and lack of judgment the average citizen displays in political matters.[22]

Fromm also turns his attention to bureaucratization, "one of the most significant phenomena in an alienated culture." [23] The reality and the spirit of bureaucracy pervade the whole of modern society—business, government, religious life, the trade union, education, the political party. More and more people earn their living as bureaucrats, and more and more people come under the sway of the bureaucracies. Bureaucratized human relations are alienated human relations. The bureaucrat deals not with real living individuals but with abstract quantities which can be manipulated in various ways. If the market has made man an article to be exchanged, bureaucracy has made him an object to be manipulated.

Some of Fromm's most telling pages are devoted to a description of alienation in the sphere of consumption. Our mass production economy is directed almost exclusively by the principle of production for profit rather than for use. As such, it devotes prodigious effort to stimulating the desire for consumption goods. Modern capitalism has been instrumental in creating what Fromm calls the principle of nonfrustration, "*the principle that every desire must be satisfied immediately, no wish must be frustrated.*" [24] Consumption is inculcated as both a duty and a right, with the consequence that we have become the most voracious consumers in history. This orgy of consumption dominates our leisure hours and fills our dreams of heaven.

> Modern man, if he dared to be articulate about his concept of heaven, would describe a vision which would look like the biggest department store in the world, showing new things and gadgets, and himself having

plenty of money with which to buy them. He would wander around open-mouthed in this heaven of gadgets and commodities, provided only that there were ever more and newer things to buy, and perhaps that his neighbors were just a little less privileged than he.[25]

The heaven of consumption, however, is in the end unsuitable for human occupation. The act of consumption should be a rich and vitally human act, an act involving all our senses, our needs, our esthetic capacities. The act of consumption should be a humanly meaningful and productive experience. In our culture, there is little of this. "Consuming is essentially the satisfaction of artificially stimulated phantasies, a phantasy performance alienated from our concrete, real selves." [26]

Fromm, in short, pushes the concept of alienation into every sector of life. Indeed, he even uses it to help account for death: he believes that many suicides are caused by "the boredom and monotony . . . which is engendered by the alienated way of living. . . ." [27] But it is not necessary to provide additional examples. Let me conclude this exposition with a few remarks on his discussion of alienation and mental health. A few remarks will do, for it follows from Fromm's view of human nature that alienated men can be neither happy nor healthy.

The core of alienated man's sickness is the loss of the sense of the self. The characteristic symptom of his sickness is anxiety. Since alienated man is worth to himself only what he thinks he is worth to others, he must ceaselessly strive for approval. This he does through conforming to the prevailing fashions. Yet, insofar as he *is* human, he cannot help straying from the herd from time to time. Hence he anxiously expects disapproval all the time, and he strives ever harder to merge with the herd. So desperate is this situation in our time that it is not excessive to say that to the degree that one is human, he will suffer the pains of acute neurosis, and to the degree that he is alienated, he will enjoy the narcotic pleasures of conformity. Fromm agrees that the proper label for our age is the "age of anxiety." He adds that this anxiety is produced by alienation, by the lack of genuine selfhood.

Another symptom of alienation is guilt, which Fromm thinks is widespread and deep-rooted in our culture. This guilt comes from two sources. The first is the feeling that one is a deviant, different from the rest, poorly adjusted. The second springs from the core of man's own true (humanistic) conscience. The voice of conscience tells alienated man that he is wasting his powers and dissipating his substance. One cannot help feeling guilty for this waste. This is the cruel rack of alienated man in an alienated society: he "feels guilty for being himself and for not being himself, for being alive and for being an automaton, for being a person and for being a thing." [28]

Despite his protestations, alienated man is unhappy. Considering the nature of man and the conditions of happiness, it could not be otherwise. "Having no faith, being deaf to the voice of conscience, and having a manipulating intelligence but little reason, he is bewildered, disquieted and willing to appoint to the position of a leader anyone who offers him a total solution." [29] This, Fromm says, is the objective state of alienated man. He concludes with a warning that we must beware of doctors of the soul who tell us that alienated man is real man, and as happy as he can be. Much of modern psychiatry is itself an alienated ideology. "Our current psychiatric definitions of mental health stress those qualities which are part of the alienated social character of our time: adjustment, cooperativeness, aggressiveness, tolerance, ambition, etc." [30] Fromm singles out Harry

Stack Sullivan's work as the most instructive example of an alienated psychiatry, but Sullivan is by no means alone. Just as Marx thought that political economy was the perfect ideological expression of alienation in his time, Fromm thinks that most modern psychiatry performs that role in his. Just as Marx thought that political economy had mistaken the shopkeeper for man, so Fromm thinks that modern psychiatry has mistaken marketing man for man.*

* The definition of marketing man (alienated man) as the man who has no self raises a hard problem for the definition of a cure in psychoanalytic work. Here I can only outline the problem, without exploring its ramifications. As I understand it, the classical definition of the role of the analyst is to help the patient strip away the accretions and repressions which cloak his identity. Through the insight thus gained one becomes aware of his true self, of the real values which make up his true identity, and of the real philosophy of life which he stands for. All this assumes an identity that was already there and that had only to be discovered. Marketing man faces the analyst with a totally different problem. Marketing man is precisely the man who *has no identity*. He comes before the analyst not because his identity has been lost but because the method of conforming to the others as a substitute for identity has failed him. If the analyst peels away the accretions and repressions of marketing man, he will discover not an identity but a vacuum. Hence the problem for marketing man is not to discover his identity, but to create one. But no psychoanalyst is equipped to do this, for psychoanalysis is a method of investigation and not a way of life. The psychoanalyst is a healer of souls, not a maker of them. Fromm would try to escape this dilemma with the aid of his essentialist notion of the humanistic conscience: there is in each of us a noble god struggling to emerge. I have already treated this idea in an earlier chapter. Here it is enough to remember Orwell's remark: in every thin man a fat man struggles to emerge.

This dilemma, which is inescapable in the Frommian system, gives the Freudian far less trouble, for the simple reason that he would not diagnose absence of self in marketing man. There *are* some clinical types which approach selflessness in the Freudian sense, but they are too few to form a social character style in Fromm's usage, and they overlap with the Frommian category of the marketing man in an apparently random fashion. The "impostor" is a case in point. Here there is good clinical evidence of an incompleteness of self; but the impostor's character orientation may be exploitative (competitive, status-seeking), hoarding (accumulating a cache by fraud and guile), or even productive (the few impostors who actually seem to transcend their limitations through their pseudo-identities, and who use these new powers skillfully and constructively; the archetype might be Thomas Mann's Felix Krull). Another example of a selfless one in Freudian diagnosis is the "as-if" personality. But these types are quite rare, and they cut across all

With this I end the exposition and turn to commentary.

The Sane Society is an ambitious work. Its scope is as broad as the question: What does it mean to live in modern society? A work so broad, even when it is directed by a leading idea and informed by a moral vision, must necessarily "fail." Even a hasty reader will easily find in it numerous blind spots, errors of fact and argument, important exclusions, areas of ignorance and prejudice, undue emphases on trivia, examples of broad positions supported by flimsy evidence, and the like. Such books are easy prey for critics. Nor need the critic be captious. A careful and orderly man, who values precision and a kind of tough intellectual responsibility, might easily be put off by such a book. It is a simple matter, for one so disposed, to take a work like *The Sane Society* and shred it into odds and ends. The thing can be made to look like the cluttered attic of a large and vigorous family—a motley jumble of discarded objects, some outworn and some that were never useful, some once whole and bright but now chipped and tarnished, some odd pieces whose history no one remembers, here and there a gem, everything fascinating because it suggests some part of the human condition—the whole adding up to nothing more than a glimpse into the disorderly history of the makers and users.

That could be easily done, but there is little reason in it. It would come down to saying that Fromm paints with a broad brush, and that, after all, is not a conclusion one

---

of Fromm's character orientations. Most of the marketing men whose selves Fromm writes out of existence would not be diagnosed as selfless ones by the Freudians. Therefore, the problem of creating, rather than liberating, identities through psychotherapy is a vastly greater one for the Frommian than it is for the Freudian.

must work toward but an impression he has from the outset. I mention these features of the book because they are
inherent in the book's character and therefore must be mentioned. It would be superfluous to build a critique around
them. There are more substantial criticisms to be made of
Fromm's account of capitalist civilization.

It is worthwhile to recall that Fromm's treatment has
both descriptive and normative aspects. Since I have already discussed his moral position, that discussion is incorporated by reference into the following pages, which will
focus on the empirical and analytic side of Fromm's treatment. I shall first indicate a couple of weaknesses in
Fromm's analysis, then argue that, granted these weaknesses, he still has much left that is valuable, and, finally,
raise the general question of a philosophical versus a sociological approach to the question of alienation.

Almost no empirical work has been done on the problem of alienation. Despite its rather long intellectual history, alienation is still a promising hypothesis and not a
verified theory. The idea has received much attention in
philosophy, in literature, and in a few works of general social
criticism, such as *The Sane Society*. What is missing is
work that would answer, presumably by the use of survey
methods and Guttman-type attitude scales, such questions
as these: What are the components of the feeling-state described as alienation? How widespread is alienation? What is
its incidence among the various classes and subgroups of
the population? Taking alienation as a dependent variable,
with what socio-structural factors is it most highly associated? Considered as an independent variable, how does it
affect behavior in various sectors of life? * Until such work

---

* I know of only one attempt to even begin this kind of work. It is Gwynn
Nettler, "A Measure of Alienation," *American Sociological Review*, Vol. 22,
(December, 1957), pp. 670–677. He built a seventeen-item scale to measure

is done, there must remain the nagging suspicion that alienation may be little more than an expression of the malaise of the intellectual, who, rejected by and in turn rejecting the larger society, projects his own fear and despair onto the broader social screen.

I am not suggesting that Fromm ought to do this kind of work. Nor do I think that alienation is nothing more than a projection of the malaise of the intellectual. I am saying only that until a fuller and different kind of evidence comes in, any discussion of alienation must be understood to have certain important limitations.

Until such evidence appears, we must make do with the evidence we have. Here, perhaps, Fromm is vulnerable, for he does not always use the best and most recent evidence available, and he sometimes selects and interprets the evidence in rather special ways. Three examples follow.

Fromm's analysis of alienation in the sphere of production centers around the concepts of the bureaucratization of the corporation, the separation of ownership from control, and the broad (and thus from the point of view of corporate control, ineffective) dispersion of stock ownership. For all these points he relies exclusively on Berle and Means's study of 1932, *The Modern Corporation and Private Property*. The broad conclusions of that pioneering work remain undisturbed, but subsequent research has

---

alienation, defined as the psychological state of a person "*who has been estranged from, made unfriendly toward, his society and the culture it carries.*" (*Ibid.*, p. 672.) Nettler's analysis of the interviews he conducted with thirty-seven alienated persons shows that his concept of alienation is peculiarly "intellectual." Thus: "The common ground beneath these estranged ones is a consistent maintenance of unpopular and averse attitudes toward familism, the mass media and mass taste, current events, popular education, conventional religion and the telic view of life, nationalism, and the voting process." (*Ibid.*, p. 674.) This unduly restricted concept of alienation renders irrelevant the large theoretical, philosophical, and psychological literature on the subject.

expanded and somewhat altered their empirical support, has suggested important revisions in the general analytic frame of reference, and has sharpened the meaning of particular analytic concepts in this area. Fromm seems unaware of these developments.[31]

Another example is his very infrequent use of the large amount of data from surveys designed to discover what and how people actually do feel and think on a broad range of topics: he cites such survey-type findings just three times. Moreover, the conclusions he draws from the findings are not always the only ones possible. For example, he cites the following data from two studies on job satisfaction: in the first study, 85 per cent of professionals and executives, 64 per cent of white collar people, and 41 per cent of factory workers expressed satisfaction with their jobs; in the second study, the percentages were 86 for professionals, 74 for managerial persons, 42 for commercial employees, 56 for skilled workers, and 48 for semi-skilled workers.[32] He concludes that these data show a "remarkably high" percentage of consciously dissatisfied and unhappy persons among factory and clerical workers. Starting from other value premises than Fromm's, some analysts might conclude that the percentages really tell us very little at all, while others might even conclude that the figures are remarkably low. Eric Hoffer, for example, once said that America was a paradise —the only one in the history of the world—for workingmen and small children. What matters is that while Fromm's reading of the data is not the only one possible, it is precisely the one we would expect from a writer who earnestly believes that every man can and ought to be happy and satisfied. Fromm also cites a poll on attitudes toward work restriction conducted by the Opinion Research Corporation in 1945, in which 49 per cent of manual workers said a man ought to turn out as much as he could in a day's work, while 41 per cent said he should not do his best but should turn out only the average amount. Fromm says these data show that job dissatisfaction and resentment are widespread. That is one way to read the findings, but again there are other ways. One might use such findings to indicate the strength of informal primary associations in the factory, an interpretation which would run counter to Fromm's theory of alienation. Or, he might remind Fromm that the 41 per cent figure is really astonishingly low: after all, the medieval guild system was dedicated to the proposition that 100 per cent of the workers ought to turn out only the average amount; and today's trade unions announce pretty much the same view.

In view of these shortcomings in both the amount and the interpretation of survey-type findings on public opinion, and considering the criticisms which can be brought against Fromm's philosophical anthropology, such a passage as the following cannot be taken seriously. "Are people happy, are they as satisfied, unconsciously, as they believe themselves to be? Considering the nature of man, and the conditions for happiness, this can hardly be so." [33]

The ambiguities suggested above stem from a more basic difficulty in Fromm's style of thought. He seems to use the term alienation in two different ways. Sometimes he uses it as a subjective, descriptive term, and sometimes as an objective, diagnostic one. That is, sometimes it is used to *describe felt* human misery, and other times it is postulated to *explain unfelt* anxiety and discontent. The failure to keep these two usages distinct presents hazards to the reader. It also permits Fromm to do some dubious things with empirical findings. When alienation is used as an objective and diagnostic category, for example, it becomes clear that Fromm would have to say that awareness of alienation goes far toward conquering it. (He in effect does say this in his discussion of the pseudo-happiness of the automaton conformist.) Starting from this, and accepting his estimate of the iniquities of modern society, it would follow that the really disturbing evidence of alienation would be that of a work-satisfaction survey which reported widespread, stated worker satisfaction, rather than widespread, stated worker dissatisfaction.

The point is that in a system such as Fromm's, which recognizes unconscious motivations, and which rests on certain ethical absolutes, empirical data can be used to support whatever proposition the writer is urging at the moment. Thus, in the example cited above Fromm rests his whole case on the premise that the workers are being deprived unconsciously, unknowingly, of fulfillment, and then supports this with survey data reporting conscious, experienced frustrations. He has his cake and eats it too: if the workers say they are dissatisfied, this shows conscious alienation; if they say they are satisfied, this shows unconscious alienation. This sort of manipulation is especially troublesome in Fromm's work because, although his system is derived largely from certain philosophic convictions, he asserts that it is based on empirical findings drawn both from social science and from his own consulting room. While the "empirical psychoanalytic" label which Fromm claims sheds no light on the validity of his underlying philosophy, it does increase the marketability of his product.

The final example of the failure to use available evidence, though evidence of a different kind from that which has so far been considered, comes from Fromm's treatment of some other writers who have dealt with the same themes. In a brief chapter dealing with "Various Other Diagnoses," he quotes isolated passages from some writers whose views seem to corroborate his own, and finds it "most remarkable that a critical view of twentieth-century society was already

held by a number of thinkers living in the nineteenth. . . ."
He finds it equally "remarkable that their critical diagnosis
and prognosis should have so much in common among
themselves and with the critics of the twentieth century." [34]
There is nothing remarkable about this at all. It is merely
a matter of finding passages that suit one's purposes. There
is a difference between evidence and illustration, and
Fromm's citation of the other diagnosticians fits the latter
category. Glance at the list: Burckhardt, Tolstoy, Proudhon,
Thoreau, London, Marx, Tawney, Mayo, Durkheim, Tannenbaum, Mumford, A. R. Heron, Huxley, Schweitzer, and
Einstein. This is a delightfully motley collection. One can
make them say the same thing only by not listening to them
very carefully and hearing only what one wants to hear.
The method of selection Fromm uses achieves exactly that.
Furthermore, the list is interesting for its omissions. It
omits, for example, practically the whole line of great nineteenth century English social critics, nearly all the great
writers whose basic position is religious, and all those who
are with more or less accuracy called Existentialists. Of
course, the list also excludes all writers who are fairly "optimistic" about the modern situation; these, almost by definition, are spokesmen for an alienated ideology. It is not
hard to find that concurrence of opinion which Fromm
finds so remarkable when you ignore all who hold a different
opinion.

Turning from these problems of the use of evidence,
one meets another type of difficulty in Fromm's analysis,
which is his loose and ambiguous use of certain important
terms. One such instance has already been presented: his
use of alienation. The only other one I shall mention here
is his use of the term capitalism.

For Fromm, capitalism is the enemy, the root of all
evil. It is of course useful to have a sovereign cause in one's

social criticism, for it makes diagnosis and prescription much easier than they might otherwise be. One pays a price for it, however, and in Fromm's case the price is high. It consists, first, in putting so many things into the word that it becomes distended, too gross for precise analysis, and, secondly, in losing sight of important factors that have little or nothing to do with capitalism, however defined. Or, sometimes, one merely gets a rather distorted perspective on things by viewing them through the lens of Fromm's capitalism. For example, the bureaucratization, quantification, routinization, and abstractification which Fromm speaks of are tendencies in modern life which appear in the economic as well as in other spheres, but which were hardly "caused" by capitalism, and which will certainly not be eradicated merely by abolishing capitalism. Fromm sometimes also seems to confuse technology with capitalism. Much of the emptiness of modern life which Fromm so movingly describes seems to me not so much a function of "commodity production" as of the "rationalization" (in Weber's sense) of life which has been developing since at least the seventeenth century. Perhaps commodity production is as much a desperate attempt to fill the emptiness of modern life which rationalization has left in its wake as it is itself a cause of the emptiness.* Certainly the disappear-

* Fromm (along with most of the rest of us) is deeply concerned over the eruption of the irrational which is so prominent and fearful a feature of our times. He regards irrationalism as a by-product of alienation: cut off from themselves and their fellows, unable to find meaning in work and life, men rise up to smash the order which mocks and maims them. Another explanation might be suggested. As Fromm himself has pointed out, ours is the first basically secular culture in history. In ages of faith, men find meaning and purpose for their lives, and their deaths, in religion. Also, religious institutions not only once had power to punish those who violated the moral sense of the community, but they also provided a channel through which both mass and individual enthusiasms, frenzies, and fanaticisms could be drained off with limited harm (and often with large benefit) to the community. With the decline of religious faith, all this disappears. For the first time in his

ance of the political community and the failure of the masses to take much interest in the affairs of the commonwealth—tendencies which Fromm along with numerous others deplores—can be traced back at least to Hobbes. Long before capitalism had become a dominant economic system, Anglo-American political thought had been fashioning a conception of politics and citizenship which saw the former as nothing but the clash of interests and the latter as a tool the individual could use in defending his own interests. Politics as a search for the good life and citizenship as a moral experience were conceptions which disappeared from political philosophy with little prompting from something called capitalism.

These necessary qualifications and criticisms made, there remains much in Fromm's diagnosis which is excellent. Fromm has earned a secure place in the splendid tradition of humanistic social criticism. He is one of the very few writers of our day about whom one would wish or dare to say that.

A society's critics are more to be valued than its treasures and monuments, more to be valued indeed than anything but its dreamers and visionaries. When a man combines the two vocations he follows the finest of all "warrant-

---

history, Western man faces the absurdity of existence without the shelter of faith. For the first time in Western history, masses of men confront death as personal annihilation rather than as the threshold of eternal life. For the first time in Western history, religious institutions lack the power of effective punishment, as well as the power to give vivid symbolization to man's irrational strivings. All that is left is the self in its temporal existence; and with this comes the despairing realization that life has only the meaning that self-assertion gives it. Nietzsche knew that with the death of God all things were possible. In this universe to which both human and divine meaning are foreign, only a few moderns have been capable of the supremely ironical courage of Bertrand Russell's *A Free Man's Worship*. Whether the masses can endure and remain pacific without the solace and discipline of ideology is still, as Renan indicated in the introduction to *The Future of Science*, the great unanswered question of the modern age.

able callings" in the open society. Such men are always in short supply; and in our day a number of tendencies conspire both to reduce the number of those who enter upon the vocation of criticism and to restrict the work of those who have entered it. Little in the way of effective social criticism can be expected to come from academic social scientists. Academics are, on the whole, a gentle breed, unfit by temper and training for the rough calling of criticism. In addition, the pathetic humility of the social scientists in the face of the "real" scientists, combined with the commendable yearning to become truly scientific, sets additional barriers in the way of social scientists who would become social critics. These barriers take a number of forms: the conviction that one must cleanse himself of all "values" before he enters the laboratory; the easy and pejorative distinction between descriptive theory and normative theory, and the cognate distinction between "journalism" and social science; the view that identifies science with rigorous method and accurate measurement, a view which has the effect of limiting the problems chosen for study to those which are manageable by such methods and measurable by such instruments; the increasing specialization within the social sciences; the growth of a technical language; the emphasis on factual or descriptive investigation of social and individual behavior. All these raise barriers between the vocation of science and the vocation of criticism. In addition, the emerging ethic of "responsibility" within social science and the growing alliance between social science on the one side, and the state, the corporation, and the foundation on the other, also reduce the likelihood of social scientists becoming social critics. The former encourages attitudes of prudence and moderation, and prudent and moderate men seldom make good critics. The latter directly affects the selection of topics for research in the direction of those which have an apparent policy application or relevance, or which concern some felt social "problem," or which are of special concern to one or another group.

Nor can we look to the men in public life for effective social criticism. The exigencies of public life in a democracy compel the politician to keep close to the realities of his constituency. His is the practical task of coping with day-to-day problems and meeting day-to-day demands. He has little time for reflection and little space for vision. Further-more, none of the great parties in any of the Western states now offers the electorate a sweeping program for a new society. One has the increasingly strong feeling that most political debate in our day is not enlightening, and that the language of politics does not include terms for the really basic concerns of mass culture and mass society. Most of our political discussion is an echo of issues that were real and pressing a generation ago—issues of social justice, of political equality, of removing unfair privilege and guaran-teeing fair shares for all within the framework of an ever expanding economy. I do not suggest that all such prob-lems have been solved; of course they have not. I only sug-gest that the language and leaders of public life seem to be falling ever farther away from what our best and most sensi-tive moralists and visionaries agree upon as the real issues of modern life.[35]

The growing shortage of social criticism and moral vision is aggravated by a number of other factors, some deep and old in our culture, some of more recent origins. A par-tial list would include the following. The success ethic and our pragmatic perspective on political, social, and moral questions make us a people little given to philosophy; if the system works, here and now, it is its own justification. Then, in a rapidly changing world, we feel increasingly beleaguered by strange and hostile forces from without. The result is a growing conservatism within, a desire to hold fast to that which we have and know, rather than to experiment with projects whose possible evils we know not of. Don't rock the boat: that slogan becomes a conviction in a restless age and a troubled world. We also still live in the clear memory of the day of McCarthy, when the feeling passed current that rocking the boat, even in a playful spirit, could be a very serious business. Add to these factors the din of the mass media pounding out their message to consume and advance and be popular, and there emerges a situation in which even when the critic raises his voice he will often go unheard.

When the critic must perform under these adverse conditions, it is high praise of a man to say that he performs very well. Fromm merits that praise. He is indisputably among the first rank of the analysts and critics of our cultural and moral crisis. He can make serious claim to being the foremost among them.

The Homeless One

To be a great social critic requires that one have a position outside society, outside all time and place; a position, if one may say it, in eternity. Fromm, I think, has failed to find that position. His critique of modern society can claim two solid achievements. First, he has given passionate and lucid *expression to the sense of alienation* in our time. Fromm has found the right words to report modern man's sense that he lives as a stranger in a world that has gone desperately wrong. He has stated again, and forcefully, the dimensions of what Katherine Anne Porter has called the "majestic and terrible failure of the life of man in the

Western world." (Although, I shall argue later that he sees too much of the terror, and too little of the majesty.) His second achievement is that he has presented a powerful *sociology of alienation*. That is, he has described the typical forms through which alienation manifests itself, and he has charted the course which alienated feeling takes in the modern epoch. These are important and durable achievements.

But Fromm's concentration on alienation as the feature of a specific era and specific social-economic conditions means that he has neglected some broader dimensions of a theory of alienation. What is currently called alienation has been a concern of Western thought, and a reality in Western life, since long before the capitalist era. It might even be suggested that the capitalism which Fromm identifies as the cause of alienation may itself be not the cause, but a product of alienated ways of thinking—though I realize that the relation between thought and social structure is never as simple as either Fromm or I have just put it. In any case, the question which must now be asked is, what difference does it make if we approach alienation from a sociological rather than from a more broadly philosophical point of view? What are the consequences of viewing alienation as the product of specific historical conditions rather than as an inherent feature of the human condition? In discussing that question, I shall not argue that it is "wrong" to build a sociology of alienation, or that Fromm should have built a philosophy of alienation. Rather, I shall argue that Fromm's sociological theory of alienation blinds him to basic dimensions of the problem of alienation, that it spares him from considering the hard question of how far social reform can heal the wounds of alienation, and that it predisposes him toward utopian solutions for problems which may have no sociological solutions at all.

I shall approach these conclusions along two paths, the one analytical, or even etymological, and the other historical and philosophical. In the first I shall try to show that self-alienation and alienation of the self from others are really very different things, and that Fromm's analysis is vitiated by his failure to keep the two apart. In the second I shall develop the Existentialist concept of human alienation and try to show that it is a significant and in some ways superior alternative to Fromm's sociological theory of alienation.

Our word self derives from the Latin reflexive pronoun *se*. This derivation suggests the notion that the self is something that is "folded back," something that looks back and reflects on the way by which it has arrived at its present state or situation. The implication of this is that the self can contemplate its own origin and history and by so doing discover, or at least refer to, its own vital essence. To put it another way, in certain realms of being a thing is not a thing until it moves, for without motion (involvement) there can be no measurement, and a thing is by definition that which has measurable qualities. A thing is that which moves. A thing's self, then, is the history of its movement. In Isak Dinesen's *Last Tales*, one of the old Cardinal Salviati's penitents, sensing in him something more than the usual vocational experience, and seeking from him something more than the usual professional wisdom, beseeches him to tell her *who* he is. The Cardinal replied that his birth was a mystery, for he was one of identical twins, which one he never knew. The only way he can identify himself is by recounting *what* he has done, and what has been done to him.

The other word which matters here is the word alien. It comes from *alius*, Latin for "other," connoting strangeness, foreignness, of different and unknown origin and nature. The alien is the strange one, the one of unknown history. To be alienated, that is, to be made alien, is to be made strange and solitary, cut off from the background of origin and history. The man who is alienated by or from some other thing or some other men has been robbed of a portion of his history, as when his membership card in some organization is torn up, and it is no longer admitted that he once belonged to the group. George Orwell found the perfect symbol for perfectly alienated men in his discussion of the robbery and replacement of histories in *1984.** It is important to add, however, that to be alienated in this sense is to be, indeed, diminished but not destroyed, because the alienated man *had* a history before being robbed of it. I shall return to this a little later. Now, in what sense can a man be alienated from himself?

It is clear that selfhood means both having a history and knowing what that history is. My history is important to me because it sets me off from all that is "not I." My history is my identity, that is, my distinction from the surroundings. In his *Pictures from an Institution*, Randall Jarrell describes the president of the institution as being so exquisitely adjusted to his environment that it was hard to tell which was president and which was environment. Jarrell's president is the perfectly identityless one.

The self is a history, but not *just* a history. It is also all that can be deduced or extrapolated from that history, especially the consciousness of the present and the contemplation of the future. The self lives in three time dimensions, and self-alienation might mean the loss of any one of the three, though the loss of the past is the most frequent and

* A discussion, it should be mentioned, which was brilliantly anticipated in Eugene Zamiatin's satirical novel *We* (written in 1920; published in 1924).

most important. Thus one could say, if he were allowed a certain looseness with the terms, that a man can alienate himself (or be alienated) from his self in the sense that he sloughs off his past, as Eric Hoffer has put it, and looks just briefly at the present, and then longingly and perhaps fearfully at the future. A more careful use of terms, however, would make it clear that such a man is not really alienated from his self. Rather, he has divided his self into two parts, the historical and the hoped-for, and has enlarged the latter by reducing the former. What is interesting here is that when this process has gone very far and one has completely cast out the historical, he has nothing left from which to deduce the future. Then he faces the future in one of three ways: he sees the future as formless, limitless, full of possibilities; he sees it as a gray and yawning emptiness; or, he turns himself over to and relies upon the dramatic program for the future offered by some leader or some mass movement.

From this it can be said that the man who has alienated himself from his self is truly destroying his self. He is not merely turning himself over to others to use as they will, as appears to be the case with the "true believer." He is, rather, actually diminishing the size and power of his self, so that henceforth he is carried along, given a history as it were, by his surroundings. This is important because it means that the self-alienated one whose alienation takes the form of the true believer cannot recover his self from the movement simply by asking for its return, as though it were something he had only loaned out. He must re-remember his history, rebuild what he had obliterated, remember what has happened in the meantime, restore connections with a past which has faded away since he last looked at it. In short, he must do what one who is under psychoanalysis does to a more intense degree. This task is difficult for exactly the same reason psychoanalysis is difficult: it is painful.

This suggests an important warning, which, although obvious, is often ignored. Since the task of reconstructing the self is both complex and painful, there is no guarantee that the one who undertakes it will succeed. He may achieve not an authentic restoration but a blemished copy. This is just another way of saying that the fact that one pays heed to his history and his feelings does not mean that he is exempt from error in his understanding or report of them. One can make mistakes about the causes of his feelings, and he can make mistakes about their real content and location. Merely paying attention to oneself, being aware of oneself, does not mean that one therefore accurately grasps his self. No man is more aware of himself than the hypochondriac, but his mistake about himself is so large and so pervasive that he confuses "real" feelings with fancied ones.

These considerations indicate the differences between self-alienation and alienation from others. Turning to the latter, it is useful to start by distinguishing it from a situation it is often confused with, that of open conflict. Two features are decisive. First, the man who is alienated from others feels *estranged* from them, cut off, detached from their affairs and concerns. Secondly, and this is only the other side of the first point, he has little or no emotional *investment* in the lives of those from whom he is alienated. The alienated one is distant from the others and has no desire to draw closer to them. In the situation of open conflict, on the other hand, not only are the two actors (individuals or groups) already very close to each other, but they also desire intensely to draw even closer, albeit for destructive purposes. (To avoid misunderstanding, it is worthwhile stating the obvious point that physical space and movement are irrelevant here.) This is the meaning of the ancient observation that love and hate are akin: "In one's friend one shall have one's best enemy," as Nietzsche put it. The closer a relationship between two actors approaches either friendship (positive investment) or open enmity (negative investment), the less appropriately can the term alienation be applied to that situation, for alienation from others means essentially estrangement from and lack of investment in their affairs and concerns.

Alienation from others may happen in two ways. First, the one may "arrange" to have others alienate him, as the saint, the aristocrat, or the intellectual (in Benda's sense) does. Or, one may become alienated from others without himself encouraging or initiating the process. Examples would be the person who is a kind of natural "misfit," or the members of certain minority groups, such as the Jews in the United States or the Negroes in the North. Those who are alienated from others might be called the strangers. The stranger may or may not have his self destroyed. It is true that some portion of a man's history is robbed by those who alienate him, but this robbery (though the coward will try to "forget" it) may come to be an important part of the man's history, as it is, for example, with the intellectual. In this case, what looked like robbery is only attempted robbery. The self endures and is often strengthened and improved by the very memorableness and violence of the event. It follows that alienation from others is by no means inherently bad or destructive of the self. It may indeed be the very anchor point of a strongly developed selfhood. This will be true especially if the stranger is fortunately endowed with a combination of guilt and curiosity: guilt to make the robbery important to him; curiosity to examine the robbery as to its style and meaning. The stranger who has both guilt and curiosity will emerge from the attempted robbery with a stronger self and a sharper perception of his environment. There *is* a sociological cure for this type of alienation—the cure of "community"—but we must remember that the price of a complete cure is a reduced number of powerful selves and sensitive, critical observers.

On the other hand, the man who alienates himself from his self always ends up with less self. This is the alienation which is always an impoverishment, and the one for which there is no known sociological cure. Selfhood is another name for self-awareness, and the search for selfhood involves a passionate concern for one's total history. Now, to have a passionate concern for one's total history is the same as having the desire and the courage to reveal and to confront all the nastiness, viciousness, and unpleasantness of one's history: the pleasant and attractive things are always easily remembered. The man who is alienated from himself is the man who will not acknowledge the taints that are within himself. (He also, unknowingly, "acknowledges" taints within himself which are not real.) He is truly the maimed one, and, it is necessary to repeat, there is no sociological remedy for his defect.

Both self-alienation and alienation from others can result from similar causes. Our times can be typified by indicating a number of these causes. First of all, the intricate division of labor and specialization of function prevent nearly all of us from expressing our total selves in our work, or from using our work as a means of self-realization. Our lives are carved up into roles, and nothing but confusion and embarrassment can come from an attempt to put the whole of our selves into a role that demands only a piece of us. Division of labor also means differences of life-experience, and this too results in the estrangement of man from man and group from group. This cause of alienation can

be cured, if we are willing to forego the pleasures and con-
veniences of the division of labor and return to a state of
rustic simplicity.

The second typical cause of alienation in our times is
to be found in the very nature of the modern history of
both peoples and individuals. The history of peoples in our
time is a history of hate and terror, of failure and chaos.
With the diffusion of the Freudian doctrine, individuals too
are coming to an awareness that their own inner history is
not pretty. From this, our era can be typified by saying:
(1) men are so discomfited by their history, public and
private, that they "contrive" to have others steal it from
them; (2) men are so discomfited by their history that they
themselves blot out portions of it, hoping thereby to destroy
it; and (3) with the growth of what William H. Whyte, Jr.,
calls the social ethic, and the growth of what Fromm calls
the marketing orientation, men who have been alienated by
others lack the courage to accept their alienation and use it
as the fulcrum of a stronger selfhood.

I conclude this section by summarizing the main
points. There are important differences between self-alienation and alienation from others which Fromm has failed
to recognize, with the result that he offers a sociological
cure for a type of alienation which does not admit of a
sociological cure. Furthermore, in his eager search for the
community of "love," he fails to appreciate the positive advantages for heightened selfhood which can result from
alienation from others. Finally, and most ironical of all,
Fromm's doctrine of universal love, under modern conditions, can only have the melancholy consequence of making
the strangers and misfits even less able to bear their estrangement from the group and transform it into a heightened
selfhood.

With these conclusions, I turn to the second path, which is a brief exposition of the Existentialist theory of alienation.

Broadly understood, alienation belongs to a group of concepts whose origins predate capitalism by a few thousand years: sin, the fall, depravity, idolatry. The opposite of alienation, which might be called harmony, belongs to an equally old family: the garden, concord, love, union, communion. The movement from alienation to harmony is described by still another set of sacramental terms: salvation, redemption, reconciliation, atonement.

A true sight of sin, warned Thomas Hooker, is hard to come by, and earnest attention to the tomes of the theologians only makes it all the harder for us to grasp the inner meaning of the dreaded idea. "It's one thing to see a disease in the book or in a man's body, another thing to find and feel it in a man's self. There is the report of it, here the malignity and venom of it." [36] The greatest writers who have struggled with sin as a hideous personal reality (Paul, Augustine, Luther, Kierkegaard) have seen its essence as the separation of the soul from its Creator, the separation of man from the ground of all being and meaning. Therein lies the "malignity and venom" of it, for when man is estranged from God, in revolt against or in flight from Him, the estrangement poisons all parts of his being. The man who is separated from God in the center of his own being must inevitably see his intellectual, moral, and esthetic capacities all become corrupted. He can attain neither the true nor the beautiful nor the good; and the harder he tries, the deeper becomes the alienation. Cut off from the source of light, his wanderings take him ever deeper into the dark.

The third set of concepts mentioned above refers to

the experience by which alienation is healed and harmony restored. Each term expresses in its own symbolic content this one act or experience of restoring a disrupted peace or harmony. Redemption indicates a buying back. Salvation refers to the process by which the soul is restored to health and cleansed of sin. Reconciliation means bringing together and making whole again. Atonement means the condition of being at one with others, the re-establishment of friendly relations between God and sinners. All these refer, in a most concrete way, to the experience of restoring a once real but now lost harmony.

The journey of restoration is a spiritual one which each man must take for himself, though of course others may encourage him and even walk with him for part of the way. Social institutions set the landscape through which the pilgrim must travel, so in each age the course of the journey will be different, but in every age the pilgrim is a stranger, at home in no society, neither very much helped nor very much hindered by its institutions. Neither the reconciled one nor the seeker, however, will be unmindful of institutions. Although they have only instrumental value, well-ordered institutions are to be valued precisely because they are useful instruments. The good society is one which aids men in the search for themselves and the meaning of their lives. But institutional arrangements cannot by themselves either heal the wounds of alienation or offer an authentic replacement for the peace of salvation. This means concretely that no institution of this world may claim total loyalty, nor must any man give it, for each of us is a stranger in the world, partially alienated from himself, his fellows, and his society. No man may expect reconciliation on the merely sociological plane. The greatest writers on sin, on alienation, have spoken on this question with one voice.

These remarks should not be interpreted as an argument that concern with and understanding of alienation in the structure of existence begins with or is limited to Christian, or even religious, thought. In a very real sense, certain Platonic themes are fundamental to all later developments in this field. At the heart of Plato's teaching lies an awareness of the human predicament as the predicament of alienation. The soul has lost its home in the realm of essences and is condemned to endure in an existential world of transitory and ephemeral appearances and opinions. This existence is in contradiction to the soul's proper participation in the eternal realm of pure essences. Plato describes in many places the "fall" from essential to existential being, and the process of ascending again from the latter to the former. His descriptions of the fall and the painful reascension are always presented in the language of mythology, for he held that only the realm of essences yields to conceptual or philosophical analysis, while the domain of existence resists such analysis. Plato's distinction between the realms of existence and essence, and his discussion of the methodology appropriate to the understanding of each realm, underlie the whole orientation of what in modern times has come to be known as Existentialism.

The existential aspect of Plato's thought, his view of the human predicament as alienation and estrangement, remained embedded in a larger essentialist ontology. The same is true of the classical Christian theology of sin and salvation mentioned above. The existential perspective conditioned the descriptions of the ambiguities and contingencies of the human condition in both Platonism and Christianity, but this perspective always operated within an essentialist frame. Thus understood, an existentialist perspective has never been entirely absent from Western thought. It can be found, to mention a few places, in Augustine's anguished soliloquies on pride and love, on sin and solidarity, in Luther's magnificent descriptions of the ambiguities of goodness and the terrors of despair, in Dante's supreme visions of human destructiveness and human creativeness, and in the nominalism of Ockham, with its irrationalism and its emphasis on particularity and contingency.

With the seventeenth century the existentialist aspect or perspective became absorbed by the new essentialism and rationalism of a scientific variety which found its first great exponent in Descartes, was fortified by Kant, and achieved its supreme expression in Hegel.* In this current of thought, man as concrete existent drowns. The man who laughs and loves, who suffers and is afraid, who knows guilt and anguish, disappears. He is replaced by the pale man of pure consciousness, *res cogitans*, the knower who is essentially separated from the world of objects. Man becomes reduced to consciousness, and his relations with the world become narrowed to those between the manipulator and the objects of manipulation.

Behind that *sum* in Descartes' formula there still lay hidden an I which is more than consciousness, an I which does more than think, an I which concretely exists within a situation of finitude and alienation. It was this I which modern Existentialism set out to liberate from the rationalism of the essentialists. Modern Existentialism, which dates from Kierkegaard, must be understood as an attempt to recover the existentialist point of view and description of

---

* At every point in this impressionistic account one is compelled to qualify. I know that the existentialist perspective did not "die out" in the seventeenth century. In some ways, it even received its finest expression to that date in Hobbes's sardonic pages on the duplicities of the human condition. But in this respect Hobbes remains in the medieval tradition, and especially, as Oakeshott has recently emphasized, in the nominalistic tradition. What I want to emphasize is that from the seventeenth century onward, essentialism increasingly crowds out the existentialist point of view.

the human condition which had remained embedded in much essentialist ontology before Descartes. When Kierkegaard inveighed against the newfangled System of Hegel, it must be granted that he was right, for the System truly was newfangled in the sense that it destroyed themes which had remained in philosophy from the beginning. Similarly, when he cried that the "lunatic postulate" of man as pure consciousness was the real modern aberration, it must again be granted that he could find strong support for his protest in the history of philosophy before Descartes.

But if Existentialism is first of all a movement of recovery, it is also a movement of revolt. In order to recover the pre-Cartesian past, it was first necessary to overthrow the Hegelian present. In this revolt, the existential aspect was liberated from essentialist ontology and made into an ontology of its own. It was no longer a question of the two themes being blended together in proper proportion: one must replace the other. We inherit the dilemma posed by the divorce between the two themes; this, indeed, might be the decisive way to define the meaning of alienation in our time.

Understood as a movement of recovery through revolt, Existentialism embraces many of the great thinkers and artists of the nineteenth and twentieth centuries. All these revolutionaries were concerned to restore "that individual" to philosophic existence. But the attack was not pressed solely on the philosophic front. The Existentialist revolutionaries realized that the disappearance of the individual from philosophy was but one aspect of a much larger process whose ultimate result must be the effective disappearance of the individual altogether, the denial of the individual as the locus of ultimate reality and the bearer of infinite significance. Kierkegaard, Schopenhauer, Nietzsche, Stirner, Marx, John Stuart Mill, Bergson, William James,

Dilthey, Simmel, Weber—all these men, each from a special point of view, each with a unique emphasis, examined the historical-social movement by which men were being transformed into things. All charted part of the process of the breakdown of accepted meanings and analyzed facets of the despair that comes from meaninglessness. All searched for ways by which personality could affirm itself under social conditions which increasingly threatened to annihilate the person and replace it with the thing. When the nineteenth century ended in 1914, the revolutionaries suddenly ceased to be isolated prophets of defeat, gloomy nay-sayers in an age of affirmation. Their work was now seen as the literal account of reality.

Since I am concerned here to pose the philosophical rather than the sociological theory of alienation, it would be beside the point to chronicle the Existentialist sociology of the nineteenth century. What must be emphasized, against the tendency of the positivist social science of our day with its bias against a philosophic view of reality as being excessively "abstract," removed from the actual and concrete realities of behavior as ascertained by empirical investigation—what must be emphasized is that the philosophic theory of alienation has always been concrete, close to reality, keenly aware of the changing forms and manifestations of alienation under varying social conditions. But with all its richness of sociological and psychological detail, the philosophical theory of alienation refuses to concede that alienation can be reduced to an exclusively sociological problem and understood solely in sociological terms.

This point made, I can move on to a brief account of the basic ideas in the modern Existentialist theory of alienation. I mainly want to show that there is a real alternative to Fromm's formulations, and to lay the groundwork for the final portion of the essay. The outlines of the Existentialist theory of alienation can be presented under four headings: (1) rejection of the separation between subject and object; (2) the way man exists in the world; (3) how the essentialist error has cut man off from being; and (4) the description of the human condition.

Subject and object. Existentialism rejects the distinction between subject and object in the cognitive act and refuses the view that the ethic of "detachment," of "objectivity," is the royal road to knowledge. This is the "lunatic postulate" that Kierkegaard had to demolish on his way toward the discovery of the "thinker in existence." What Tillich calls the existential attitude can be generally defined as "the attitude of participating with one's own existence in some other existence." It means "participating in a situation, especially a cognitive situation, with the whole of one's existence." [37]

There are of course realms of reality where detachment and objectivity are the only acceptable methods. But there are other realms where another method must be followed, a method which seeks not the separation of thought from its object, but their most intimate union. You cannot, for example, know another person by detaching yourself from him. To do that is to convert the other into a thing, thereby destroying the very element which makes a self something other than a thing. To know another self you must participate in it, must share in its existence. But by participating in it you change it. Hence the act of knowing changes both the subject and the object. In existential knowledge, a new meaning is created, and this creation is the joint product of the knower and the known. In this way Existentialism hopes to lead men "back to the objects" and heal the divorce between the knower and his world, a divorce which has impoverished both by making man a mere *res cogitans* and his world a mere object to be manipulated. Existentialism would return to Emerson's definition of the philosopher as "man thinking."

The way man exists in the world.   The Existentialist argues that the essentialist separation between the spectator and the world has produced a grievous misunderstanding of the structure of human existence. This misunderstanding centers on the attempt, in both naturalistic social science and essentialist philosophy, to conceive of man as one object among others.

Man's existence is not merely spatial and temporal, like that of an object. Objects are determined by their properties; that is, the object is its properties. Hence, objects can be defined without inquiring into their existences. It is sufficient to know their properties, which are their essences. The case is different with man, for what a man is, is determined not by his properties but by his choices. It is impossible to ascribe an essence to the self for the self is able to transcend its properties and break away from its past.

So the core of human existence is possibility. Man is the being who is able to transcend himself, to project himself toward a future which will exist only when and because he makes it. Hence we cannot say that man is, but only that he *exists*, and that he is on the way to being this or that. In Sartre's formulation, "man's essence is his existence." This is the meaning of Existentialist freedom and the core of the Existentialist analysis of the structure of human existence.

How the essentialist error has alienated man from knowledge of being.   Man's existence in the world is such that he is involved in the world, concerned with it, interlocked with it. Thus some Existentialists argue that man has a kind of primordial understanding of the structure of being which comes from the fact that he is involved in the world and that he handles and uses and lives with things and other men. But for centuries the essentialist error of separating man from the objects of knowledge has grown until today we no longer are able to realize that knowing means acting and participating. We have lost our primordial understanding of being and have become completely alienated from the ground and meaning of human existence. Heidegger, especially, emphasized this aspect of human alienation and searched for methods of overcoming it without embracing an authoritarian religious creed. In the background of his thought there always lurked a vague and even mystical conception of being, and he tried tirelessly to find the path which would lead men beyond the realm of appearances into the realm of the ground of being. Other writers, of whom Sartre is the most powerful, rejected this mystical restriction and pushed the analysis of the separation between man and being to the radical and consistent conclusions which are identified with his name and which make of him the symbol and foremost spokesman of modern "atheistic" Existentialism.

The description of the human condition. Here the voices are so many that merely to list them would be to make a catalog of most of the leading philosophers and literary men of our day. All, however, emphasize certain themes in their picture of man in the world. Man lives in a world without transcendental values. Whatever moral values there are, are developed by man in his infinite freedom and responsibility. Man is free, within certain limits imposed by his social and physical environment, to choose what he shall be and do. Human nature is not fixed and permanent. It is what man makes it, and it differs from age to age. The meaning of a man's life is found in his choices and in his relations with others; for, though ultimately alone, each life has meaning only in its relationships to the lives of others. Hence the individual must "engage" himself, but no engagement is final. In their concrete descriptions of the feeling states which each man experiences in this situation, the Existentialists emphasize freedom, finitude, estrangement and loneliness, guilt, care, concern, anxiety, and despair. Any nonreligious reader with some knowledge of history who reads the Existentialist descriptions of the human condition might conclude, perhaps with some surprise, that he has been an Existentialist all along.

At this point, one distinction should be made. A few pages back I used the figure of the pilgrim to symbolize the enduring Christian concern with alienation. But there is a difference between the pilgrim and the man of modern Existentialism: the former has a goal; the latter wanders. Bunyan's Christian moved toward a certain destination, and from the start of his journey he was guided and encouraged by the clear voice of Evangelist. The modern has neither goal nor guide. For him, in Heidegger's phrase, existence is "wandering in need." He wanders in a maze of forest trails leading nowhere; and at each turning he is assailed again by the despair which comes from his own sense of finitude and isolation, and by the anxiety which comes from his loss of the gods. One of Camus' images captures both this sense of wandering and the haunting memory of a time which had direction.

> You are wrong, *cher*, the boat is going at full speed. But the Zuyderzee is a dead sea, or almost. With its flat shores, lost in the fog, there's no knowing where it begins or ends. So we are steaming along without any landmark; we can't gauge our speed. We are making progress and yet nothing is changing. It's not navigation but dreaming.
>
> In the Greek archipelago I had the contrary feeling. Constantly new islands would appear on the horizon. Their treeless backbone marked the limit of the

sky and their rocky shore contrasted sharply with the sea. No confusion possible; in the sharp light everything was a landmark. And from one island to another . . . I felt as if we were scudding along, night and day, on the crest of the short, cool waves in a race full of spray and laughter. Since then, Greece itself drifts somewhere within me, on the edge of my memory, tirelessly . . . Hold on, I too am drifting. . . .

By the way, do you know Greece? No? So much the better, What should we do there, I ask you? There it requires pure hearts. . . .[38]

Before concluding this sketch, it should at least be mentioned that there are "schools" and divisions within Existentialism. Perhaps the three main tendencies are: (1) the Christian Existentialism of Kierkegaard, which has been developed theologically by Barth and Tillich, and psychologically by Jaspers and Marcel; (2) the atheistic Existentialism of Heidegger and Sartre, which has had an enormous literary development; and (3) the specifically Thomistic Christian Existentialism expounded by Maritain. All, however, share the views that the starting point of philosophy is the problem of existence, that detached reason alone will not achieve the knowledge necessary to the solution of basic moral and human problems, that freedom is the condition and anguish the emotion of men as they confront the problems of life, and that the development of morality requires positive action and participation by the individual.

Kierkegaard developed these ideas within a religious framework. He started from the conviction that the intellect alone will not resolve the paradoxes which confront man, and that it is these paradoxes which engender the anguish which characterizes human life. For Kierkegaard, the tension is resolved through the leap to God, for in Him the finite and the infinite are one. Each takes the leap alone. Tillich preserves the integrity of this lonely vision, while Jaspers seems to recommend a flight to the security of a philosophical faith, and Marcel comes close to advocating a return to something like medieval communalism and collectivism.

Sartre gives no quarter to the absolute: for him, God is dead and man can never again revive Him. Since no Creator exists, there is no model of human nature, no essential nature of man. Man is what he wills and chooses to be, and as all his efforts to find inherent meaning in the world result in failure, he comes to see the world as alien to him, absurd. A stranger in this world, man's entrance upon life and exit from it are both accidental events in a meaningless universe. But aloneness gives absolute freedom, accompanied by absolute responsibility. Man becomes as God, able to choose without dependence. For this freedom, man must pay in anguish and despair. He is always strongly tempted to escape his "dreadful freedom" and submit to some alien force, be it a party, an ideology, or a vested authority. But this escape brings in its train even greater despair, the despair of "bad consciousness," the despair of choosing to be what one is not. The only choice man cannot make is choosing not to choose.

Maritain's Thomistic Existentialism also starts from a definition of the human condition as one of finitude and anguish. In Maritain's thought, man's desire to realize his being can be reconciled with his anguish over the possibility of nothingness only through faith in the Free Existent. This faith restores one's ties with humanity and develops in one the strength to practice the Christian virtues of love and charity.

What matters for present purposes is that all these

writers stress finitude and estrangement as inherent in the human condition. Any solution to them must be metaphysical, not sociological.

It would be wrong to conclude that the theory of alienation outlined above implies a counsel of quietism toward the concerns of social existence. On the contrary: all Existentialist thought starts from the premise that man is deeply and necessarily involved in the affairs of this world. Driven by the anguish of existential paradoxes, man strives incessantly for solutions to his problems. He seeks these solutions on the sociological as well as on the metaphysical plane. The Existentialist conception of man as the being who projects, who throws himself forward into an unknown future, implies not a social quietism but the most vigorous kind of social activism. Existential man, indeed, is committed to only one thing: change. He is the permanent revolutionary, the one who is forever striking out toward a new stage, even while the old one comes within his grasp.

What the theory does imply is a certain skepticism of all plans even while recognizing that plans are necessary, a certain disloyalty to all social schemes and ends even while recognizing that human existence is always social existence. This implies that human effort is at one and the same time an essay in creativity and a meditation on failure. There may be in the end no answer but failure, but man must nonetheless gather unto himself the courage of despair and seek without end for ends. He must realize that every end is only a stage to be transcended, not the goal at which action stops. The important point, in short, is that the metaphysical theory of alienation implies not social quietism but the recognition that all thought and action must in a sense end in failure. In this framework, the basic perspective on social action is the perspective of cautious and continuous experimentation, combined with the basic understanding that no man or party can make claims on any other man or party which would impair the freedom to experiment. This is a radicalism, to be sure, but a radicalism which hopes for little success and which acknowledges the legitimacy as well as the inevitability of disloyalty against the established order.

This is the orientation that Fromm rejects. Time and again he comes close to it, and, as was emphasized in the first chapter, he shares more with the Existentialists than he seems aware of or cares to acknowledge. But he always returns to the plane of naturalism and offers a total solution through sociology. Starting as he does with a view of man as the stranger, the freak of the universe, he never seriously considers the question as to how far and under what conditions the stranger can find a home in society. He never considers the question as to just how far social transformation can heal the wounds of alienation. This, which should be the deepest problem in Fromm's thought, is in the end simply ignored. In the end, he puts the freak of the universe in the cage of society, and says simply that if we build the cage to proper specifications the freak will be happy and comfortable. What should be a radical dichotomy in Fromm's thought, a dichotomy requiring the most painful consideration, is dismissed. It is resolved by the drive of temperament. In the language of Existentialism, Fromm lacks the courage of despair. He will acknowledge no problems that cannot be solved here and now, by the methods of reason and the powers of man. Again Fromm is faithful to the eighteenth century.

But not the eighteenth alone. As the brilliant Simmel suggested, each age that is truly an Age is guided by a sovereign idea. All the energies of the age are shaped by this idea and appear as manifestations of it: it is to the energies of the age as form is to content. In the Middle Ages, Simmel shows, the sovereign idea was God. For the Renaissance it was nature. During the seventeenth century the ideas of an ordered universe governed by natural laws dominated intellectual and artistic life, while in the eighteenth century the concept of the rational individual became dominant. The sovereign category of the twentieth century is life. What matters is living, here and now, living as a process, the process of expressing all one's powers and living to the fullness all of one's capacities. Our age is an age of revolt against form in favor of life. This revolt expresses itself in all sectors: in art, religion, philosophy, marriage and the family, and the consumption-oriented economy. Everywhere the call goes up that one should have what he wants and do as he wishes. In its purest form, this tendency is expressed in Existential philosophy, with its unwillingness to see man subjected to abstract categories and its courage to face up to loneliness and meaninglessness. In its most morbid form, the tendency appears in the economic realm, where man is regarded as a creature of desires whose main right and purpose is the consumption of more and more goods and the enjoyment of more and more pleasures.

Fromm's work is informed by one special feature of this cult of life, namely, the idea that man can do what he wants to do. Our age is an age of vast power. We have unlocked the energies of nature and turned them to our purposes. The entire globe is being made over, covered by concrete and steel, transformed, as it were, into an artifact. In the industrial civilizations, even the poorest and weakest men see all around them the immense powers at man's disposal, seemingly limitless power to shape the environment in a human form. Armed with such power, men become impatient with restrictions, unwilling to believe that anything is forbidden or impossible. This leads to a desire for final solutions—on this earth, here and now.

One brutal paradox forces our attention. Do we not observe that as the cult of life gathers strength in our time, the actual respect for human life diminishes? Life not dedicated to a purpose larger than itself is empty; why respect it? Life which demands immediate fulfillment of its desires is life without morality; for does not morality mean a disciplined renunciation of some desires? The older religious faith, with its promise not of immediate but of ultimate salvation, could afford a policy of trying to save and purify the sinners. We learn from the messianic political movements of our day that promises of immediate salvation end in attempts to exterminate the sinners.

I am not arguing that Fromm advocates any of these measures. He does not. I am arguing only that he expresses the modern cult of life and power in extreme terms, and that this cult easily ends in destruction. I am arguing that the cult of life and the faith in human power are basic both to his whole sociological theory of alienation and to his proposed remedy for the sickness of alienation, to which I now turn.

CHAPTER IV

The Good Society

Just as Fromm concluded his criticism of present-day ethical and psychological theory with a portrait of the good man, so does he conclude his criticism of present-day society with a constitution for the good society. Before turning to this part of his work, two preliminary clarifications should be made. The first concerns the nature of his constitution for the new society. The second concerns a certain objection that is often brought against Frommian utopianism as such.

Concerning the first, it is enough to say that Fromm's constitution is just that, a constitution and not a book of statutes. Since Fromm undertakes to present only the most general principles of the sane society, criticism must remain on the same "constitutional" level. A critical attack based on the strategy of "what about this, what about that" would be a waste of time, for it would saddle Fromm with a burden he explicitly rejects. To abuse John Marshall's dictum, the critic must remember that it is a constitution he is expounding, not a statute or an administrative order. In fact, if we accept Napoleon's judgment that the best con-

236

stitution is one which is brief and obscure, then we must grant that Fromm's is very good indeed.

The second comment is more important. Most of the critics of Fromm's constitution for the good society rest their case on the conviction that Fromm overestimates the potential rationality of man. This misses the point. The whole debate about man's "inherent" rationality or irrationality is quite irrelevant to Fromm's thesis, which is that men become rational only under specific social conditions. What is wrong with Fromm's view of man is not his generous estimate of man's rational powers but his shallow explanation of man's destructiveness and irrationality.

There is another reason why criticisms which rest on Fromm's alleged overestimation of human rationality are beside the point. Even if he did not believe that all or most men could become rational and productive, Fromm would still have solid justification for describing the good man and the good society. He believes, rightly, that the very absence of ideal visions is itself a cause of the destructiveness, authoritarianism, and contempt for man which characterize the present age. Utopian schemes are justified if they do no more than remind readers that decent solutions to some of our problems are possible and worth striving for. In this sense, Fromm's utopia rests on the premise that if men do not struggle toward light they fall into darkness. "Where there is no vision," it was said in the Proverbs, "the people perish."

Fromm's Place in the Utopian Tradition

Frequently in these pages Fromm has been called a utopian. It is now time to inspect that label more closely. I shall start with a reminder that utopianism generically considered is broader than the works of avowedly utopian

writers, move on to a few comments on the utopian tradition strictly so-called, and then place Fromm within the
general utopian tradition and indicate the distinctive characteristics of his approach.

Utopianism is by no means the monopoly of a class of
writers called utopians. It is not even confined to those who
explicitly address themselves to the theme of social reconstruction. In a general way, every educated and sensitive
man is a utopian. Each possesses in his imagination a sanctu-
ary to which he can retreat from the despairs and perplexi-
ties of everyday life. Often enough, the clash between the
agreeable fantasy and the disagreeable reality provides the
sadness and the drama in the works and lives of such men.
It is also noteworthy that gaping distances between fancy
and reality are as common among literary men as among
those who are usually, and disdainfully, called utopians.
One can find many examples among, to limit the field,
famous Americans from Mark Twain's time to the present.
Twain had his dream of small towns and great rivers, where
boys lived in truth and harmony with nature: too bad boys
become men. Henry Adams had his exclusive club, where
gentlemen talked of literature and politics: why must there
be the servant problem? For Eugene O'Neill the perfect
world seemed to be one in which the primitive religious
instinct was still in communion with gods powerful enough
to work tragedy: Freud and rationalism undermined all
that. Fitzgerald built his utopia of international hotel rooms
and Riviera villas, where shimmering flappers and hand-
some youths reveled in grace and champagne: but three
o'clock in the morning always had to come. Sherwood
Anderson longed for a world where buoyant young people
shared a sunny love, expressed in bountiful natural sexual
intercourse: but the Winesburgs of this world are always
oppressed by convention and haunted by lonely misfits. Dos

Passos for a while dreamed of redemption by the legions of history's only noble army, the proletariat: too bad the workers took to Fords rather than to the barricades. William Faulkner dreams of a plantation world of brave gentlemen and gracious ladies, served by loyal old retainers and obedient fieldhands: but in 1865 the South spawned the Snopeses and the NAACP soon followed. Ernest Hemingway still recalls that world where Manolete faces his death alone and with grace each afternoon: is there an arena left where they do not file the horns of the sons of Islero? Mr. T. S. Eliot has retreated to a world where devout churchmen write urbane prose, and the masses know their place in a moral universe defined by the king, the bishops, and their own simple piety: it is sad that neither the classes nor the masses any longer put much stock in the Trinity and the apostolic succession. If the visions of the previously mentioned writers are all hopelessly anachronistic, those of the modern Capotes and Salingers are so fragile and private that it would be coarse to invade them. Unwilling to do that, I turn to the public world of utopian thought strictly so-called.[1]

The starting point of utopian thought is the conviction that man has reached a point in the historical journey where the ascending trail, once so broad and smooth, has abruptly narrowed to a thin ledge and come to a dead end above an abyss. Crouched on the ledge, too cramped to turn around, he sees above him a broad shelf beckoning on up the mountain in another direction. With every passing moment, fear and fatigue sap his strength, and all his equipment, which before had seemed so light and useful, now drags him down and threatens his balance. He must leap, and he knows he can make the leap if he does it now while strength is still his and the light is still clear. That is to say, the utopian orientation is a complex blend of a sense of crisis, a peculiar courage based upon knowledge and faith, and a vision of salvation.

The utopian begins with the sense that his is a time of total crisis, a time when what is in question is not just this or that feature of society but the whole of man's life in the world. The old structure is near total collapse; great sections of it already lie in rubble. This total crisis demands a total act, a leap into a new mode of life. The total act that is demanded of us, however, must be based upon the fullest and most earnest knowledge of our present condition and of our own resources, human and material, for building a new order. Only that knowledge can give men the faith in themselves which they will need for the leap into the future. The leap itself is both encouraged and guided by the vision of a future perfection.

The utopian is at once a critic and a dreamer, and the great utopian works are a rich blend of logic and poetry, a compound of lucid criticism and glowing prophecy. But the utopian dream is not a private one, nor do its origins lie in the primitive unconscious. Rather, the utopian wish must be made concrete in symbols which have objective and shared meanings, and it must be expressed in the public language of social justice. The utopian, at bottom, expresses the deep human cry for harmony, community, brotherhood, and love. Hence his vision is essentially a moral and esthetic one, and his achievement is to be measured by standards drawn from those spheres.

There are a number of important distinctions within the utopian style. First, there is the distinction between moderate and radical utopianism. The former, which is almost synonymous with the "social planning" mentality, consists in looking at recent history and using the knowledge thus gained to exercise more-or-less control over short-range future developments. The moderate utopian is not out of step with the present time nor in revolt against it. He wants only to harness the power and control the pace of current social-economic tendencies. The radical utopian, on the other hand, is entirely out of step with the current movements of society. He would go back to the root of the malady and work basic changes in the foundations of the social order. He is the one who, even while he crouches on the narrow ledge, insists that we must retrace in thought the whole trail back to the point where the first wrong choice was made, the choice which culminated in the present catastrophe.

There is also an important difference of technique between the moderate and the radical utopian. The former employs the gentle arts of public relations and administrative manipulation. The latter relies on the spread of enlightenment and the enlargement of moral vision for the foundation of the new society, and calls for direct popular action in order to achieve it.

A second distinction within the utopian style is that between mechanicism and organicism. The former, which is displayed best in the work of Bentham and Fourier, flows from an abstract imagination which first lays down a theory of human nature and then deduces from it a universal social order. This social order is a lifeless mechanism, a machine which solves all problems by the same operation. The blueprint of the new society, which pretends to be a grand work of social architecture, is really nothing more than an abstract form imposed upon disparate living human beings and social forces.

The organic style, represented by Kropotkin and Proudhon, flows from a willingness to look into the hidden tendencies of the present social order, to probe there for the forces which, though for the present obscured, are yet working toward the transformation of society. This organic

242 Escape from Authority

style attempts to seek out and encourage those underlying tendencies in the social system which can overcome and transform present contradictions and tensions. Above all, the organic style starts from a realization of *society*, rather than from an abstract theory of human nature, and works first to inaugurate real changes within the organic structure of society.

The next distinction is that between technological and sociological utopianism. The former seeks social transformation through some technical gimmick. It paints glossy pictures of "techtopia," brittle paradises in which the machine is the instrument of salvation. This style of utopian thinking is now the dominant one, for it appeals to the distinctively modern pride of control over nature through technology. Numerous such utopias crowd the second-rate science fiction of our day, and the one thing they have in common is a lack of the grand and humane imagination that went into the great utopias of previous eras.

In contrast to this, sociological utopianism centers upon the transformation of social institutions and ideas. It insists upon changes in the social rather than in the technical system. Change must be rooted in society itself, and not just in the tools that society uses to subdue nature. In this style, the chief task is that of seeking the social and cultural transformations which can convert the present vicious social order into one which is right and just.

The final distinction within the utopian style is that between voluntarism and determinism. In the first, which includes all those writers whom Marx and Engels scornfully called Utopians, men are the active agents of their own fate. They must make the choice and perform the deed. Voluntaristic utopianism is thus the precise secular analogue of the prophetic strand in Jewish and Christian eschatology. The prophet addresses a people each one of whom has the power to participate by his own will and choice in the birth of the redeemed society. The choice lies with men as to whether and how they will work for the right social order, which the prophet only foretells and outlines in prodigious images. The deterministic strand, on the other hand, works from the premise that the process of social change has been foreordained in all details. Men are merely the agents and tools of what is already immutably fixed. The outcome may be revealed to them, and each may be assigned his special role in the drama of salvation, but the acts of the drama, including its final scene, have been prepared by forces outside man. Marxist scientific socialism represents most clearly this style of utopianism. It is the secular analogue of the apocalyptic strand in Jewish and Christian eschatology.

Closely related to this is a distinction concerning when and how utopia is to be achieved. Here again Marx and the Utopians represent the two orientations. For the former, utopia is to be achieved after the revolution. For the latter, utopia is to be realized gradually during the revolutionary process itself. Buber's formulation of the issue is excellent:

> It may be contended that the Marxist objective is not essentially different . . . [from the Utopian objective of freedom, individuality, and diversity]; but at this point a yawning chasm opens out before us . . . a chasm between, on the one side, the transformation to be consummated sometime in the future—no one knows how long after the final victory of the Revolution— and, on the other, the road to the Revolution and beyond it, which road is characterized by a far-reaching centralization that permits no individual features and no individual initiative. Uniformity as a means is to change miraculously into multiplicity as an end; compulsion into freedom. As against this the "utopian" or non-marxist socialist desires a means commensurate

with his ends; he refuses to believe that in our reliance on the future "leap" we have to do now the direct opposite of what we are striving for; he believes rather that we must create here and now the space *now* possible for the thing for which we are striving, so that it may come to fulfillment *then*; he does not believe in the post-revolutionary leap, but he does believe in revolutionary continuity. To put it more precisely: he believes in a continuity within which revolution is only the accomplishment, the setting free and extension of a reality that has already grown to its true possibilities.[2]

Using the terms developed above, Fromm's utopianism may be described as radical, mechanistic (though with a strain toward the organic), sociological, voluntaristic, and gradualistic (though with a strain toward the revolutionary). All such labels, quite obviously, are crude; and they can sometimes conceal more than they reveal. Still, they are of some use in placing Fromm in the utopian tradition and in indicating the general characteristics of his thought.

In addition to these general categories, Fromm's utopianism can be defined by three special characteristics which give his work a peculiar tone and stamp it as uniquely his. Added to the five general features, they provide a sufficient description of the nature of Fromm's utopianism.

The first special component of Fromm's utopianism is his belief that destructiveness and evil are not inherent in man but are the results either of economic shortages or of bad social institutions and relationships. This means that Fromm's discussion of corruption and regeneration proceeds neither in the language of the Jewish-Christian tradition nor in the language of Freudianism, but in the language of social reform. Specifically, Fromm looks back to the nineteenth century Utopian socialists for most of the articles of what he calls humanistic democratic socialism or communitarian socialism. Given his view of the origins of evil and destructiveness, it follows that there is nothing inherent in human nature to keep men from attaining a perfectly good society.

The second aspect of Fromm's utopianism consists in his view that it is possible for men to achieve the knowledge necessary for the construction of the perfect society. Indeed, that form of words is not sufficiently emphatic: he believes not just that such knowledge is attainable, but that it is easily attainable. At one point in *The Sane Society* Fromm replies to the fainthearted ones in words which capture the very spirit of the utopian confidence and the utopian courage. "Yet it is quite beyond doubt that the problems of social transformation are not as difficult to solve —theoretically and practically—as the technical problems our chemists and physicists have solved. . . . Even a fraction of the reason and practical sense used in the natural sciences, applied to human problems, will permit the continuation of the task our ancestors of the eighteenth century were so proud of." [3] And, one would add, the Gnostics before them.

Hence the requisite knowledge for successful utopian transformation is either already available or else can easily be secured. (It is not entirely clear which of these Fromm thinks is the case.) Nor is the knowledge available to us knowledge of means only, and not of ends. The ends of the good society and the good life have already been discovered.

> We do not need new ideals or new spiritual goals. The great teachers of the human race have postulated the norms for sane living. To be sure, they . . . have emphasized different aspects and have had different views on certain subjects. But, altogether, these differences were small. . . . In every center of culture . . . the same insights were discovered, the same ideals were

preached. We, today, who have easy access to all these ideas, who are still the immediate heirs to the great humanistic teachings, we are not in need of new knowledge of how to live sanely—but in bitter need of taking seriously what we believe, what we preach and teach.[4]

Given this faith in man's goodness and in the power of human reason, the third feature follows as a matter of course. Fromm will take a radical attitude toward problems of social improvement. He will advocate sweeping changes, changes that go to the roots. In Fromm's thought this radicalism expresses itself not only in matters of program but also in what may be called the "law of simultaneous advance." This is the principle that reform must proceed simultaneously on all fronts. The revolution must not be merely, or even primarily, economic or political or moral or philosophical. Rather, it must sweep across all these sectors simultaneously: a prairie fire of progress. Mere "isolated progress," as Fromm calls it, mere tinkering or cautious experimentation with one or another aspect of life at a time can at best lead to very slight improvement and will at worst end in disastrous failure.

> . . . sanity and mental health can be attained only by simultaneous changes in the spheres of industrial and political organization, of spiritual and philosophical orientation, of character structure, and of cultural activities. The concentration of effort in any of these spheres, to the exclusion or neglect of others, is destructive of *all* change. In fact, here seems to lie one of the most important obstacles to the progress of mankind. . . . Each of [the] great reform movements of the last two thousand years has emphasized one sector of life to the exclusion of the others; their proposals for reform and renewal were radical—but their results were almost

complete failure. The preaching of the Gospel led to the establishment of the Catholic Church; the teachings of the rationalists of the eighteenth century to Robespierre and Napoleon; the doctrines of Marx to Stalin. The results could hardly have been different. . . . Undoubtedly *one* step of integrated progress in all spheres of life will have more far-reaching and more lasting results for the progress of the human race than a hundred steps preached—and even for a short while lived—in only one isolated sphere.[5] *

These three elements—belief in the natural goodness of man, faith in the power of reason, and advocacy of the principle of simultaneous advance—are themselves a sufficient definition of a certain style of utopianism. Fromm the reformer drops the language of both Marx and Freud and speaks in the tones of the eighteenth century. The nostalgic remoteness of those tones is a measure of how far we are from that golden age.

Communitarian Socialism

The major articles of Fromm's constitution for the new society can be set forth under four headings: (1) ethical and moral foundations of the new order; (2) economic transformation; (3) political transformation; and (4) cultural transformation.†

* That Fromm thoroughly misunderstands "the great reform movements of the last two thousand years" is devastatingly apparent from this passage.

† Fromm's account, which I shall follow closely, appears in *The Sane Society*, pp. 283–352. Only extensive quotations will be given precise citations. In the summer of 1959, Fromm gave an address entitled "A Proposed Socialist Manifesto" before a convention of the Socialist Party-Social Democratic Federation. This essay has been distributed rather widely in mimeograph form, but it has not, to my knowledge, been published. It is an excellent summary statement of Fromm's position.

Ethical and moral foundations.   The supreme value is man, and every man is to be treated always as an end and never as a means. No man may, by virtue of his wealth or social position, exercise power over any other man. All authority must be based on competence and must be exercised in the interests of those subject to it. All are equal, and all are equally free. The purpose of society is to provide the conditions for the fullest development of man's capacity to reason, to love, and to produce. All instruments of coercion must disappear, and the state must be replaced by a free association of all citizens bound together by their common interests and their sense of brotherhood. Each individual must be brought to understand his solidarity with all mankind. In sum, the principles of the good society are liberty, equality, and fraternity.

Economic transformation.   The great aim of communitarian socialism is to achieve an economic system in which *"every working person would be an active and responsible participant, where work would be attractive and meaningful, where capital would not employ labor, but labor would employ capital."* [6]   To achieve this aim, all economic activity must be put on a new moral footing: production for use, not for profit. The rights of the owners of capital do not include management of the industry. Capitalists are entitled only to a fair payment for the use of their capital. Although communitarian socialism is not opposed to private ownership or enterprise as such, any enterprise whose proper social functioning is not compatible with profit must be socialized. Also, the state must found new enterprises in all areas of the economy which are not now adequately served by private enterprises. Industries which influence taste and morals, such as communications and entertainment, must be socially regulated to whatever extent is necessary to produce a healthy cultural environment for the people. All attempts to stimulate artificial needs by the methods of mass persuasion must be stopped.

These technical problems of ownership and regulation in the public interest solved, Fromm turns to the more important question of how industry should be governed. The answer is, by the principles of "co-management and workers' participation." Industrial government must be democratic government. All who have an interest in the industry must have a voice in it. The principle, Fromm thinks,

> . . . can be worked out in such a way that the responsibility for management is divided between the central leadership and the rank and file. Well-informed small groups discuss matters of their own work situation and of the whole enterprise; their decisions would be channelled to the management and form the basis for a real co-management. As a third participant, the consumer would have to participate in the decision making and planning in some form.[7]

This may seem a little vague, but Fromm is confident that the details can be worked out. After all, "in constitutional law we have solved similar problems with regard to the respective rights of various branches of government. . . ." (True, we have; but the comparison seems an unhappy one, for we have not solved the jurisdictional problems of separation of powers by democratic methods. The Supreme Court is not a democratic institution.)

Only if the workers achieve full participation in the government of industry will alienation from work, which is the root of all alienation, be healed. But we must also take steps to see that the new industrial rulers rule competently. The workers must be educated to a "wider knowledge of all the technical problems involved in the production of the

whole product" and each must also be trained to an understanding of the place of his enterprise in the national and
world economy. All this knowledge will be disseminated by
a system of free industrial schools and continuous on-the-
job instruction. The worker will of course continue to earn
while he learns.

These reforms will do much to make work meaningful
and attractive. In addition, informal social organization
must be encouraged in the workplace. There must be a
real "community of work," but this must be counterbal-
anced by measures which will teach the members of each
particular community of work to overcome parochial loyal-
ties in favor of the "one truly social orientation," which is
"solidarity with mankind." When it becomes clear to all
that "the primary purpose of any work is to serve people,
and not to make a profit," the motivations for work will
change from money, power, prestige, and status, to motives
of interest in the work, participation in the community, and
the building of an independent economic existence. Those
who think that money and power are the strongest incentives
driving people to work forget that this is true only of alienated men. Happy, productive, integrated men are not lazy.
They are eager to work, and they work not for money and
power but for self-fulfillment and service to the community.

Democracy in industry and meaning in work are the
necessary but not the sufficient conditions of individual
liberty and human solidarity. To them must be added certain measures of economic equality and security. Concerning the former, Fromm says that while all incomes need
not be equal, "inequalities . . . must not transcend the
point where differences in income lead to differences in the
experience of life." [8] Concerning the latter, he advocates,
in addition to a full system of social security for sickness,
unemployment, and old age, a "universal subsistence guar-

antee." This would mean that any individual could at any time and for any reason claim a minimum subsistence sum from the state. Fromm thinks this should be limited to, perhaps, two years, "so as to avoid the fostering of a neurotic attitude which refuses any kind of social obligation." The cost of such a scheme "would hardly be more than what big states have spent for the maintenance of armies in the last decades. . . ." Furthermore, the increased cost would be more than balanced by the increased output of the happy workers.

Political proposals. The citizen needs help. Alienated from political life, poorly informed, and manipulated by powerful propaganda machines, he brings to politics a stock of shabby prejudices, hackneyed stereotypes, and garbled slogans. He has an abundance of likes and hatreds but little sound knowledge and less effective volition. His vote is not much more than an abdication of responsibility. Democratic elections take on more and more of the characteristics of a plebiscite in which the citizens surrender their political will to one or the other of the political machines. In this age of conformity, the very idea of majority rule has become an instrument of alienation and abstractification. Originally, Fromm says, majority rule "did not mean that the majority was *right*; it meant that it is better for the majority to be wrong than for a minority to impose its will on the majority." Now the majority is regarded as right, and the minority is by definition wrong.

Sound decisions cannot be made in the atmosphere of mass voting. They require informed discussion within small face-to-face groups. Sound decisions also must be based on sound information. Therefore, a way must be found to supply the citizens with full and objective information on all the questions which come before them for decision. Finally, the decisions of the small groups "must have a direct influence on the decision-making exercised by a centrally elected parliamentary executive."

These goals can be achieved by a pleasingly simple reform: revive the town meeting and adapt it to modern conditions. The population would be organized into groups of about five hundred persons each on the basis of residence or place of work. These groups would meet regularly, say once a month, and would choose their own officials and committees, which would change every year. The groups would discuss the main political issues of national and local concern. They would receive objective information prepared by a politically independent cultural agency composed of "personalities from the fields of art, sciences, religion, business, politics, whose outstanding achievements and moral integrity are beyond doubt. . . ." After discussion and decision, the five-hundreds would forward their votes to the central seat of government, where the over-all result would be computed and registered. The decision thus arrived at would be regarded as the decision of the "true 'House of Commons,'" which would share power with the house of universally elected representatives and a universally elected executive." Through this procedure, "the process of alienation in which the individual citizen surrenders his political will by the ritual of voting to powers beyond him would be reversed, and each individual would take back into himself his role as a participant in the life of the community." *

Cultural proposals. First of all, "we do not need new ideals or new spiritual goals," for "the great teachers of

---

* In the lecture cited above, Fromm has increased the work and power of the five-hundreds. They would meet weekly, and more often in cases of emergency. The collective decision of this "lower house" would have "eventual predominance" over the decisions of the national Congress. It seems to me that Fromm has here, unwittingly, solved the problem of the use of leisure time in the abundant society.

the human race have postulated the norms for sane living."
What we need is not new wisdom but richer understanding
of, and more serious dedication to, the old wisdom.

The task of impressing on men the guiding ideals is the
task of education. We must abolish the concept of education as a process of training people to adjust to the social
machine and devote our schools to the development of
the human powers. Schools should strive to impart to their
students the taste for critical thought, and to give them
character traits "which correspond to the professed ideals of
our civilization." We must erase the harmful separation
between theoretical and practical knowledge, for "this very
separation is part of the alienation of work and thought."
From the beginning, theoretical instruction and practical
work must be combined. No primary education would be
complete "before the student has a grasp of the fundamental technical processes of our industry." The high school
"ought to combine practical work of a handicraft and of
modern industrial technique with theoretical instruction."
The system of adult education must be enormously expanded.

We must develop collective art and rituals which will
help us "*respond to the world with our senses in a meaningful, skilled, productive, active, shared way.*" This "will begin
with the children's games in kindergarten, be continued in
school, then in later life. We shall have common dances,
choirs, plays, music, bands. . . ." Not a word about foot-
ball.

What about religion? It is likely that within the next
few hundred years a new humanistic and universalistic religion will develop. In the meantime, we can unite in firm
negation of the idolatries of the state, of power, of the
machine, and of success. In this negation we shall find more
of a common faith than in any "affirmative statements

254 Escape from Authority

about God." We can also, religionists and nonreligionists alike, take seriously the Jewish and Christian ethical teachings of the dignity of man, of love, of reason, and of the supremacy of spiritual values.

This completes the constitution of utopia. When all these things are done, Rousseau's problem will have been solved. Men will have "succeeded in building a society in which the interest of 'society' has become identical with that of all its members." [9]

Utopia is at once a vision of the good and a program of action. The utopian appeals to the freedom of the future against the prison of the present. His work begins with the destruction of the actual so that imagination can be free for the flight into the possible. Hence the utopian demands two things of his reader: he requires that the reader also liberate himself from the present; and he requires that the reader conceive of man as the fantastic one, the being who routinely does the prodigious and is insulted by the merely practical. If the reader will not meet these two obligations, the utopian builds in vain. In a very important sense, then, the only really adequate critique of a utopia is the construction of a counter-utopia. Above all, the whole line of criticism of utopia which takes the form of saying "it isn't practical, because men and things just are not that way" is beside the point.

Governed by these canons, I shall comment on two features of communitarian socialism. The first, and briefer, set of remarks will treat the question of whether, within the framework of Fromm's theory of man, utopia is possible. The argument here will attempt to show that Fromm's optimistic and generous view of man leads necessarily to pessimistic conclusions on the possibility of utopia, conclusions which might have been avoided had Fromm shown a little less pity for man's sufferings and weaknesses, and a little more respect for his perversity and toughness. Another way to put the thesis would be to say that, by making individual goodness and badness almost entirely a function of social conditions, Fromm makes it almost impossible for men to reform society. The second set of remarks will concern Fromm's views on a basic substantive question, the transformation of work and authority. Here I shall argue that the trouble with his utopia is that it is not utopian enough, that he fails to escape the confines of the present.

Can Robots Revolt?

I am not concerned to comment on the futility either of utopianism or of rationalism. That has been done often enough; and, more often than not, by men of small courage and imagination who would spare themselves the pain of thought and failure by calling themselves realists and everybody else idealists. There is no more distressing symptom of our failure of nerve than the power of this word "realist" in recent political discussion. The realist, we must suppose, is one who realistically faces up to "reality." Without accepting solipsism, I think Vladimir Nabokov is right when he says that "reality" is one of the very few words which mean nothing without quotes. In the intellectual currency of our day, however, it has taken on some precise values. The political realist divides all "reality" into two parts, interest and power. The first is what you are after, and the second is what you use to get it. Since every path has obstacles, the realists' wisdom comes down to the precept, takes the path of least resistance. That is why it is so hard to follow realists; they turn aside, double back, and strike out anew with dazzling dexterity. No wonder they are always bumping into themselves and into each other. Of all perceptions of "reality," the realists' is the most impoverished.

So I do not intend to enter the standard realistic objections against utopianism. I take as premises for the following discussion of the possibility of achieving the Frommian utopia these points: (1) survival and physical comfort are not the goal of human life, but only its animal bases—men build societies not merely to live, but to achieve the good life; (2) there are occasions when men and civilizations must choose between life and death, and this choice is not best understood as one between physical life and death but as one between the maintenance and advancement of moral and cultural values, and the decline into barbarism or meaninglessness; (3) so long as men can think and plan there is always the possibility of meaningful moral action, even in the face of the most desperate situations. As a utopian, Fromm appreciates the power of these elementary considerations.

In considering the possibility of achieving utopia, it must be said at once that Fromm himself does not think the prospects are sanguine. He judges that "the most likely possibility" for the future "is that of atomic war," the result of which must be either "the regression of the world to a primitive agrarian level" or the emergence of a single "centralized state based on force—and it would make little difference whether Moscow or Washington were the seat of government." If we escape this doom, the outlook still is not bright. "In the development of both capitalism and of communism as we can visualize them in the next fifty or a hundred years, the process of automatization and alienation will proceed." [10]

Assuming we escape both war and robotism, the road to communitarian socialism will still be long and tough. Fromm recognizes that institutional change by itself is barren. He denies himself the easy postponement of spiritual regeneration to some indefinite time after the political and economic revolutions are fulfilled. We must first put down our own pessimism and cynicism and break the idols of money and power; only then can we start the institutional reforms which will restore humanity. Above all, Fromm refuses to assign the mission of redemption to a chosen class. He knows that the proletarians, along with the rest of us, have to lose a lot more than their chains before they can build the sane society.

What, then, are the possibilities of achieving the good society? It is consistent with Fromm's whole analysis of human nature (specifically, his concept of the basic human needs, his concept of the humanistic conscience, and his thesis that destructiveness is not an inherent quality of man) to say, the possibilities are pretty good. If destructiveness is not an inherent quality of men, if men do have a humanistic conscience, and if we know the goals of the good life, then it is theoretically possible for men to achieve the communitarian socialist utopia.

But to say that may be to say something that does not have much practical meaning. Two questions must be asked: (1) Can men, from their present fallen condition, rise to the acts that will create the conditions necessary for the good society? (2) Can men maintain such a society once they have achieved it? * I shall confine the discussion within the framework of Fromm's system, for I want to show that his own optimistic premises compel pessimistic answers to both questions.

1. Can fallen men redeem society? Fromm has described us as automatons, on the way to becoming robots.

---

* It is worth noting that these are the only two questions which need be considered in discussing the possibility of Fromm's utopia, for he rejects *chance* and rests his whole case on intelligently directed human abilities.

Can robots revolt? In a certain way, yes: they can destroy their world, but they cannot build a better one. The revolution of the robots is the revolution of nihilism. "But given man's nature, robots cannot live and remain sane, they become 'Golems,' they will destroy their world and themselves because they cannot stand any longer the boredom of a meaningless life." [11]

Men have become automatons. Automatons are on the way to becoming robots. Robots turn into Golems. How can this catastrophic progress be stopped? If I understand Fromm correctly, it cannot, for he has introduced no braking mechanism into his social analysis. His whole thesis is that under bad social conditions men can move in only one direction, toward destructiveness. A vicious circle is set in motion: as social conditions deteriorate, destructiveness increases; as destructiveness increases, social conditions deteriorate even more . . . and so on, to nihilism. This is one of the unpleasant conclusions that must flow from any theory which, like Fromm's, sees human goodness as a function of social goodness. It is a conclusion which was present from the beginning in the optimistic thesis that man is "primarily" productive and his "secondary" destructive potential is actualized only under evil social conditions. The other side of that thesis is the grim conclusion that once evil has entered society destructiveness must follow. Given Fromm's logic, I see no way to escape this conclusion. It is ironical how the premises of the optimist turn into the conclusions of the pessimist. (Fromm, of course, does not accept this conclusion. I am only arguing that he must accept it, if he is to be true to his argument.)

A second feature of the system leads in the same direction. Just as Fromm has no brake against destructiveness, so has he no starter for productiveness. It is true that for Fromm the taint that keeps us from perfection is not in ourselves. For Fromm, man is not a creature inherently depraved and weak but a creature whose strongest urge is toward goodness and productiveness. Thus the problem is, how can the great moral powers of man be unchained, set free to perform their wondrous work of redemption? I think the problem is insoluble within the framework of Fromm's social analysis. First, it was argued in the above paragraphs that once man has fallen he can only fall farther. Secondly, Fromm, unlike Marx, or Mannheim, sets up no class which, by virtue of its special social-economic position, can act as the redemptive force for the whole of society and all of the classes.

If I understand Fromm correctly, the initial power can come only from a source outside the social system: the prophet, the hero, the leader. Conditions such as those we live under, according to Fromm, are the spawning grounds of charismatic leaders and mass movements: the weak, the maimed, and the bored look for leaders and movements.* Therefore, there is no doubt that the motive power for vast social change could come from such a leader at the head of such a movement. But the prophet can speak for hate as well as for love, for destruction as well as for communitarian socialism, and there is not the slightest bit of evidence to give us confidence that his power will more likely be used for good rather than evil. Under social conditions such as those which Fromm thinks prevail in the United States today, there is every reason to fear that only evil can result from mass movements and magical leaders. Alienated men know only that they are hurt and need help. Men who do not love themselves cannot love

---

* This, in fact, is one of the dominant and most capably developed of all Fromm's themes in *Escape from Freedom*. The only work of comparable quality on the theme is the brilliant essay by Eric Hoffer, *The True Believer: Thoughts on the Nature of Mass Movements* (New York: Harper, 1951).

others. Men who hate themselves also hate others. From self-contempt, as Pascal said, come "the most unjust and criminal passions imaginable." Such men are less likely to be moved by prophets of love and construction than by prophets of hate and destruction.

Before leaving this question of the possibility of achieving the sane society, one other point ought to be made. Here again it is a matter of spelling out the implications of Fromm's position. The corollary of the law of simultaneous advance is the proposition that failure to advance in one sector of society threatens the advances made in all other sectors. Put in its extreme form, the corollary asserts that one recalcitrant class or interest (for example, the owners and managers of capital, though it is as likely to be the workers, who do not seem to realize how unhappy they really are) can thwart all progress toward utopia. Given the diversity and perversity of men, the general insecurity and fear aroused by sweeping social change, and the tenacity of the vested interests of all kinds, it is inevitable that many more than one segment of society would refuse to march with Fromm toward the sane society. This means that Fromm's revolutionaries would very promptly be confronted with the choice of watching the revolution fail or attempting to establish more and more control over society. The communitarians would soon have their Lenin. Fromm's thought on this matter stops at the level of the slogan: the revolution must be accomplished by peaceful means. His failure to probe much beneath this shows, I think, his shortcomings as a political thinker.

This raises a question which one must always come to when dealing with a moralist and ideologist: what is the writer's audience? If one asks, whence come the heroes who will lead men to the sane society, the answer must be, from among the followers of Erich Fromm. This suggests that

Fromm is really addressing two audiences. The first is the small band of productives and near-productives; men who, like Fromm himself, are either already healthy or else capable of healing themselves. These fortunate few, for reasons only poorly understood, either have escaped the plague of social insanity or else have thoroughly recovered from it. Having risen above their age, they can see the sickness of the masses beneath them, just as they can see the way toward cure. To this group Fromm the prophet speaks in the language of program and action. The second group consists of all the rest of us, the legions of the nonproductives —marketers, receptives, hoarders, exploiters. These are the followers, those who will, each for his own unhealthy reason, accept the direction of the healthy few. They will, presumably, follow in the same style that they do everything else, that is, as robots. Their great hope is that they may become healed in the sane society. What matters here, however, is that Fromm addresses these people not in the language of action but in the language of hope and comfort. All he can achieve with them is to persuade them that the Frommians are on their side.

The thin line of the productives, I have argued, is a very flimsy barrier against the catastrophic movement which is inherent in Fromm's whole analysis, the movement from human to robot to Golem. Even if we grant that the strength of each of the productives is as the strength of ten, because his psyche is healthy, only an incorrigible optimist could have confidence in their ability to withstand the hordes of the nonproductives. Indeed, the more one reads Fromm, the more one comes to marvel at the way he always puts down the gloomy implications of his own analysis and comes up with a shout of affirmation. In this, he reminds one of the despairing-triumphant Walt Whitman of the *Democratic Vistas*.

And yet, there is an obscure and ambiguous note in this social optimism of Fromm's. If we think of him as the prophet, the one who sees past his age into the possibilities beyond, we must also see him as the one who seeks followers. Running counter to this, however, is a current of mysticism and irrationalism which has been present in his thought from the beginning. His recent flirtations with Zen, which will be discussed more fully below, represent the latest and strongest manifestation of this tendency. Mysticism, of course, means a turning away from society in the search for salvation. It means pessimism rather than optimism concerning the possibilities of social change. Does the inclination toward Zen suggest a certain despair concerning the possibilities of social transformation? Or does it indicate a fervent, though clandestine, search for disciples? If the latter, this is surely the acme of optimism, for it is hard to imagine a rosier hope than that of organizing Zen Buddhists for social action. I leave the question there—unanswered.

2. Can the sane society, once achieved, be maintained? If the foregoing analysis is sound, this question is purely academic. But a brief treatment of it will reveal some additional facets of Fromm's thought.

The possibility of maintaining utopia would depend upon the ability of men to withstand deviations from utopia. If men cannot tolerate severe and prolonged deficiencies in their environment, then the first large deviation would shatter the whole structure. Fromm's theory of human nature compels the conclusion that the margin of tolerable deviation is small, for the productiveness-destructiveness balance is very fragile. Frustration of man's natural creative powers—failure to satisfy the basic psychic needs— immediately transforms man's energies into destructive forces. Such frustrations could come from many sources—war, cold war, economic imbalance or deprivation, natural catastrophe, and so forth.

Once destructiveness appears, a kind of multiplier effect comes into play. Destructiveness spreads outward from its source at an accelerating pace, contaminating one area of society and character after another, until all are infected. This progress would continue until all the five basic human needs were twisted into unhealthy forms. Then the natural restorative powers of human nature would rise up either to smash the corrupt social order or else to arrest the forces of destruction and begin the hard task of reconstruction. But the arrest obviously would come too late to save utopia. It would come just in time to present the reformer with the problem which Machiavelli formulated: How can a community restore itself when its members are radically corrupt? Fromm nowhere faces the terrible possibility that perhaps Machiavelli's problem can be solved only by Machiavelli's means.

A final point. The law of simultaneous advance has a second corollary which bears on the question of the maintenance of utopia. This corollary implies that any lag or relapse in one part of society will be followed by lags and relapses in related sectors. This is just another way of putting the multiplier effect mentioned above, but this formulation suggests the kinds of questions concerning the application of state power which the communitarians would soon have to face. Under what conditions should political power be used to spur the efforts of recalcitrant classes and interests? Under what conditions should political power be used to arrest the retrograde tendencies of one or another class or interest? Fromm has offered no discussion of these questions.

The Organization of Work

Fromm's scheme for the transformation of work is a simple one, consisting of one dominant goal, one ethical principle, and two major procedural recommendations. The goal is the restoration of meaning and dignity in work. To achieve this, the economy must be guided by the principle of production for use rather than for profit. In addition, work must be governed democratically, that is, by the practices of co-management and worker's participation. Finally, each worker must be educated to an understanding of his role in the process of production. When these things are done, we shall have healed the wound of alienation from work, which is the core of all alienation.

I shall discuss this formulation and solution to the problem of work under two headings. In the first part of the discussion, I shall challenge the inarticulate major assumption of Fromm's treatment of work. In the second part I shall proceed as though the first had not been written; that is, I shall accept, for the purposes of discussion, Fromm's major assumption and go on to argue that both his formulation and his solution of the problem of meaning in work are inadequate, lacking in imaginativeness and depth. This second part of the discussion is based upon the canon of criticism which was laid down earlier, the canon that "the only really adequate critique of a utopia is the construction of a counter-utopia." I shall be arguing in effect that the trouble with Fromm's utopian solution to the problem of work is that it is not utopian enough, that he has failed to escape the confines of the present.

Fromm formulates the problem of work as a problem of *restoration*. His discussion rests upon the implicit assumption that once upon a time men found meaning and dignity in work, but that now, owing largely to the institutions and the ideology of capitalism, this has been lost, and men are chained to meaningless and degrading tasks. There is no evidence known to me that such a golden age ever existed.

From the very beginning, the Western cultures have regarded work as at best a painful necessity for some people and at worst a debasement of human life. Antiquity despised the laboring activities which provided the animal bases of human life. Aristotle, for example, described only three ways of life which were truly human, because they could be chosen and followed in freedom. For the rest, neither the coerced labor of the slave nor the more "free" labor of the artisan and merchants was considered to possess sufficient dignity and freedom to be judged an authentically human life at all. Those who worked merely produced the essential and useful bases of a human life, but they did not themselves live a truly human life. The Biblical story begins with a description of work as a painful servitude imposed on man as punishment for original sin. Subsequent Christian emphasis on equality and on the sacredness of all human life freed work from some of the contempt which antiquity had fixed on it, but in none of the premodern Christian writers will there be found a glorification of work as the meaning of life. Premodern Christian thinkers recommended work as a protection against the temptations of idleness, as a means to ward off otiosity, or as a duty which must be performed by those who had no other means of keeping themselves alive. Even in the last justification the real duty lay in keeping oneself alive, and not in working as such: if one could live by begging, that was as good as working. Finally, the ethics of all aristocratic cultures—that is to say, of all but the most modern cultures—despise work and regard it as brutalizing and degrading. To talk about "restoring" meaning in work in the sense that Fromm has in

mind is to talk about restoring something that never existed.
The attitude toward work which Fromm appears to hold is
a very modern one.

The fact seems to be that only a very few men have
ever found deep meaning in work as such; and the work
that they have done has been work of a very special kind.
The poets, the writers, the teachers, the painters, the philosophers—those for whom to work is to create with the
whole of their intellectual and spiritual powers—these are
the privileged few for whom work has deep and inherent
meaning. If work is to be meaningful in the only sense that
matters, it must be work of a kind that demands very special talents. The individual who finds meaning in work must
himself have talent: there are aristocrats of work as of
everything else. It is hardly necessary to point out that most
men lack creative talent and that most "jobs" do not require it.

The aristocrats of work, then, can under certain circumstances find meaning in it. What of the masses, those millions for whom Fromm would prescribe? I would suggest
that the notion of meaning in work, as he uses it, does not
apply to them, but that perhaps his notion of dignity in
work does, with some modifications. The masses have not
found meaning *in* work, but they have under certain conditions derived satisfactions *from* it. One of these satisfactions has been the belief that there is a dignity in work.
What I have in mind here is the fact that, from the earliest
times, servile work—work which is necessary to the perpetuation and comfort of life—has been rationalized and
justified by ideologies which, in one or another way, assure
the workers that their lot is a dignified and virtuous as well
as a necessary one. Ideology has lightened and dignified
work by giving the worker the satisfaction of feeling that
what he does is valuable and meaningful both to himself

and to others. In this sense, the masses *have* found meaning and dignity in work, the meaning and dignity which come from ideologies of justification, ideologies which explain how work is related to the achievement of the good life. But to regard work itself as the meaning of the good life, as Fromm does in his concept of the productive man, is a specifically modern derangement of the sectors of life, a putting of last things first, which has no precedent in previous ages.

Work-justifying ideologies usually have two parts. One part explains the value of work to the community. Examples can be drawn from many times and places: The feudal myth of the sturdy yeoman, who by his work and obedience freed other sectors of the community for fighting and praying; the Puritan notion of the "warrantable calling," with its emphasis on service to the community; the Stakhanovite, who builds socialism with tractors. The other part explains how work benefits and ennobles the individual worker himself. Here also examples are easy to find: the Christian conception of work as a penance for wrongdoing and a barrier against temptation; the feudal notion of the dignity of faithful service; the Lockean concept of labor as the source of property; the Jeffersonian glorification of the farmer as the most virtuous of men and the most favored of God; the Franklin-Alger myth of honest work as the key to success and happiness.

The modern ideology of consumption is in form and function no different from any of these older ideologies of work. For in a time when the community measures its health by the size of and the rate of increase in the gross national product, and the good life is equated with the life of bountiful consumption, the ideology of work-as-the-key-to-consumption is precisely suited to provide men with a sense of satisfaction and "meaning in work."

In conclusion, Fromm's program for the restoration of meaning in work rests on a premise which never existed in reality. I now want to proceed as though this premise were sound, and argue that even within his own terms of reference, his solution to the problem of work is not utopian enough.

Most writers who deal with work today start with a very limited view of man. Man is seen as motivated by desires for prestige, economic well-being, and security. These things are in fact what most workers do want—if we may trust the major research findings. This modest view of economic man leads to equally modest proposals for reform, which are usually either of the "human relations in industry" variety of the Mayo-Homans-Drucker-Whyte school, or of the "workers' control" variety of Fromm and some of the English Socialists.[12]

A truly radical solution to the problem of meaning in work under the conditions of high technology, intricate specialization of labor, and mass production, must start from truly radical premises, for the drag of the system is so strong that you must start far away from it in order to escape being drawn into it. If you start, for example, from the premise that the worker is seeking security and status you will be drawn ineluctably to the "human relations" kind of conclusion. If you start from the premise that the worker is seeking dignity you will be drawn either to a very conservative conclusion of the trade union as a community,[13] or to the workers' control type of conclusion of Fromm, which can really mean little more than a perpetuation of the present bureaucratic control of industry, modified by a rhetoric of democracy.

Banish these prosaic premises and introduce some others. Start, for example, from the premise that man is a sloth and work is a drudge. Take seriously the view that men work to live, and not the other way round. This premise would provide a solid justification for the economy of bountiful consumption which now exists, and about which we are so ambivalent, and it would provide guidelines for future development. It would unburden the national mind of its guilt about "materialism," and it would provide both business and labor with a respectable ideology of the pleasures of consumption in place of the present hypocritical slogans of defense against inflation on the one side and living wages for the workers on the other. The workers would be relieved of the burden of feeling that they ought to enjoy their work. We could in good conscience extol some of the very real virtues of modern work about which we now feel ambivalent: the fact that the worker is basically free of responsibility for judging the quality, quantity, and social utility of the article he produces; the fact that when the worker is on the job he is freed of his family; the fact that when the day is over he is free of work; the fact that routine, simple, repetitive tasks leave his mind free for creative reverie.

The premise of sloth would also provide a blueprint for the future. We could unchain our technical genius and apply it without restriction to the construction of techtopia. It would not take long to realize the one condition which Aristotle thought would abolish the need for managers to have subordinates and masters to have slaves—the condition that machines be able to do their work at the signal of command and regulate their own actions through intelligent participation: "as if a shuttle should weave of itself, and a plectrum should do its own harp-playing." Within a generation, say, human work outside the artistic and intellectual spheres would all but disappear. Perhaps no more than an hour or two of work per day would be required of each of us. There is no reason why even that work would have to be very hard or heavy. Many of the hard manual jobs which, owing to their nature, could not be performed by machines, might well be done by trained apes, who would of course be treated well and fed the finest bananas. The rest of us would spend our days meeting the problems and enjoying the pleasures we choose for ourselves.

Or, if the premise of sloth seems to lead too directly to the "air conditioned nightmare," reject it and choose another. Start from the premise of Promethean man. Take seriously the view that man is the creature who will storm the universe regardless of personal cost or prospect of success. Explore the implications of the glaring contrast between man at work under the conditions of industrialism and man seeking his own ends through activities freely chosen by him. Look closely at these two portraits of man. First, the man drawn by industrial sociology: bored with his job, taking little interest or pleasure in it, thinking up all kinds of diversions to give meaning to his day, engaging in extreme forms of work restriction, indulging himself in escapist reverie, resentful, little interested in his union or his community, often absenting himself from work, touchy about the slightest encroachments on his "rights," and suspicious of even slight changes in the work situation. Secondly, a few men whom all of us know: the young writer who sacrifices health and comfort for his work; the devoted scholar and teacher who cannot find time for half the things he wants to do; the explorer who thirsts for an expedition to the extreme corners of the earth; the hunter who rises before dawn to tramp all day through the roughest country and the harshest weather; the man who hates his job at office or factory but who works in his garden until the sweat streams from his face and his back cracks. What is apparent here is that men who are working for their own satisfaction at a job that challenges them are utterly careless of fatigue.

They want no talk of seven-hour days and pleasant conditions. Put these men in a factory and they will shortly look like the man of the industrial sociologists.

Anyone who deplores alienation from work and who believes in the dignity and worth of the individual must think seriously about this contrast between industrial man and free man. Such thought ought to start from the recognition that nothing will replace the individual's need for and satisfaction in the creation of a whole product which he deems worthy and good, or for contributing his best efforts to a common task which he has accepted and which he understands in its entirety. If these goals are not compatible with the profitable, or efficient, operation of a huge industrial enterprise or a massive bureaucratic administrative and business structure, then perhaps the huge factory and the massive bureaucracy ought to be dismantled.

Jeremy Bentham, for utilitarian motives, spent many laborious hours perfecting the design for a remarkable building to be known as the Panopticon. It was to be a star-shaped structure, half-factory and half-prison, so nicely built that each inmate would pass his days in perfect isolation from his fellows and under the perpetual eye of a warder stationed at the center. Bentham's Panopticon, as Sir Leslie Stephen said, was a mill excellently designed "to grind rogues honest, and idle men industrious."

Radical thought on the problem of meaning in work ought to start from the premise that the Panopticon has become a reality. The modern worker works at a task and a pace neither of which he sets himself. He is kept under constant surveillance not by a human warder (who might, after all, be subject to the humanizing influences of bribery and friendship) but by the nonhuman logics of time and efficiency. His performance is judged and his rewards allotted by intricate computing machines capable of juggling complex performance equations made up of numerous standard terms for energy, cost, time, motion, and the like. That the trade unions agree to this panopticonic system is just another index of how far we have come from any real understanding of dignity and freedom in work. It is certainly true that unions have greatly reduced the brutal exploitation of the workers and have achieved something like a constitutional order of fair play in industry. But when we see the union agreeing to piecework schemes, standard norms and rates of work, duties and rewards determined by time-motion principles, and the like, we must ask whether this is fair play for real human beings, or whether it is fair play for men who are treated as though they were machines which must be handled carefully and maintained properly if they are to perform at their fullest capacity. The unions have entirely accepted the principles of efficiency and productivity as the criteria of economic effectiveness, and ask only that the worker get a fair share of the rewards. Indeed, the one feature of the Panopticon which most modern factories and bureaucracies lack is the conviction that work has a moral meaning, the belief that through diligent labor the rogues can be made honest and the idle industrious. Bentham's Panopticon, after all, was not merely a prison but a *penitent*iary, a place where bad men paid for their sins and thus were made good. Work has no such reforming and disciplining function for modern man. It is something he does because he needs the money to buy the things which his society tells him are identical with the good life. The modern worker enters the Panopticon not because he has transgressed against society, but precisely because, having accepted society's values, he becomes society's slave—a fact which makes the work go more smoothly and reduces the demand for warders.

Thought which is truly radical would give these premises serious consideration. Certainly Fromm is right when he says that the principle of profit and efficiency must be replaced by the principle of use and satisfaction. But the acceptance of this principle entails some consequences which Fromm has given no sign of recognizing. His panacea is co-management and workers' participation. There is really very little to be said about this, mainly because it is so amorphous. But, vague as it is, it seems to me to run in the wrong direction. First of all, if the idea means worker control of the whole economy, it ought to be challenged as merely another form of interest domination. Secondly, if the idea means worker control in specific industries, it ought to be rejected as a technique which would in effect make labor an auxiliary of capital. As Bell has pointed out, worker participation in management "tends to minimize the separate interests of workers from management, and to rob the workers of an independent status in the plant." [14]

The idea of workers' control can be given a concrete meaning and does have valuable applications in one place—the immediate workplace itself. The worker should be given the fullest democratic voice over all the matters which directly affect workaday life in his particular shop. He should have a check on the bureaucratic power over him, and he should have the strongest voice in setting the pace and conditions of work. He also should have a voice in setting just standards of pay.

But all these things do not go very far. They are at most small techniques, and they may not even be the best ones which can be designed. What is needed is a basic change of attitude. If the radical says that the worker is not a commodity, he should go on to accept the implications of the statement. Those implications go far beyond Fromm's co-management and co-participation. They entail a thorough rejection of the cult of efficiency and a thorough acceptance of the principle that the only cost of production that matters is the human cost, and that the test of an economic system is not how many cars it makes but what kind of men it makes.*

This means that the modern utopian who started from

* There is an important moral principle at stake here. Throughout his discussion of work, Fromm asserts that the democratization of work will increase the workers' output. Thus, one of his major justifications of workers' participation is still the justification on grounds of efficiency. Actually, it is not at all certain that increased participation in decision-making will result in increased productivity. A recent study suggests the opposite. See Nancy C. Morse and Everett C. Riemer, "The Experimental Change of a Major Organizational Variable," *Journal of Abnormal and Social Psychology* (Vol. 52, January, 1956), pp. 120–129. In this study, which was conducted in a large insurance company over a period of a year and a half, the researchers hypothesized, following the doctrine of Kurt Lewin, that increased participation in decision-making would increase motivation to produce. Two groups of clerks were set up on the basis of democratic principles: the clerks were given wide latitude in deciding how the work should be arranged and how the group should be governed. Two other groups, similar in duties and composition to the first two, were governed by "authoritarian" principles: superiors made and enforced the rules. Two groups to whom nothing was done were used as control groups. The researchers found that people liked fun better than work. The hierarchical groups showed greater productivity gains than the democratic groups, while members of both types of group expressed strong preference for the self-governing group. Members of the self-governing groups showed smaller productivity gains than the hierarchical groups but liked their work far more. Which value should have priority, pleasure or productivity? One who accepts the "labor is not a commodity" principle would of course stress the satisfaction of the immediate work group. This would seem to call for a syndicalist organization of work, even at the expense of decreased efficiency and productivity. Decreased efficiency and productivity would of course result in higher prices for goods and services. Why should the consumer bear these costs of the workers' satisfaction in work? Fromm has not faced up to these problems because he asserts, with little or no supporting evidence, that workers' participation in decision-making will result in greater productivity. For additional recent studies showing the absence of a clear and consistent relationship between productivity on the one side and such variables as morale, satisfaction, and group cohesion on the other, see M. S. Vitales, *Motivation and Morale in Industry* (New York: Norton, 1953); and A. H. Brayfield and W. H. Crockett, "Employee Attitudes and Employee Performance," *Psychological Bulletin* (Vol. 52, September, 1955), pp. 396–424. The unkindest blow of all to the happiness-in-work ethic has been the discovery that high morale is not a sufficient condition for high productivity, and that, in fact, high morale does not necessarily lead to higher productivity than low morale.

the values of socialist humanitarianism would take seriously
Thoreau's command to simplify. Under the conditions of
surplus technology, mass production, and the consumption
orientation, this might require such proposals as the following (the list is suggestive, not exhaustive): the advocacy of
a nonmaterialistic ethic, an ethic which stresses intellectual,
esthetic, and recreational pursuits, rather than economic
ones; a rigorous abolition of all the economic goods and
services which we could just as well do without; vigorous
criticism of the ideology of limitless consumption; en-
couragement of every variety of individual effort and do-it-
yourself enterprise; an extensive educational campaign to
encourage voluntary population control; reduction in the
size of the great urban centers; a massive program of de-
centralization of industry and administration; recognition
that the worker, or the small group of workers, should, to
the fullest extent possible, make a whole product, even if
this means a sacrifice of "efficiency"; acceptance of the principle that the pace and tempo of work shall be set by the
workers, and not by the marketplace and the abstract imperatives of efficiency, again even at the price of increased
costs of production; rapid introduction of automation techniques into all jobs which must be done, but which the
society deems monotonous and unchallenging; and full application of the principles that each man shall do the thing
he likes best, and that no man shall be so poorly paid that
he cannot leave his job at any time and prepare himself for
one he likes better. Such measures as these seem to be im-
plied in any serious intention to give meaning and dignity to
work. At least, they get at the problem in a way that the
slogan of co-management and workers' participation never
can.

Fromm's slogan of co-management and workers' participation is a hangover from the simpler days when Social-

ists could believe that utopia would arrive when the last capitalist had been sent to join the last priest. What is needed now is not a slogan of technique but a program of content, a new vision of the moral purpose of work and life. Most of the slogans which rattle through the windy spaces of the national mind today are legacies from a time which knew what the ideals meant because the realities so utterly denied them. Full employment, prosperity and comfort, protection for the rights of labor and the underprivileged, social justice—these ideals meant something in the context of a social order characterized by drastic unemployment, depression, exploitation of the workers, neglect of the underprivileged, and social injustice. But today, when we have come closer to these goals than any other society ever has, they no longer provide much guidance nor have much meaning. When Henry Wallace spoke not so long ago of "sixty million jobs," he was derided as a visionary. Today, if there were only sixty million jobs we would declare a national emergency. Nor is this only, or even mainly, because the population has increased. It is primarily due to the fact that we have just kept on demanding and producing more and more material wealth without any clear idea of what end it is we are seeking. Only a very few men have even begun to think about the need for new goals in the uses of wealth.[15]

Under present conditions, co-management and workers' participation would, most probably, mean only an acceleration of the present powerful tendencies toward materialism and what Fromm calls alienated consumption, for the workers have no conception of any moral or esthetic order beyond the present one. What has to be recognized is that the workers have been "corrupted," tamed. And they have been tamed to the harness of meaningless work not by the stick of hunger, but by the carrot of limitless consumption, by the vision of utopia offered by the ad-men and sold on the installment plan. Only if this is kept in mind can one explain the astonishing fact that organized business and organized labor have combined to make productivity, profit, and "full" employment—that is, work in its inescapable modern meaninglessness—the dominant and almost the sole aim and function of the community's internal political life. The principal feature of our political life is the use of truly prodigious means for paltry ends. After all, the expenditure of a very small proportion (the Goodmans estimate one-seventh) of our available resources of labor, time, money, and materials would provide all Americans with a very solid "subsistence." The remainder goes for luxury and emulative consumption goods—as though we had already thought through to a solution the profound political and moral question of the relation between standard of living and quality of life.

It was once believed that men would not work unless they were hungry. William Townsend's *Dissertation on the Poor Laws* (1786) drew some conclusions from the fable of the "natural" balance of the goats and dogs which were to have an enormous impact on nineteenth century thought. According to the fable, Juan Fernandez landed a few goats on an island off the Chilean coast. The goats multiplied at a lavish rate, thereby providing a convenient meat supply for the English privateers who were plundering the Spanish trade. In a flash of pre-Darwinian insight, the Spanish authorities then landed a dog and a bitch on the island. They too increased and fed on the abundant supply of goats which nature and Juan Fernandez had provided. "Then," wrote Townsend, "a new kind of balance was restored. The weakest of both species were among the first to pay the debt of nature; the most active and vigorous preserved their lives." From this theorem, Townsend drew some maxims which not only showed the futility and vice of the Poor Law but which also, first through Malthus and the Political Economists, then through Darwin and the Social Darwinists, have had an enormous impact on modern society. "Hunger," Townsend wrote, "will tame the fiercest animals, it will teach decency and civility, obedience and subjection, to the most perverse." And men, are they not animals? Not just *like* animals, but *only* animals? "In general it is only hunger which can spur and goad [the poor] on to labor. . . . The laws . . . have likewise said, they shall be compelled to work. But then legal constraint is attended with much trouble, violence and noise; creates ill will, and never can be productive of good and acceptable service: whereas hunger is not only peaceable, silent, unremitting pressure, but, as the most natural motive to industry and labor, it calls forth the most powerful exertions; and, when satisfied by the free bounty of another, lays lasting and sure foundations for good will and gratitude." [16]

Townsend's maxims soon became the accepted doctrine. The Reverend Thomas Malthus and a host of lesser divines made it canonical; Herbert Spencer and his epigoni made it scientific: blunt the goad of hunger as an incentive to work, and the most damnable licentiousness, incivility, and indolence will result. The centuries-old Christian view of work as a duty to the community, a punishment for sin, and an agency of salvation disappeared.

It has remained for our time to discover a new motivation for work. We have learned how much more powerfully men can be driven by the promise of "more and more" than by the threat of "not enough." In the United States, the poor and hungry are few and getting fewer, but still the American works; and he works harder and better than the poor and hungry masses of less-favored nations. The American worker has been tamed even beyond the measure proposed by the stern Malthus. What has tamed him, however, is neither the discipline of the machine nor the threat of starvation but the dream of more and more, the dream of the heaven of consumption so alluringly drawn by the advertisers, the dream which can be his through frequent and generous increases in his present wage, augmented, of course, by the second income of his working wife, and multiplied at a Biblical rate by the magic of credit. "In dreams begin responsibilities." Delmore Schwartz's line, written with a different intention, is cruelly relevant here, for the American worker has freely accepted the slavish responsibilities of his dream of consumption.*

To this point, I have argued in effect that Fromm's proposal for the reorganization of work fails to achieve a sufficient imaginative distance from both the past and the present. I have argued that the principle of co-management and workers' participation is a hangover from the past and that, if applied in the present, it would probably result in more of what we already have—a consummation which Fromm does not devoutly wish for. If the principle leads anywhere, it probably would lead in the wrong direction, for it is based on the implicit conviction that the workers have a noble moral vision which the capitalists and man-

---

* Some support for this conclusion on the probable uses of workers' power is provided by a couple of interesting facts reported in a recent acute essay on the political vocation. See Stimson Bullitt, *To Be a Politician* (Garden City, New York: Doubleday, 1959), p. 111. Bullitt reports that voters are most receptive to the candidate's brief personal appeal in two situations: outside the factory gates as the morning shift comes on; and in the suburban shopping center. There may be a basic law of American politics here. The officers of the state, far from being regarded as the executive committee of the exploiting class, are those charged with seeing that the drudgeries of work are translated into the delights of consumption. Mr. Bullitt also remarks that it is useless, and a little dangerous, to approach the prospective voter in a bar or at a racetrack. The drinkers and gamblers intend to reach heaven by their own efforts; or, perhaps, they hope for a special grace.

agers lack. There is at present little evidence for that, and there is little reason to expect that the future will provide more. At the risk of being very wrong I would suggest that the tendency may be in the other direction.

In the United States, the principle of equality of opportunity meets no significant resistance on the plane of official ideology. There is of course more resistance on the plane of institutions and popular sentiment, but here too equality demolishes one after another of the artificial barriers to ability. Inherited titles disappeared long ago, and in recent years the barriers of race, creed, and inherited wealth have been greatly reduced. The tendency of the age is toward the career open to talent.

There is no reason to think that the quantities and proportions of various talents in a human population change markedly over short (long?) periods of time. But while the total quantity of talents remains roughly constant over time, their distribution among the classes and sectors of the population may change rapidly. In a society where the class and status system is rigid, permitting little movement up or down the social ladder, talented persons will appear among all the classes. We may postulate that in such a society there will be proportionately as many talented persons among the lower (say, peasant and proletariat) classes as among the upper (say, noble or wealthy) classes. Of course, the talented persons among the lower classes will usually lack the means to develop and manifest their abilities, but the abilities are nonetheless there. But where there are few barriers to the development of socially desired talent, the situation is very different. No longer will talented persons be scattered randomly throughout society. We will approach a social order where men enjoy the status to which their abilities, as judged and valued by society, entitle them. Put another way, when artificial barriers to the development of talent are removed, a man's ability can be judged by his rank. The man who enjoys a high station can take full credit for it, and the man who occupies a low station cannot blame society for it. Jefferson's vision approaches fulfillment: the natural aristocracy and the social aristocracy become virtually identical. And when every worker carries an executive's badge in his lunchpail, we must conclude that the executives deserve to be executives and the workers deserve to be workers.

In no society is the correspondence between rank and ability perfect, but the open and mobile society approaches this condition. Furthermore, this model of society is certainly the goal and to some unknown but high (and increasing) degree the reality in the United States. We are already well beyond the first stages of this revolution of ability; and, despite the urgent denials of Professor C. Wright Mills, the revolution will henceforth proceed apace. Two forces are driving it. The first is a dual movement of continuing reduction of various impediments (race, family, creed) to the development of talent, combined with an increase in social assistance to the needy and worthy. The second is increasing leisure. The latter is the truly revolutionary factor, for with increased leisure, those who have talent will be able to develop it, while no amount of leisure time will develop the talents of those who have none. Hence the talented will draw ever farther away from the untalented. Projecting this tendency into the future, one can envision a social order in which the lower classes are in fact made up of the untalented, the defective, the chronic misfits, and those who have few or no abilities much valued by society. Undoubtedly, some of the members of this class would have talent, but no desire to develop it. From the social point of view, however, this amounts to about the same thing as having no talent. Such a lower class would be stagnant, uncreative, barren of indigenous leadership, and resentful.

It hardly seems necessary to draw the implications of this for a theory of authority in work and politics. It is enough to suggest that to implement the principle of democracy in all sectors of life under such conditions is to invite rule by the masses in exactly the sense that Ortega had in mind when he defined the masses as "those who demand nothing special of themselves, but for whom to live is to be every moment what they already are, without imposing on themselves any effort towards perfection; mere buoys that float on the waves." [17]

This small fable of the talent state—the Meritocracy, as Michael Young aptly calls it—must not be taken literally. All I wanted to point out was that all parties officially accept the ideology of the opportunity state, and that more and more social policies look toward the end of the rainbow where talent will be the sole passport to advancement, and where all men will have equal opportunity to develop their talents. But when the word becomes flesh, it must undergo the corruptions of the flesh. At least three strong barriers stand in the way of the pure talent state.

The first is the power of the family, which is bound together by carnal and erotic bonds, not by the ties of talent. The family is the ancient fortress of favoritism and nepotism; and as long as the family unit remains, talent will never be the sole passport to position. Private virtue becomes public vice: parents protect the weak, the slow, and the ungifted as fiercely as they do the strong, the fleet, and the gifted. A true talent state would have to destroy or greatly weaken the philo-progenitive family and model itself after, say, the Society of Jesus, which is masculine and celibate. The masses show no readiness for a program of poverty, chastity, and obedience.

The second barrier is the large and growing number of elderly people in the population. Their vice is their age;

and the medicine they ask is not the purgative of competition and struggle, but the anodyne of insulation and security. No party dare ignore them.

The third barrier is nothing other than the temper of the mass itself. For centuries the masses lived in societies which were essentially noncompetitive. These societies, of course, had room for talent, but mainly for those few who were born into privileged positions. The industrial revolution destroyed the status societies and threw the masses into the market, where "merit," which meant the ability to survive the competitive struggle, was the law of life. But ever since the industrial revolution, the masses have struggled to destroy the market society and restore the status society, with the one great difference that now the masses also demand their fair share of the comforts and privileges which once were enjoyed exclusively by the elites.

So the apparent movement toward a real talent state is largely an illusion. The masses are willing to use the slogans of opportunity—indeed, politicians dare talk in no other language—but what they really desire is a social order which will give the ungifted millions assured security and comfort. The talented few will be permitted, even encouraged, to rise, but they will not be permitted to build a state in their own image or to build a social order which imposes elite values on the masses. They will not be permitted to build a social order which dissolves all familial and status bonds in the giddy and limitless flux of talent, a social order which has no place and no esteem for the common people. This will be a Meritocracy of a sort: a Meritocracy which has no choice but to assure and to advance the comfort and security of the masses. Under such conditions, it is a nice question to determine who rules whom—which is precisely the question Ortega asks and Fromm ignores.

CHAPTER V

Behold, the Man . . .

Ortega's remark introduces the closing themes of this critique. All that remains to be done is to set forth some of the basic perspectives which have guided my appraisal of Fromm's work. Nothing here will be new: it is a matter of making explicit and general what has thus far only been suggested. The primary perspectives which have guided this appraisal, the perspectives which lie at the base of my differences with Fromm on questions of the second and third order, can be treated under two headings. The first concerns the basic political categories of liberty and authority. The second concerns one moral and one esthetic question. Under the first heading I shall argue that Fromm misunderstands both the nature of liberty and authority and the functions they perform in the lives of individuals and communities. Under the second I shall try to show how certain of Fromm's settled tendencies and orientations effectively blind him to certain dimensions of the meaning of beauty and the good life.

A preliminary caution. To talk about settled tendencies and orientations in the work of a writer whose thought is

284

still changing may seem a risky enterprise. In Fromm's case, however, thanks to the recent appearance of an essay on "Psychoanalysis and Zen Buddhism," the enterprise can be approached with a fair measure of confidence.*

The recent essay comes at a convenient time for my purposes because it is at once an arrival and a departure: Fromm has broken through the confines of Freudian rationalism and taken a bold step toward intuitionism and mysticism. In this respect, his intellectual biography resembles that of John Stuart Mill, who also started out the prisoner of a disciplined system and spent most of his life trying to escape it. Mill began with the rigors of Utilitarian logic and ended with the frivolity of female suffrage, an advocacy which was as "advanced" for his day as Zen is for ours. The essay on Zen also expresses emphatically some themes which, although present in the earlier work, had appeared there in subdued tones. The essay still contains some of the ambivalences present in Fromm's earlier writings, so it seems reasonable to regard them as permanent features of his work. An epilogue which will tie this latest essay to the earlier work now seems both necessary and possible.

Fromm's writing, the earlier more than the later, has power because he faces up to the reality that to live in our day is to feel lost. He faces up to the felt condition that something has gone wrong, that everything in our life, even our guilt, is problematic. Of course, it will be said, men

---

* The essay appears in a book which originated, Fromm reports, "in a workshop on Zen Buddhism and Psychoanalysis," held during August of 1957 in Cuernavaca, Mexico. A *workshop* on Zen—there is a true marvel. Many things can be done in the singular Western institution of the workshop, but it is hard to include Zen among them. Workshops are for work, not for contemplation, and they are busy, noisy places. The typical posture of the workshop delegate is not that of the lotus position. Will Zen survive the din? Can Zen be retooled, given more zip and chrome, shined up and packaged for the American consumer?

have always felt this; and to an extent this is true, especially in politics, where men are always assaulted by unique situations, which means confusion and doubt.

But if other men in other ages have also felt the anxiety of the problematic, what is special about our own age? In respect to the problematic, nothing. In respect to our fear of where the problematic is heading, perhaps a great deal. Our age fears, as few others have, that the problematic seems headed toward the chaotic. We fear shipwreck; and we know that this time the disaster could be total. This sense Fromm has caught, and not to see that he has offered us a description of how men react to the possibility of shipwreck is to miss a chief value of his work. He has shown us three basic styles of response to shipwreck. Some persons break into the ship's stores and abandon themselves in drink and revelry, one last party before the end. Others give themselves to a leader who claims to have a secret chart and an unsinkable boat. Still others, and these the greatest number, look on life numbly and go through it aimlessly, afraid to confront the catastrophe, but unable to ignore it either.

In a time like our own the ideas of the shipwrecked are the ideas most worth reading, for any man who today does not know he is lost is lost beyond hope. He will never find himself or guide others. The Liberal epoch has run its course. In our own day we have seen the superannuation of the purposes and premises which inspired liberal thought and action through the 1930's, and we are now compelled to confront without blinkers the full tragic crisis of the concrete present. It can no longer be denied that Western man, for all his restlessness, his dynamism, his craving for movement, does not know what he really wants. Lacking that knowledge, and therefore lacking the power to gain fulfillments, Western man now shows himself hostile to life, and perhaps prepared to destroy it.

Fromm has recognized much of this and has sought for something of value beyond it. It is this affirmative part of his work that makes it appealing to those of us who are temperamentally unable to accept the politics of cynicism and despair, and who are morally committed to the liberal conviction that intellect ought to enlighten the human condition, not lament it, and that learning ought to ennoble the human estate, not mock it.

While Fromm has added nothing to the poetry and philosophy of shipwreck, he has told us something of its sociology. While he has added nothing to the great literature of the personal styles of facing shipwreck—of which there are basically only two, the way of Montaigne and the way of Pascal—he has offered us a healing doctrine. Fromm's doctrine follows the way of Pascal, though his solution is secular and social, while Pascal's was religious and personal. Furthermore, although he follows the way of Pascal, he does so without Pascal's anguish, beauty, and fierce concentration. Now, when Pascal is made secular and social, he looks like Rousseau. Start with Rousseau's sentiments; then, strip away the poetry; next, translate him into the modern American idiom, emphasizing the themes of work, activism, and equality; finally, add a lot of material on specifically modern conditions and problems, taking care to use wherever possible the standard terms of social science— and the result will be Frommism. Fromm's solution reads in substance: since we lack faith, and know not where to go, let us cleave to one another in love, while we search for ourselves in our work.

Much of Fromm's power, then, lies in his courage to face shipwreck, his grasp of what shipwreck looks like under modern conditions, and his offer of warmth and work to replace coldness and boredom. I have tried to show throughout this essay that while this is much, it is far from enough.

Fromm's work is weakened by his misunderstanding of the two fundamental problems, the problem of authority and the problem of liberty.

Fromm thinks that the malaise of modern times is a consequence of the invasion of our world by irrational authority. In a sense, this is surely true. But it is not fundamental. The fundamental trouble is not the presence of irrational authority, but the absence of all authority properly so-called. Irrational authority rushes in to fill the vacuum left by the flight of rational authority. These two formulations may seem close together, and they are, but it makes an enormous difference which way the problem is stated.

Fromm thinks that if we can only banish the irrational authorities—tradition, superstition, convention, authoritarian monotheism, social and economic class limitations, advertising and propaganda, charismatic leaders, bureaucracy —reason and beauty will flourish. This is just not enough. Men will be ruled. The majority of men lack the power to form their own conceptions of the real and the ideal. Therefore, there must be guiding ideals, and there must be uniform and authoritative rules based on the guiding ideals. There must also be men who represent and embody the ideals, and who make and enforce the rules based on them.

When one says that authority has fled, in this sense, he sets the discussion in a very old context. Saint Jerome wrote the following passage over fifteen centuries ago:

> Shame on us, the world is falling in ruins, but our sins still flourish. The glorious city that was the head of the Roman Empire has been engulfed in one terrific blaze. There is no part of the earth where exiles from Rome are not to be found. Churches once held sacred have fallen into dust and ashes, and still we set our hearts greedily on money. We live as though we were

doomed to death on the morrow, but we build houses as though we were going to live for ever in this world. Our walls glitter with gold, gold gleams upon our ceilings and upon the capitals of our pillars; yet Christ is dying at our doors in the persons of His poor, naked and hungry. . . . Flocks and shepherds perish together, because the priest is now even as the people.[1]

The guiding ideals dim, and men live by taste and desire. Meaning and commitment go out of life, to be replaced by frivolousness and boredom. To have deep convictions, strong principles, becomes almost a matter for embarrassment. A kind of skepticism or even cynicism saps all intentions and movements. The great thing is to keep cool, stay loose, be uncommitted. But it must never be forgotten that men, and especially young men, stay loose because they can see nothing in the dominant social order worth attaching themselves to. That is part of the meaning of the flight of authority, and it seems to be the largest meaning behind the currently felt concern about the "silent generation" and juvenile delinquency. The refusal of the young to commit themselves, and the rise in delinquent behavior—even, as the surprised and pained expression goes, among young people who come from good homes where they have everything—are implicit proof for the proposition that the young find little in the culture about them that attracts or merits their commitment and that, furthermore, they are not very sure their parents do either.

The film *The Wild One* stated the themes that matter here. In this movie, whose imagery was based upon an actual event, a club of motorcyclists—chewing gum, drinking beer, and dressed American style in their black leather jackets bearing the club emblem of a death's head and crossed rods and pistons—roar into a small town and hold it in terror.

At one point there occurred between a sweet young girl of the town and the leader of the club an exchange which epitomizes my theme. The girl asked: "What are you rebelling against?" Reply: "What have you got?" The authority of the leader over his band was absolute, because he was the coolest and most accomplished nihilist among them.

The mocking and almost casual destructiveness of the motorcyclists was so upsetting to the viewer just because it was directed against the values and symbols which inform our lives, but in which we are unable to believe very deeply, suspecting them to be hollow at the center. The citizens of this typical American small town were defenseless precisely because their culture of platitudinous morality, high living standards, and Hollywood tinsel was not worth defending. The town cop, the enforcer of the rules, was a caricature of authority: weak, indecisive, alcoholic. The violence of the motorcyclists could be met only by the violence of the brutal men of the town, the dispensers of justice by force, and then by the state police, the impersonal and efficient wielders of superior power. Beyond this, however, the film's terror came from its power to make one realize that the promiscuous destructiveness of the motorcyclists endangered not only the sham values and the mock authorities but real human values as well. The sham values of the town were contemptible, but it is possible that more noble values might lie beneath them; and it is certain that if noble values are to arise, they must arise from the town. The cyclists would destroy the town.

Now, to say that is to say that a discussion of the breakdown of authority must be embedded in a context even older and deeper than that provided by the lament of St. Jerome. Jerome wrote of the death of an actual city, great Rome, the reality and the symbol of the authority that ordered an Empire. But if even great Rome can fall, then what city is ever safe? Authority is always in jeopardy.

At the dawn of civilization, men lived closer to the deepest realities of communal life than we ever can. Knowledge which they grasped immediately, almost physically, we grasp only by the hardest work and thought; and, even then, our grasp sometimes seems weak and our vision narrow, when set alongside theirs. Hobbes's intellectual destruction of the civil state, for example, and his lucid re-creation of the state of nature, powerful feats of the imaginative reason though both were, seem pale and weak when compared with any of a number of ancient myths and folktales dealing with the same themes. The men of the first cities each day could see the high wall which separated their city from the chaos of nature outside it. They knew their city and its defining wall were works of art, not products of nature, tiny islands of order surrounded by nature's vast wildness. Being so close to experience, they could report their knowledge in the vivid concrete language of experience, as poets still do, rather than in the drier, more remote language of the detached and observing intellect that Hobbes had to use.

The men of the early cities, long before and for quite some time after systematic political philosophy came to be written, put their knowledge in wonderful folktales, haunting myths, rich clusters of imagery and symbol. They typically set aside special periods during which their knowledge was acted out in ritual and ceremony. Many of these myths and rituals concerned the guilt man felt for violating nature, for hacking open the earth, subjecting it to slavery, and forcing it to yield up its living fruit. For this violation, man had to ask nature's pardon; and he also had to pay nature's debt, often through the sacrifice of one of his own kind, the mankind, the kind that alone among the creatures forced nature to his will.

But these men of the dawn-cities knew that nature existed inside the walls of the city as well as beyond them. Inside the walls, nature existed in the breast of every man. And just as the nature beyond the frail walls threatened the city from without, so did the nature inside each man threaten the city from within. So, the defense of the city also required that the nature within the breast of man be chained, and perhaps violated; and what violated this aspect of nature was authority. From numerous myths and tales concerning this theme, many of them conveniently collected in *The Golden Bough*, we may rediscover the deepest of all political insights: authority is a sin; its guilt is order itself; and the guilty are those who through their authority impose order.

In all social orders the individual suffers a split of attitude. Society nurtures and strengthens men, and men (who are neither gods nor beasts) require an ordered society for the unfolding of their finest powers; still, men feel the constraints and pressures of social order and fear even that order may unman them. On the one side, there is the lunging animal drive for unlimited satisfaction, the pulse of nature which throbs in the vitals of the city and yearns to disrupt it; on the other, the realization that order is necessary for the fulfillment of the human potentialities. This is the dilemma of both man and the state. It is a struggle within the breast of the polity itself, and the sin of authority is that it must, in the name of order, judge the passions guilty. For this sin, authority must make expiation. But just as there is the sin of authority, so is there the sin against authority. Men do realize that without authority they would be as beasts; so even while authority is challenged, the challengers feel the guilt which comes from denying a necessary part of themselves. That is the deep truth of the Proverb: "The fear of a king is as the roaring of a lion: whoso provoketh him to anger sinneth against his own soul." [2]

Out of this double sin, the sin of authority and the sin against it, has come the whole dark folklore and symbolism of the dying king, the mock king, the king as fool. In some of the legends the king himself had to die a ritual death after a fixed reign. In others, the real king evaded death by appointing a scapegoat who died in his place, always after a period during which he could employ his tragic power in the enjoyment of all pleasures. Sometimes a mock king would reign for a period during which all authority was mocked. In a thousand variations, the ancients acted out the tragedy of kingship, the tragedy of presuming to impose order on the wild and chaotic forces of nature. All these variations had one theme, the theme of the king who must die for the sin of order, and the theme of the fierce and guilty pleasure of the populace at the death of the king.

Many ancient peoples gave anarchy its due but still retained for everyday life the benefits of order by setting aside a fixed period of license during which authority lapsed. Then law and morality were set aside and all things were permitted. Work stopped, the markets closed, slaves became masters, the populace abandoned itself to revelry, and the darker passions enjoyed a license which could never be theirs in the course of normal life. Of all these holidays, the one which is most familiar to us, and the one which has given the name to the rest, was the Roman Saturnalia. The Saturnalia was not merely a symbol; it was a literal acting out of the lapse of authority. It is significant that the Saturnalia was popularly supposed to commemorate the lusty and merry reign of Saturn, god of sowing and husbandry, who was king during the fabled Golden Age, when all men were free and all fields were fertile; that is, the Saturnalia was the revenge of nature against order.* This custom of the ancients was a wise one, for restraint is always unbearable to some people, and conventional virtue is felt as a heavy burden. And all of us yearn at times for the life which is natural and free.

When the problem of authority is formulated in this way it becomes clear that every solution of it is in a basic sense both artificial, that is, a work of art and will rather than a work of nature, and false, that is, an attempt to solve a dilemma which is insoluble because it is inherent in man and polity. When the problem is formulated in this way it also becomes clear that any attempted solution of it demands a positive conception of duty and goodness, for, unless they are offered this in return for renouncing their passions, men will see the whole working of authority as an unnatural imposition. They will then rise against it actively, or mock and ignore it passively. The result in both cases is the submersion of the individual in society, pure fellowship and warmth, and from there the regress to nature, the free expression of the instinctual desires.

The main point of my critique is that Fromm's solu-

---

* There seems little doubt that in the earliest days the King of the Saturnalia was killed at the end of his reign, as were a garish array of similar comical yet tragic figures from other lands and ages, who, wearing their mock crowns and gorgeous costumes, went to a violent death after a few days of pranks and pleasures. In the remoter and cruder parts of the Empire, the practice of killing the mock king may have continued well into the Christian era. Frazer reports a well-documented case of a Roman garrison in Lower Moesia which was performing the ceremony in the ancient way as late as A.D. 303. Each year the soldiers selected by lot one to play the part. For thirty days the chosen one, attended by a mob, went in public and enjoyed absolute license. His merry reign ended abruptly on the thirtieth day, when he was made to cut his own throat on the altar of the god he had impersonated. The practice was more quickly civilized in the metropolis, so that by the time of Augustus the ludicrous, doomed figure has become merely the lusty, ribald Lord of Misrule depicted by the classical writers.

tion to the problem of authority does not offer these positive conceptions. His solution reads simply: liberate men
from irrational authorities. But if you liberate men in this
way, that is, without helping them toward a conception of
what liberty is for, you only lead them into deeper slavery,
the slavery of the social. The man of today is led, to be sure,
but he is led by fashion and opinion, by the taste and desire
of the many at the moment. And it is significant, as Fromm
himself has shown, that the desire which increasingly wells
up from society is the desire for the gratification of all
demands, the desire which Fromm has accurately called
the "principle of nonfrustration." Moral philosophers have
always known that there is no greater slavery than the
slavery of unlimited desire. As that principle permeates
more and more sectors of society, it becomes clear that to
advocate, as Fromm does, the extension of the democratic
principle into every sector of life is in effect to advocate government by desire. And what is desired is defined by fashion
and opinion. Fashion is a severe dictator, for it is government not by rule but by whim. The regime of fashion is
not constitutional.

The greatest failure of Fromm's thought is that he cannot see this. He cannot see that when authority is lacking
fashion reigns. He cannot see that authority must rest upon
positive conceptions of duty and the good life. He cannot
see that his advocacy of the democratic principle, as he has
defined it, is really an advocacy of fashion and passion, made
attractive by the understanding that all men have an equal
right to see their desires gratified. He advocates, in effect,
the unrestricted development of the mass democracy of our
day; and this mass democracy can be best defined, I think,
as that style of government in which every man gets what
he desires, while nobody can be blamed for the fact that
our communities seem ever more adrift, the larger affairs of

life increasingly beyond control, and the conception of the good life itself ever more a vague and hazy, almost anachronistic myth.

All this comes down to saying that Fromm lacks a clear and accurate conception of the political. Lacking that, his reasoning on political subjects becomes clouded. Political life occupies a middle terrain between the sheer givens of nature and society on the one side, and the transcendental ends toward which men aspire on the other. Political action is that type of action through which men publicly attempt to order and to transform the givens of nature and society by the light of values which are above or outside the order of the givens. Political authority is that authority which defines the ideal aims of the community and which tries to shape and direct nature and society in accordance with these ends. Just as the father in the family has the twofold task of restraining the children from regressing to the comforts of infantilism and of urging them upward toward the acceptance of mature human standards and obligations, so the authority in the polity has the twofold task of restraining the citizens from regressing to nature and society and of urging them upward toward the achievement of ideal ends. The task of restraining the citizens from regressing to nature is beautifully symbolized by the city's wall, which it is the special duty of authority to maintain, and which, it must not be forgotten, not only limits entry into the city but also restrains escape from the city back to nature. The task of restraining the citizens from regressing to society is embodied in all those rules and regulations which order life within the city, and which are maintained by authority. Within the ordered human space established by the laws and guaranteed by authority, men can live together in trust and friendship and can cooperate in the give-and-take of political activity properly so-called. Through this political activity, men come to realize themselves by working out their destinies with others. And that leads to the third task of authority, which is that of enabling men to order their lives toward ideal aims. This function of authority is completely captured in Aristotle's two deepest ideas: man is a political animal; and men form societies not just to live but to live well.

In summary, it is the ambiguous fate of politics to be "contaminated" by nature and society even as it aspires toward the ideal. Political reasoning is the hardest and most subtle kind of reasoning, for, when the political theorist is reasoning about anything other than trivial questions, he is reasoning about questions which lie at the two boundaries of the political: the basic political-philosophical problems are "boundary exchange" problems. This means that the theorist always runs the risk of transgressing the boundaries of the political and either reducing politics to nature and society, or else denaturing politics entirely and substituting for political thought pure and uncontaminated metaphysics. But to make either error is to destroy politics. Fromm makes the first error: he deals with political subjects only in order to end politics and begin the reign of nature.

My criticism of Fromm's formulation of the problem of freedom has followed the same lines. Considered from the aspect of freedom, human life presents a strange dilemma. The dilemma is that while each of us must live his life alone, by and for himself, if one does not live his life toward some goal outside his own life, his life will lack tension and power, achievement and meaning. This is the dilemma which has flayed the souls of sensitive men for centuries; and it will continue to do so, for it is ineluctable. One escapes it only at the price of slavery, the form of which depends on the side of the dilemma one embraces. If one stops with the self, he becomes his own slave. If he emphasizes only the external end, he becomes the victim of external forces, "even," as Augustine put it, "unto contempt of self."

Fromm commits the first kind of error. He defines freedom as the expansion of life, the unfolding of all one's powers, the fuller living of life. Life becomes its own end and product, the goal and good in itself. I have indicated that Fromm embraces this conception for good and worthy motives—a hatred of all unjust and irrational authorities and ends imposed on man—but the consequences of the position are the same, regardless of the motives which led to its acceptance. A life which merely turns round and round within itself is lost in its own labyrinth. The directed life requires a goal. And this goal is not the living of life, not the motion and fever of living, but an end outside the self toward which the motion is aimed. A life whose imperative is "live for living" is aimless, adrift in its own existence. A life given over to itself is empty, with nothing to occupy it but the invention of frivolities and busynesses—as though these could fill the void left by lack of purpose.

This is why Fromm's notion of self-fulfillment must seem a mockery to the person who earnestly seeks the meaning of freedom. One can be many things; that is, he can choose to fulfill any of a number of possible conceptions of his self. But to live is to choose, and that means to choose one part of one's powers and desires over others. Often this choice is made at the greatest pain, for one realizes that when he chooses to follow one path he at the same time chooses not to follow others, which may also be very attractive. Thus freedom always means a disciplined and reasoned rejection of some alternatives in favor of others, a domination of some of one's powers and desires by others. If this choice is not made in the light of a conception of the good life, which is to say a conception which helps man understand that not *all* his powers ought to be actualized, but only those which are *properly and uniquely* man's glories, then it is a choice made in the darkness of egoism. Fromm's doctrine leads to the omnipotent I who is chained by his own energy.

These are some of the personal consequences of trying to escape the dilemma of liberty by embracing only its first half. But liberty is rarely an exclusively personal matter. It nearly always involves other persons, as the root of the word indicates. (*Liber* and *Libera* were ancient Italian deities of fructification and increase, often associated by the Roman poets with the Greek Bacchus. The goddess *Libertas*, to whom several temples were erected at Rome, originally personified personal freedom, but in imperial times she represented constitutional government.) Fromm has given virtually no consideration to the problem of liberty on the social level. He is silent on the question of what happens when two omnipotent I's, rushing through the dark, bump into each other. This is no oversight in his work, no mere failure to remember to deal with the problem. Rather, it is a position which he must hold as a consequence of his thesis that truly productive men will never harm each other but will always relate to each other through love and knowledge. It is a consequence of his thesis that there are no real conflicts of interest between men that will not disappear in the sane society. "Men, let them but once clearly understand one another, will not be long ere they agree." Jeremy Bentham said it, and Erich Fromm believes it.

Taken seriously, Fromm's doctrine would drown all true individuality in a sea of brotherhood. It would erase the distinction which lies at the heart of any social philosophy which is also moral: the conviction that the good man is never the same as the good citizen, not even the good citizen of the good society; the conviction that the best men always transcend the standards of the city, and are the critics and teachers of the city, even while they benefit from it and perform their duties to it. It would abolish politics, and it would convert individual or minority disagreement with the community into a species of sin, which for Fromm is the same as mental sickness. Along with many writers of the utopian bent, Fromm has apparently forgotten the central teaching of the history of the struggle for constitutional government: the most important article of any plan for the good society is the article which defines the limits of the plan's own power to control the lives of men.

So far, I have argued generally that Fromm misunderstands both the nature of authority and liberty and their functions in the lives of individuals and societies. Now I want to remove the discussion from that general context and examine authority and liberty specifically within the structure of Fromm's thought. This will require an examination of the relationships between his notions of liberty and authority on the one side, and his conception of human nature and his vision of the good society on the other. This examination will lead to conclusions very similar to those of the more general discussion, but there may be some value in showing how these conclusions are built right into the structure of his thought.

Let me start with a rough division of all social theorists into three classes. Writers of the first class take a generally pessimistic view of man. They may agree largely with Swift's judgment of Homo sapiens as "the most pernicious race of little odious vermin that nature ever suffered to crawl upon the surface of the earth." Or they may, with Hobbes, see man as *homo homini lupus*, the most formidable of the beasts of prey, the only one that systematically preys on its own species. Or perhaps the writer sees man as only the child grown large, but the child still—impulsive, often unaware of his own real interest, mindless of the interests of others, still in need of restraint. What matters is that the writers of this class accept some variation on the theme that man is weak, evil, sinful. Writers of the second class take a generally optimistic view of man and see him as essentially good and pure. They might agree with the Rousseau of the early essays, in which man appeared as the noble savage. Perhaps with Kropotkin they stress the sympathetic faculty in human nature. Finally, theorists of the third class paint a picture of man that falls somewhere between the two extremes. For them, man is a marvelous compound of many elements—weakness and strength, good and evil. A little lower than the angels and a little higher than the animals, he has something of each in his nature. Man may be nature's weakest reed, but he is also, as Pascal wrote, a thinking reed. He may be in part a gorilla, but he is also, in Renan's description, a Good Gorilla.

Corresponding to each view of human nature is an attitude toward institutions. Writers of the first class emphasize order, hierarchy, the need for authority and restraint. On the whole, they look at social policy as a body of measures designed to advance culture and civilization by restraining the forces of evil and destructiveness in men. Writers of the second class emphasize freedom, equality, opportunity. They think that culture and civilization can best be advanced by measures which lift restraints from man and promote personal freedom, self-expression, and creativity. Writers of the third class live in a more complex institutional world than do those of either of the first two classes. For these writers, institutions must both promote and restrain. Social policies can advance culture sometimes by restraining malevolent tendencies and sometimes by promoting benevolent ones.

I would feel very uncomfortable with this caricature if Fromm did not fit so neatly into one of its compartments. Fromm falls—he need not be pushed—squarely into the camp of Rousseau. His faith in man reborn is unlimited. His vision of man as the spontaneous creator is clouded by no melancholy reflections on the pages of history that have been written in blood. Pride, hate, destructiveness—these are only secondary potentialities which emerge when the primary potentialities are thwarted. The great thing is to lift the false restraints, to free man from the burdens of the irrational authorities, the stupid customs, the authoritarian ideologies, and the false religions which bend him down and pervert his powers. Fromm has a faith in the noble savage which makes Rousseau's faith seem a pale negation by comparison.

Given this view of man, it is all but impossible for Fromm to come to terms with the restraining institutions of a society. In his view, practically all institutional restraints are either unnecessary or demonstrably harmful to man's finest powers. Fromm wants to abolish the authority of one man over another. This theme, the fear and hatred of authority, runs through all his work and makes it almost impossible for him to build a meaningful *political* theory. In England, Fromm's first book appeared under the title *Fear of Freedom*. If ever his writings are collected and published in a uniform edition, they might be issued under the title *Fear of Authority*.

There is an irony in this. Fromm's faith in man and his desire to see man freed from restraints would, in the end, turn the individual over to the worst tyranny of all— the tyranny of the neighbors. This appears most sharply in his utopia: that warm and friendly community would bring men so closely together and expose them so nakedly to the influences of their neighbors that it is doubtful whether any really free and creative spirit would survive the ordeal. So eager is Fromm to break down the barriers between men that he forgets that barriers are defenses against the encroachments of the outsiders as well as separations from them. Freedom and creativity, and dignity too, require law and restraint, formal procedures which a man can use to keep a safe distance between himself and the others. Sometimes the others, pressing together for warmth, may forget that around each man there must be an empty space, a territory of considerate neglect, a private backyard in which one may roam as he wishes, unobserved and unchallenged even by his friends. Schopenhauer once said that men are like porcupines: if they stand too far apart they freeze to death; if they huddle too closely together they stick each other with their quills. We would all stick each other in Fromm's community, for there would be no institutional barriers and authorities to keep us a safe distance apart.

All I am saying is that freedom grows only in civilization and that civilization requires justice and order as well as mercy and love. I am not saying that civilization is *all* order, nor that we must keep order above all, even if that means calling out the military. It just seems to me that Fromm is incapable of coming to terms with the first problem of political philosophy, the problem of order.

If the analysis is sound to this point, it must be carried farther. If you take Fromm's radically optimistic view of man, combine with that his hatred of authority, and then add a third element which has not been considered in this context, it may turn out that Fromm is led to a position which virtually denies the possibility of ordered society—not just institutions of restraint and denial, but ordered society itself. The third element is Fromm's conception of the good.

For Fromm, it will be remembered, good is the affirmation of life. It is the unfolding of one's powers according to the laws of his being. Life itself is the great principle. There is no other beyond it by which to judge or explain it. The creative and mature person recognizes *"that there is only one meaning of life: the act of living itself."* [3] This introduces the dithyramb in honor of spontaneity.

Spontaneity. It is hard for Fromm to describe, but whatever it may be, it is the greatest and most truly human experience, the hallmark of the liberated and creative man. It involves total knowledge and acceptance of one's self and all its emotional, sensuous, and intellectual capacities. The spontaneous act is one that is not thought out. It comes on the spur of the moment and wells up from the center of the soul; the authentic and unrehearsed expression of all one's powers. In acts of spontaneity one affirms himself and the whole world in love. The truly spontaneous person realizes that in living, "what matters is the activity as such, the process and not the result." If man lives for the future rather than in the present, if he plans and strives and denies himself for tomorrow and does not relish each moment of today, he misses "the only satisfaction that can give him real happiness—the experience of the activity of the present moment—and chases after a phantom that leaves him disappointed as soon as he believes he has caught it—the illusory happiness called success." [4] Unfortunately, Fromm complains, spontaneity is dismally scarce in our alienated and achievement-oriented society, but we crippled ones can at least get a glimpse of its beauties by observing the human types which have the most of it, artists and small children. "And a little child shall lead them. . . ."

It is unpleasant to have to put a damper on such

enthusiasm. Certainly, acts which proceed from an inner impulse and express one's whole feeling without inhibition are among the richest experiences of life, and they can bring great joy both to the one who acts and to the one who beholds. But no man could hold that pace forever, and even spontaneity can become monotonous. Life would be a dull business without some moodiness, some gloom, and even some downright nastiness. Furthermore, I doubt whether the view of spontaneity as including the total affirmation of self, and the view of productivity or creativity as the hallmark of the sane mind, has any merit at all. One cannot read far in the biographies of the writers who have told us the most about the self or the soul without discovering that, almost to a man, they were profoundly disturbed about their own souls. And many of the great creators have had more than a slight touch of madness. If spontaneity means total affirmation of the self, and if productivity means sanity, what shall we do with Van Gogh and Dylan Thomas, and a host of others?

> Swift had pains in his head.
> Johnson dying in bed
> Tapped the dropsy himself.
> Blake saw a flea and an elf.
> Tennyson could hear the shriek
> Of a bat. Pope was a freak.
> Emily Dickinson stayed
> Indoors for a decade.
> Water inflated the belly
> Of Hart Crane, and of Shelley.
> Coleridge was a dope.
> Southwell died on a rope.
> Byron had a round white foot.
> Smart and Cowper were put
> Away. Lawrence was a fidget.

Keats was almost a midget.
Donne, alive in his shroud,
Shakespeare, in the coil of a cloud,
Saw death very well as he
Came crab-wise, dark and massy.
I envy not only their talents
And fertile lack of balance
But the appearance of choice
In their sad and fatal voice.[5]

There is another difficulty with this notion of spontaneity in the moral life.[6] Along with a number of related words, such as authenticity, autonomy, individuality, and sincerity, spontaneity is one of the most attractive and most frequently used words in moral discourse today. What has to be pointed out is that all these terms are instrumental. They may suggest criteria for judging how an act should be done, but they provide no guides for evaluating the ends of action. Spontaneity may be a lovely and virtuous feeling-state, but in the realm of moral discourse this is only half of what matters. One can spontaneously commit homicide, smash windows, or push the button which sends an atomic missile on its journey of death. Spontaneity may be a necessary condition of the virtuousness of an act but it is not sufficient. The act must also have a virtuous content and objective. This requires a positive morality and a philosophy of authority, neither of which the ethic of spontaneity provides.

In fact, the tendency of the ethic of spontaneity is to draw attention away from the aims of action, which come to seem paltry and almost irrelevant, and concentrate it upon the will to live itself. When authority disappears, all things are allowed. And when everything is allowed, everything is equal. It seems foolish to try to establish a scale of values among one's experiences: what matters is experience itself. As Camus put it in his analysis of the ideal of the absurd man, "what counts is not the best living but the most living." [7] In contradistinction to this ethic of spontaneity, a really distinguished code of ethics must rest upon a rule of authority and obedience, a rule which Nietzsche stated with the finest lucidity:

> It clearly seems that the chief thing in heaven and on earth is to *obey* at length and in a single direction: in the long run there results something for which it is worth the trouble of living on this earth as, for example, virtue, art, music, the dance, reason, the mind—something that transfigures, something delicate, mad, or divine. [8]

The ethic of spontaneity, then, emphasizes the form of life and neglects its substance and aim. Seen from this point of view, Fromm's idea appears as one current in the much larger modern stream of technicism or instrumentalism. Many writers have commented on the various manifestations of this theme, and on the growing power of the theme itself, in modern life. Some writers have noted the displacement of "substantive reason," which evaluates the validity of goals, by "instrumental reason," which evaluates only the efficacy of techniques for achieving preset goals. Many writers have commented on the tendency of academic ethical writers to deal more and more with the logical analysis of ethical propositions and less and less with substantive ethical questions: philosophers do not try to define the good life; rather, they construct treatises on the many senses in which the term "good" has been used. Even the popular manuals of ethics take on an increasingly instrumentalist character: how to get along with your neighbors; how to be successful; how to reduce your tensions and guilts. (What if your neighbor is not worth getting along with? What if you in fact have committed a crime?) This technicism, it seems, pervades more and more areas of life: methodology replaces substance; why and what for are swallowed by how. Without stopping to examine it carefully, I would remind the reader of Spengler's warning that technicism is one of the marks of a declining civilization.

What should be examined more carefully, though the examination need not take long for the problem is a simple one, is the prescription of spontaneity as the antidote to conformity. Fromm, along with a host of other writers, is disturbed by the prevalence of conformity in our society. I am not concerned with the question of how widespread conformity is, or whether it is spreading, but I am concerned with what seems to me a radical and widespread error of thought, an error shared by Fromm, on this matter. What makes conformity seem such a danger is not conformity itself, not the mere fact of conformity, but the fact that what we conform to seems so banal, so trivial, so humanly unappealing. That this is the case will appear if one reflects for a moment on the simple truth that no one objects to conformity with others *in a good cause.* Then conformity is regarded as a great value, a term of praise. What we have to fear is not conformity as such, but conformity for the sheer sake of conformity, and conformity toward trivial or contemptible ends. When the "problem" of conformity is stated this way, it becomes evident that it is really an expression of a deeper problem, the lack of any positive and compelling visions of the good to fill the emptiness of modern life. Thus the "answer" to conformity is not spontaneity but the construction of and the dedication to such visions of the good for man and society. The ethic of spontaneity provides no help in this task; rather, it is a way of evading the task.

The glorification of spontaneity is not new with Fromm

nor does his expression of it differ essentially from many older expressions: one thinks immediately of the Romantic cult of genius. Nor is it surprising that the notion itself, and others like it, should be so appealing today. A certain tension which may be inherent in civilization itself underlies such patterns of thought and makes them a recurrent feature of an intellectual tradition. In any community which has reached an advanced and complex state of civilization, or which has moved in a rather short time from a condition of relative simplicity and freedom to a condition of relative sophistication and restraint, there will appear an urge to return to a style of life which is more passionate and unfettered than the style permitted by the current conditions. The Greeks had their memory of the tribal past, which was enshrined even in the greatest cities in the cult of Dionysus. America has her national memory of the virgin continent and the limitless frontier. In a day when civilization seems to tower over man, observing and regulating his smallest acts, it is to be expected that the call for spontaneity should come forth from many writers, and that it should appeal to many men. All of us yearn to express ourselves; and when complex social conditions demand so many things from each of us, and forbid so many others, it is easy to feel that what matters above all is expression itself, free and self-generated action, regardless of content.

This is fine, so long as the tendency is kept within some limits. Civilization rests upon restraint and needs compulsion. The chief difference between the civilized man and the savage (or the child) is that the civilized man has cultivated the habit of prudence and accepted the discipline of forethought. He does not act only on impulse and he does not live only for the moment. He takes thought for the future and performs many tasks not because they please him today but because he reasons that they will profit him in the long tomorrow. He knows that life is more than the pleasure of the moment. It is in debt to the past and responsible to the future. The worship of Saturn is for holidays.

These things are obvious to any one who thinks for even a moment about the first man who planted seeds in the ground and anxiously worked and waited for the harvest. Fromm's praise of spontaneity tells half the story. His view of human nature blinds him to the rest.

In the latest essay on "Psychoanalysis and Zen Buddhism" Fromm expresses these tendencies toward the primitive more emphatically than in any of his earlier writings. In this essay, he says that *the* question of life is: "How can we overcome the suffering, the imprisonment, the shame which the *experience of separateness* creates; how can we find union within ourselves, with our fellowman, with nature?" [9] In discussing this question, society is always regarded as the separating and stultifying force. The "socially conditioned filter" of language, logic, and taboo limits the kind of experience which can enter awareness and deprives men of a full "awareness of reality." The result is that the social I, the I of consciousness, is crippled, debased, a corruption of the real man. "We might say . . . that the content of consciousness is mostly fictional and delusional. . . . [Most] of what is in our consciousness is 'false consciousness' and . . . it is essentially society that fills us with these fictitious and unreal notions." [10] Whereas consciousness represents only the social (partial) man, unconsciousness represents universal man. It represents "the whole man, rooted in the Cosmos; it represents the plant in him, the animal in him, the spirit in him; it represents his past down to the dawn of human existence, and it represents his future to the day when man will have become fully human, and when nature will be humanized as man will be 'naturalized.' " [11] The great tragedy is that the "socially conditioned filter" not only limits what enters consciousness but also limits our awareness and corrupts our perception of the commands of "the 'humanistic conscience,' that voice which speaks in the name of the full development of our person." Society blocks the realization "of the immanent evolutionary goals inherent in the chromosomes from which [one] develops. . . ." [12] The great aim of therapy, then, as humanistic psychoanalysis uses the term, is to transform *the mere idea of the universality of man into the living experience of this universality: it is the experiential realization of humanism."* [13] All the limitations which evil societies have imposed on universal man must be removed, so that he can realize his universality and live according to his conscience. When this is done, men will have conquered the separateness which societies impose. Each will realize himself as a true citizen of the world, a brother of all who live.

With these formulations, Fromm in effect converts all known social orders into so many prisons, places in which each individual is locked in his own cell, isolated from his fellows by the delusions of consciousness, and brought into a vicious and alienated contact with the "community" only during the scheduled periods of collective recreation and work. Gone is the earlier understanding that society aids as well as impedes the growth of the human powers. Fromm here sees society only as a force which cripples, corrupts, confines. Any collective smaller than the universal brotherhood of love is too small for universal man.

There is really very little to be said about this. Fromm is of course correct when he says that the "socially conditioned filter" cramps awareness of reality, but he quite forgets that it also permits awareness of reality: men are both blinded and given vision by their social spectacles; and even if their social spectacles were removed, their vision would still be restricted, as Kant took pains to show some time ago, by factors internal to themselves. Our societies are like our clothes. They do sometimes conceal our beauties, impede our movements, make us arrogant, even make us ridiculous. But that is no reason for throwing them all away, at least not while we cannot remain forever young and straight and graceful, and pass all of our days in Tahiti. Our social clothes protect and beautify as well as impede and conceal.

Fromm's universalism gives great comfort in an age which has suffered much from cruel and stupid nationalisms. But the answer to nationalism is not the obliteration of all differences in the universal church of mankind. Indeed, the answer we need is not religious at all, but political. We need to develop political methods and attitudes which while permitting—and even encouraging—national and other differences can yet fashion them into a mutual strength and glory, orchestrate the diverse themes into one harmonious composition. The Frommian answer sacrifices too much. Any developed culture and civilization is a unique and irreplaceable creation, not to be cast down merely because it limits the vision of its members. And any social order worthy of memory has created bonds among its members which are more precious to them than all talk of mankind. The whole reply to Fromm's promiscuous universalism is contained in the question asked by a citizen of Rome a very long time ago: "When all men are brothers, what then can brotherhood mean?"

The earlier themes of spontaneity and productiveness also receive a special expression in the latest essay. The unconscious must be made fully conscious, not to the end that it may be understood and thus mastered, but so that it may be fully liberated. Fromm's program here advocates the elimination of all convention and inhibition—all discipline,

no matter how imposed. The natural man must be released
from the social prison so he can fulfill the destiny which is
"inherent in his chromosomes." The implications of this
are clear and terrifying. Hobbes and Freud may not have
had the whole truth about the nature of "savage lust" and
the forces of the *id*, but they certainly had a piece of it,
and, I think, a greater piece than Fromm. There is a hidden
elemental wildness in man, a "heart of darkness," as Conrad
called it, and civilization with its parliaments and police
forces, its temples and taboos, is still sometimes unable to
restrain it. In this smoldering power there are both salvation and damnation, and not just the former, as Fromm
would have us believe.[14]

One more comment on this theme. In the latest essay
Fromm returns to the subject of authority, and this time
the tendency of his thought toward the irrational and the
prepolitical becomes explicit.

Fromm opens the discussion with his favorite distinction, that between rational and irrational authority. This
time the meaning of rational authority is personified in the
Zen master.

> The attitude of the Zen master to his student is be-
> wildering to the modern Western reader who is caught
> in the alternative between an irrational authority which
> limits freedom and exploits its object, and a laissez-faire
> absence of any authority. Zen represents another form
> of authority, that of "rational authority." The master
> does not call the student; he wants nothing from him
> . . . ; the student comes [and goes] of his own free
> will. . . . But inasmuch as he wants to learn from the
> master, the fact has to be recognized that . . . the
> master knows what the student wants to know. . . .
> The Zen master is characterized at the same time by

the complete lack of irrational authority and by the equally strong affirmation of that undemanding authority, the source of which is genuine experience.[15]

This is revealing in a number of ways. First of all, it emphasizes authority as an intensely personal and private relationship, bound by no rules and subject to no public scrutiny: no constitution stands between master and pupil.

More important, Fromm overlooks all those elements in the relationship which, to my myopic Western eyes, hint at the deepest kind of irrationality and arbitrariness. Consider these incidents. The Indian master Bodhidharma, seeking to test the seriousness of Shen-kuang, who wished to come to him for training, for a long time refused even to grant an audience to the suppliant. Shen-kuang kept returning and even stood one whole night in snow to his knees. At dawn, Bodhidharma received him, only to warn him that the way was hard and not to be undertaken by those lacking in perseverance. To attest his seriousness, the suppliant hacked off his left arm with a sword and presented it to the master, who then accepted him as a student.[16] De Martino relates how the young Zen students, made desperate and fearful by their struggles with the *koan* (a kind of question or problem), may have to be "spurred, inspired, goaded or even driven by the master." The frantic student may try to avoid the master and may even refuse to go to the master for compulsory sessions: "he has sometimes to be beaten, pulled, dragged, or, as once was actually witnessed, forcibly carried by four other monks out of the meditation hall and into the interview." [17] The master asks his student a question, and tells him he must answer yes or no. Then he says, "thirty blows whether you affirm or negate." [18]

Subject a man to enough of this and there is no doubt

that he will become enlightened. He will surely learn to break through his old ways of seeing and discover new ones. This process can be described in a number of vocabularies, of which Zen is only one. It might be called brainwashing. It might be called the annihilation of the ego. It might be called the destruction of reason and will. In any language, it is clear that the student has been subjected to an intolerable burden of frustration which his anguished spirit must somehow escape, even if that means leaping out of itself. This is indeed a method well designed to teach one to "know and apprehend who one is beyond the 'fold of reason,' that is, beyond the subject-object structure of intellection." [19] It does this simply by destroying the instrument and the capacity for intellection. That Fromm accepts this goal is indicated by one of the most remarkable of his sentences. "The cerebrating person is the alienated person, the person in the cave who, as in Plato's allegory, sees only shadows and mistakes them for immediate reality." [20] (It hardly needs to be said that this is not quite what Plato had in mind.) In this same essay, Fromm finds still another remarkable expression for his conviction that intellection alienates and enslaves: "He [modern man] *thinks* of God, instead of experiencing *being* God." [21]

In short, this rational authority seems to lead to the destruction of reason. And when reason falls, all those restraints which prudent men have always put on authority also fall. It is clear that by "rational authority" Fromm means something other than the limited, rule-bound, predictable, responsible exercise of power which the thinkers of the West have meant by rational authority. I only repeat the obvious: we have learned by grim experience not to submit ourselves totally to the ministrations of any "teacher," no matter how wise or merciful. Zen is always presented to us of the West in glowing terms. I wonder how many victims of the "rational authority" of the Zen masters are to be found dragging their crippled spirits around the courtyards of Zen enlightenment. Is it entirely wrong to see that sad tale of Bodhidharma and Shen-kuang in terms of the priests of Cybele, who also had to mutilate themselves before they were admitted to the mysteries?

These Zen themes, together with some others from Existentialism, attest Fromm's passionate desire to see man overcome alienation and achieve spontaneity and wholeness. But there may be danger in this eagerness to transcend the human condition. In these concluding pages, I shall try to show how certain tendencies and orientations in Fromm's thought effectively blind him to certain large ethical perspectives and sectors of experience.

Fromm touches the dominant theme of modern Existentialism when he accepts finitude and estrangement as the central categories of the human condition. Existentialism sees the world we live in as a disrupted unity, a rubble of fragments and ruins. Man, the stranger, stumbles among the ruins and, driven by his very finitude, strives to restore even small heaps of the rubble to order. From man's finitude comes the *Angst* which compels him to action, but this action only leads to greater anxiety, for even as he strives he senses the world is alien. The action brings only deeper anxiety, then despair, and finally guilt as man faces the realization that he is really trying to escape the human condition, which is finitude. Man becomes alienated from his guilty self. He knows too that the real experiences of his life are unique to him. Death, guilt, fear, anxiety—these cannot be shared, hardly even communicated. Each lives in his own prison. In public one talks only of public things, and often he tries to escape the private things by covering them over with public action. But in the end he knows he is alone, and he escapes only at the price of a bad conscience.

Thus man is also cut off from other men as well as from himself. Existentialism accepts the relation between finitude and estrangement as necessary and inescapable.

That is precisely the relation Fromm will not accept. He begins with the Existentialists by accepting finitude as the basic feature of the human condition. He goes on to describe man's loneliness and his estrangement from himself and others. But he will not accept the Existentialist thesis of the necessary connection between finitude on the one side and loneliness and estrangement on the other. Fromm believes that estrangement (which he usually calls alienation) can be overcome in a new world. He will not see that every man, almost to the extent that he is an authentic and integral person, is lonely, for to be an individual means to recognize that one is different and in some ways cut off from all the others around him. He believes that loneliness arises from present evil social conditions, and that it will disappear when a decent human community is built. Another way to put the point is to say that for Fromm the category of alienation is at bottom a category of sociology rather than of metaphysics.

This makes Fromm's work attractively simple. And in its simplicity lies its charm and its power to persuade. Fromm believes that the only problem left in the destiny of mankind is to bring individual and social needs and purposes into harmony. To be sure, this is a big problem, but for Fromm it is a manageable one because he thinks he understands the basic needs of human nature and he sees no irreconcilable conflict between the needs of man's nature and the principles of a just and productive social order. Therefore, all that is required to bring society into harmony with human nature is a creative act of will. Fromm has banished mystery and guilt, terror and tragedy from the center of human affairs and relegated them to the pe-

ripheral status of grievous accidents, grievous precisely because they are so unnecessary. This places him squarely in
the tradition of optimistic liberalism and separates him
from all writers who have understood tragedy. For Fromm,
all conflicts are mistaken, and the good man is at once the
good citizen of the good society. In the latest essay, the good
society is finally revealed as nothing less than the restoration of the garden on a universal scale. Fromm restores the
harmony of the garden, but only at the price of oversimpli-
fying reality and denying two of the oldest and richest
themes of ethical thought.

This notion of estrangement is of course not new with
the Existentialists. In one form or another, under one name
or another, it is as old as moral philosophy. But the writer
can either accept estrangement as a necessary part of the
human condition or he can, as Fromm does, believe that it
can be vanquished. The view one takes of this matter makes
an enormous difference to his moral philosophy. Those who
hold the first view often accept something like the courage
to affirm life in the face of despair or the practice of the
intellectual virtues as the highest good. Here, for example,
is Burnet's summary of the ethic of Pythagoras:

> We are strangers in this world, and the body is the tomb
> of the soul, and yet we must not seek to escape by self-
> murder; for we are the chattels of God who is our herds-
> man, and without his command we have no right to
> make our escape. In this life there are three kinds of
> men, just as there are three sorts of people who come
> to the Olympic Games. The lowest class is made up
> of those who come to buy and sell, and next above them
> are those who come to compete. Best of all, however,
> are those who come to look on. . . . The greatest puri-
> fication of all is, therefore, science and it is the man
> who devotes himself to that, the true philosopher, who

has most effectually released himself from the "wheel of birth." [22]

Those who went to the Olympic games to buy and sell, those who went to compete, and those who went to look on have their counterparts in all times and places. Pythagoras admired the true philosophers, those who "only" looked on. They see life as a wonderful spectacle—half glorious and half sordid, half religious and half secular, half beautiful and half ugly, half victory and half defeat. The great danger is that one too easily gets caught up by the spectacle and lost in it. The great virtue is to understand and appreciate. Among all who go to the games, those who understand are the happiest and the dearest to the gods, for only in the life of contemplation does man at once gain safety from the transient pleasures of the game and exercise the faculty that makes him akin to the gods. Fromm claims the authority of Aristotle for his ethical views but I doubt whether he could ever appreciate Aristotle's supreme ethical conception, for to embrace the contemplative life as the noblest life requires an acceptance of the essential estrangement of man from man and man from society which Fromm could never make. Fromm's optimism, his meliorism, and his desire to reconcile conflicts result in an ethical activism which precludes a full appreciation of the contemplative style of life.

The same characteristics of Fromm's thought make it impossible for him to appreciate what Unamuno has called the tragic sense of life. Fromm talks often of the "tragedy" of modern life, but he uses the word to cover loosely any situation in which a chance has been lost, a pain suffered, a hope defeated. The sense of tragedy, the tragic sense of life, is finer than that. It involves more than deep sympathy for the defeated. *Katharsis.* This is what the Greeks called the state of feeling produced by the dramatic tragedy. It meant the stillness at the center of one's being which comes after pity and fear have been burned out. The soul is purified and calmed, freed from the violent passions. *Hybris* is broken, just as it was broken in the drama. Chastened and freed from the bondage of passion, the mind grasps newer and deeper meanings in reality. The spirit, now strengthened and deepened, gravely prepares for new duties and the courageous acceptance of whatever fate brings.

This state of mind, which is produced in its most intense and exalted form by the spectacle of the tragedy, can also be maintained as an orientation toward life. But that requires a fuller acceptance of the discontinuities of existence than Fromm is willing to make. Out of the tension between man's capacity for a self-transcending freedom and the essential limitations of his creatureliness come the desire and anxiety which urge him to pride and self-inflation. (I of course mean pride here in the theological sense: "And the Lord God said, Behold, the man is become as one of us, to know good and evil. . . .") This pride enlists all man's biological talents and energies in its cause and bends other men and social institutions to its purposes, but is itself the product neither of biological drives, as Freud would have us believe, nor of social institutions, as Fromm would have us believe. It comes from the self in the existential situation.

Once this is grasped, we sense vividly the limitations of all human achievement and the ambiguity of all human virtue. We can no longer believe in the innocence of man nor call every defeat of his highest aspirations a "tragedy," for we know that man lacks the power to do all he wishes, and that he will always wish to do more than he can. Great pride and talent are needed for great attempts, and all attempts are but preparations for the greatest attempt of all, which is to become God. But the attempt is doomed from the outset for the tragic flaw is already there. Still, we shall always try, for the origins of pride are in the human situation. Only one thing is certain: the nobler the effort and the closer the victory, the more catastrophic will be the final defeat. "And now, lest he put forth his hand, and take also of the tree of life, and eat, and live for ever. . . ." Here is man's glory and misery, the fate he cannot escape.

This image of life, with its own understanding of the moral problem, is inaccessible to Fromm. He starts his analysis of the human condition by insisting that finitude is its defining category, but he will not accept the stern imperatives of the analysis. Fromm agrees with the Existentialist and the Christian that finitude is man's fate and that man is driven to attempt to transcend this finitude, but he seems to make the agreement only so he can hurry on to say that man *can* escape his fate and overcome his finitude. For the works of man, Fromm has much praise. But man himself he cannot praise. He scolds the very being whose work he so admires.

> Man has created a new world with its own laws and destiny. Looking at his creation, he can say, truly, it is good.
> But looking at himself what can he say? Has he come closer to the realization of another dream of mankind, that of the perfection of *man?* Of man loving his neighbor, doing justice, speaking truth, and realizing that which he potentially is, an image of God? [23]

This is to argue that Fromm first accepts the definition of man as the finite creature who wishes to be the infinite creator, and then goes on to assert that man can be what he wishes. Fromm will tolerate no unbridgeable gap between the two categories. He will not for long abide the existential dichotomy. This craving for wholeness has blinded Fromm to the prodigious history of pride and made it impossible for him to apply his own powerful talents to an understanding of the psychology of pride.

What I am arguing, in summary, is that very different moral systems than Fromm's own can be built on the base of his own analysis of the human condition. Had he accepted the full implications of his own view of man as the stranger, he might have gone on to build an ethical system in which the contemplative life is the best life. Had he accepted the full implications of his own view of man as the creature who strives to depose the creator, he might have gone on to build an ethical system around the tragic sense of life. I am not arguing that any vision of the moral problem which cannot encompass these perspectives is simply wrong, but I am arguing that it is narrow. The ultimate choices which guide an ethical system are esthetic and temperamental, and I am willing to put my differences with Fromm on these grounds. I think Fromm's ethical outlook will do for the days of our youth, when life is all richness and promise, but it will not serve for the whole of life, during which we must watch our powers wane and see our hopes defeated, and know that the highest state man can achieve in this world is still a state of qualified unhappiness.

Fromm's work has a resonance in this time of small hopes and little beauty because it is a work undertaken in favor of man. Fromm's pages are alive with expressions of love and compassion for all mankind. His work is in the splendid tradition of those who have shown man a vision of life as beauty and creativity. Much of Fromm's own vision of that good life is noble, and many of his expressions of it achieve beauty in their simplicity and clarity. It is no pleasant task to criticize writers who give us so much. Still, one must express reservations. For if life would be poorer without such writers, they also have the talent of making us forget that the life we have is not all poor. So this is a question of self-defense. The utopian's love for the beauty that does not yet exist sometimes dims his appreciation of the beauty that does exist. We must take care that the utopian does not rob us of what we have by dazzling us with his offer of so much more.

The utopian desires perfection. Nothing else will do. So avidly does he gaze upon the shining "city on the hill" that its light blinds him to the beauty that is present even in the lives of those who dwell in the plains below. Earthly beauties pale and become tawdry in the light of the beauties above. The utopian often cannot see that "mere" earthly beauties are all the more wondrous precisely because they have been wrested from ugliness and affirmed in the face of terror and absurdity. That is the meaning of human beauty, although the utopian cannot see it. Emerson caught the point in his judgment of the utopians of his day:

> The philosophers at Fruitlands have such an image of
> virtue before their eyes, that the poetry of man and
> nature they never see; the poetry that is in man's life,
> the poorest pastoral clownish life; the light that shines
> on a man's hat, in a child's spoon, the sparkle on every
> wave and on every mote of dust, they see not.[24]

Fromm suffers some of the handicaps of the utopian blindness. He leaps too quickly from the ugly present to the beautiful future. So perilous is this leap from finitude to perfection that he can attempt it only with his eyes closed. It is not solely that Fromm judges modern man and his civilization harshly—though he does that too—but that he ignores so much of the good that men win every day from evil, so much of the beauty that men every day create and affirm

in spite of ugliness. In his eagerness to see Prometheus unbound, Fromm fails to see the beauties and nobilities that
are Prometheus's only while he suffers. It is a cruel judgment
which decides that man must be "healthy" and "happy" before he can be human and create beauty. Some writers, Mann
and Verlaine, for example, even postulated that the beautiful
had its roots in the morbid. It is not necessary to accept this
whole theory to recognize, at least, that the beautiful and the
morbid are intimately related. Some part of the deep secret
of human beings lies in the fact that they can combine the
sacred and the obscene. Some part of the mystery and
grandeur of human beings lies in the fact that they make
paintings on the walls of miserable caves and write poetry
and philosophy in the midst of hunger and filth. For
Fromm, these things, which some of us judge noble precisely because they have been built at the price of great
sacrifice and in the face of great risks, are just not good or
beautiful enough. In his eagerness to see man reborn,
Fromm fails to see the beauties and nobilities which man
achieves even—no, only—in the fallen state.

References

CHAPTER I

1. *The Ethics of Aristotle*, tr. by J. A. K. Thomson (London: Penguin, 1955), pp. 27–28 (*Ethics*, Bk. I, chap. 3, 1094 ᵇ).
2. David Hume, *A Treatise of Human Nature* (1739), Introduction.
3. Sigmund Freud, *Civilization and Its Discontents*, tr. by Joan Riviere (Garden City, N.Y.: Doubleday Anchor, 1958), p. 61.
4. Erich Fromm, *Escape from Freedom* (New York: Rinehart, 1941), frontispiece.
5. Erich Fromm, *Man for Himself: An Inquiry into the Psychology of Ethics* (New York: Rinehart, 1947), p. 13.
6. *Ibid.*, pp. 12–13.
7. *Ibid.*, p. 20.
8. Erich Fromm, *The Sane Society* (New York: Rinehart, 1955), p. 30.
9. *Ibid.*, pp. 359–360.
10. Ecclesiastes 12:13.
11. Job 1:1.
12. *Man for Himself*, p. 18. (Footnote omitted.)
13. *Ibid.*, pp. 19–20.
14. *Ibid.*, p. 18.
15. *Ibid.*, pp. 25–26.
16. *The Sane Society*, p. 13.
17. *Loc. cit.*

18. *Man for Himself*, p. 23.
19. T. S. Eliot, "Gerontion," *The Complete Poems and Plays* (New York: Harcourt, Brace, 1952), pp. 21–23.
20. *The Sane Society*, p. 69.
21. "Man is not a Thing," *Saturday Review of Literature*, March 16, 1957, pp. 9–11. See also Erich Fromm, *The Art of Loving* (New York: Harper, 1956), pp. 29–32.
22. "Man is not a Thing," *op. cit.*, p. 10.
23. *Loc. cit.*
24. Hume, *loc. cit.*
25. *The Sane Society*, p. 30.
26. *Ibid.*, p. 25.
27. Matthew 6:26, 28–29.
28. *The Sane Society*, p. 23.
29. *Ibid.*, pp. 23–24. An identical formulation appears in *Man for Himself*, p. 40.
30. *The Sane Society*, p. 27.
31. *Ibid.*, p. 25.
32. *Escape from Freedom*, p. 19.
33. *The Sane Society*, pp. 30–66.
34. *Ibid.*, p. 30.
35. See Fromm's analysis of symbiotic relatedness in *Escape from Freedom*, pp. 141 ff.
36. *The Art of Loving*, p. 25.
37. *Man for Himself*, pp. 96 ff.; *The Art of Loving*, pp. 26 ff.
38. *The Sane Society*, p. 37.
39. *Ibid.*, p. 38.
40. *Man for Himself*, p. 216.
41. *The Sane Society*, p. 60.
42. *Ibid.*, p. 66.
43. D. T. Suzuki, Erich Fromm, and Richard De Martino, *Zen Buddhism and Psychoanalysis* (New York: Harper, 1960), p. 87.
44. *Ibid.*, p. 109.
45. *Man for Himself*, pp. 43–45.
46. *The Sane Society*, p. 72.

47. All from Erich Fromm, *Psychoanalysis and Religion* (New Haven: Yale University Press, 1950), p. 7.
48. *The Sane Society*, p. 63.
49. Hume, *op. cit.*, Book I, Part IV, Section VI.
50. Kant's analysis appears in the *Critique of Pure Reason* (1781), Second Division, Book II, Chapter I.
51. Bertrand Russell, *A History of Western Philosophy* (New York: Simon and Schuster, 1945), p. 167.
52. "Handle with Care" (March, 1936). Quoted here from F. Scott Fitzgerald, *The Crack-Up*, Edmund Wilson, ed. (New York: New Directions Paperbook, 1956), p. 79.
53. Charles Horton Cooley, *Human Nature and the Social Order* (New York: Scribner's, 1902), p. 152.
54. George H. Mead, *Mind, Self and Society* (Chicago, Ill.: University of Chicago Press, 1934), p. 138. For similar or equivalent formulations, see also pp. 151–156, 193–194.
55. Peter F. Drucker, *Concept of the Corporation* (New York: John Day, 1946), p. 152.
56. Nowhere has this theme been treated more emphatically than in Philip Selznick's *Leadership in Administration: A Sociological Interpretation* (Evanston, Ill.: Row, Peterson, 1957).
57. This scheme is set forth in David Riesman's *The Lonely Crowd: A Study of the Changing American Character* (New Haven: Yale University Press, 1950), Chap. I.

CHAPTER II

1. *The Ethics of Aristotle, op. cit.*, p. 27.
2. *Man for Himself*, p. 33.
3. *Ibid.*, p. 50.
4. *Loc. cit.*
5. *Ibid.*, pp. 50–51.
6. *Escape from Freedom*, p. 13.
7. *Ibid.*, p. 290.

8. The first is from *Escape from Freedom*, p. 278, and the second is from *Man for Himself*, p. 59.
9. *Escape from Freedom*, p. 18.
10. *Man for Himself*, p. 60. See also *Escape from Freedom*, p. 287.
11. The first formulation is from *Man for Himself*, p. 60. The second is from *Escape from Freedom*, p. 277.
12. I borrowed this figure of the scale from Patrick Mullahy, *Oedipus: Myth and Complex* (New York: Grove Press, 1955), p. 259.
13. *Escape from Freedom*, p. 283.
14. *Man for Himself*, p. 60.
15. *Escape from Freedom*, p. 284.
16. C. Wright Mills, *The Sociological Imagination* (New York: Oxford University Press, 1959), esp. pp. 3–15.
17. The example is drawn from *Escape from Freedom*, pp. 280–281. Incidentally, Fromm vacillated on this question of the workers. In the place just cited, he attributes their failure to their authoritarianism. On p. 209 he says it was "due mainly to a state of inner tiredness and resignation, which . . . is characteristic of the individual in the present era even in democratic countries."
18. The characterology is set forth most fully in *Man for Himself*, pp. 62–117. My exposition will draw heavily from those pages.
19. Adapted from *Man for Himself*, *p*. 111.
20. *Ibid.*, p. 67.
21. *Ibid.*, p. 75.
22. *Ibid.*, p. 83.
23. *Ibid.*, p. 84. Fromm also says that the concept of productiveness is an elaboration of the concept of spontaneity which was presented in *Escape from Freedom*.
24. *Man for Himself*, p. 85.
25. *Ibid.*, p. 91.
26. *Ibid.*, pp. 143–144.
27. *Ibid.*, p. 144.

28. *Ibid.*, p. 158.
29. *Ibid.*, p. 159.
30. *Ibid.*, p. 129.
31. *Ibid.*, p. 130.
32. *Psychoanalysis and Religion*, p. 37.
33. *Ibid.*, p. 76.
34. Jean-Jacques Rousseau, *Emile, or Education*, tr. by Barbara Foxley (London: Everyman's Library, 1911), p. 259.
35. Lawrence Lipton, *The Holy Barbarians* (New York: Julian Messner, 1959), p. 172.
36. *Escape from Freedom*, p. viii.
37. Carl R. Rogers, "Becoming a Person," *Pastoral Psychology*, Vol. 7, February 1956, pp. 9–13; Vol. 7, April 1956, pp. 16–26.
38. Rousseau, *op. cit.*, p. 252.
39. Thomas Jefferson, Letter to Peter Carr, August 10, 1789. Quoted here from Adrienne Koch and William Peden, eds., *The Life and Selected Writings of Thomas Jefferson* (New York: Modern Library, 1944), pp. 430–431.
40. *Man for Himself*, p. 167.
41. *Ibid.*, pp. 229–230.
42. William James, "What Pragmatism Means," in *Pragmatism: A New Name for Some Old Ways of Thinking* (New York: Longmans, Green, 1907), pp. 43–81. All the following quotations from James are from this essay.
43. *Psychoanalysis and Religion*, p. 114.
44. *Ibid.*, p. 21.
45. See *Ibid.*, esp. pp. 85–86.
46. *Ibid.*, p. 94, footnote.
47. Quoted from Evelyn Underhill, *Mysticism: A Study in the Nature and Development of Man's Spiritual Consciousness*, 12th ed., 1930 (New York: Noonday Press, 1955), p. 48.
48. *The Art of Loving*, p. 59.
49. *Ibid.*, p. 53.
50. *Ibid.*, p. 55.
51. John 3:16.
52. *The Art of Loving*, p. 47.

53. Søren Kierkegaard, *Works of Love*, tr. by David. F. Swenson and Lillian Marvin Swenson, introduction by Douglas V. Steere (Princeton: Princeton University Press, 1949), p. 8.
54. Matthew 22:36–40.
55. Sigmund Freud, *Civilization and Its Discontents*, tr. by Joan Riviere (Garden City, N. Y.: Doubleday Anchor, 1958), pp. 57–60 *passim*.
56. *The Art of Loving*, p. 35.
57. *Ibid.*, p. 29.
58. *Ibid.*, p. 31.
59. *Ibid.*, p. 32.
60. Evelyn Underhill, *op. cit.*, p. 75.
61. *Man for Himself*, p. 191.
62. Thomas Hobbes, *Leviathan* (1651), edited and with Introduction by Michael Oakeshott (Oxford: Blackwell, 1946), Part I, chap. II, p. 64.
63. *Man for Himself*, p. 191.
64. *Ibid.*, p. 173.
65. E. A. Shils and Morris Janowitz, "Cohesion and Disintegration of the *Wehrmacht* in World War II," *Public Opinion Quarterly*, Vol. XII, 1948, pp. 280–315.
66. W. H. Auden, "Letter to Lord Byron," Part IV, in W. H. Auden and Louis Macneice, *Letters from Iceland* (New York: Random House, 1937), p. 211.

CHAPTER III

1. For another writer who shares this general perspective with Fromm, see R. E. Money-Kyrle, *Psychoanalysis and Politics: A Contribution to the Psychology of Politics and Morals* (New York: Norton, 1951).
2. *The Sane Society*, p. 69. Italics omitted. See also *ibid.*, p. 275.
3. *Ibid.*, pp. 72–73. See also *ibid.*, p. 276.
4. *Ibid.*, p. 273.
5. *Ibid.*, p. 79.
6. *Ibid.*, p. 83.

7. For a brilliant presentation of capitalism as a utopia, see Karl Polanyi, *The Great Transformation: The Political and Economic Origins of Our Time* (New York: Rinehart, 1944).
8. *The Sane Society*, p. 102.
9. *Ibid.*, p. 110.
10. *Ibid.*, p. 124.
11. G. W. F. Hegel, *The Phenomenology of Mind*, tr. by J. B. Baillie (London: Swann Sonnenschein & Co.; New York: Macmillan, 1910), Vol. I, p. 10.
12. *Ibid.*, pp. 197–198.
13. Karl Marx, *Economic and Philosophic Manuscripts of 1844*, Marx-Engels *Gesamtausgabe*, Abt. I, Bd. 3, tr. by Martin Milligan (Moscow: Foreign Languages Publishing House, n.d.), p. 151. See also pp. 149–150.
14. T. B. Bottomore and Maximilien Rubel, *Karl Marx: Selected Writings in Sociology and Social Philosophy* (London: Watts and Co., 1956), p. 97.
15. Marx, *op. cit.*, p. 72.
16. Bottomore and Rubel, *op. cit.*, p. 170. See also Marx, *op cit.*, p. 70.
17. Bottomore and Rubel, *op. cit.*, p. 175.
18. *Ibid.*, p. 231.
19. *The Sane Society*, p. 124.
20. *Ibid.*, p. 176.
21. *Ibid.*, p. 123.
22. See Joseph A. Schumpeter, *Capitalism, Socialism, and Democracy* (New York: Harper, 1947), esp. pp. 250, 261–263, 269.
23. *The Sane Society*, p. 126.
24. *Ibid.*, p. 164.
25. *Ibid.*, p. 135.
26. *Ibid.*, p. 134.
27. *Ibid.*, p. 151.
28. *Ibid.*, p. 205.
29. *Ibid.*, p. 206.
30. *Ibid.*, p. 193.
31. I have in mind especially these works: Temporary National

Economic Committee, *The Distribution of Ownership in the 200 Largest Non-Financial Corporations* (Washington, D.C.: Government Printing Office, 1941); and Robert Aaron Gordon, *Business Leadership in the Large Corporation* (Washington, D.C.: Brookings Institution, 1945).

32. Cited from C. Wright Mills, *White Collar* (New York: Oxford University Press, 1951), p. 229. Fromm's discussion appears in *The Sane Society*, pp. 296–297.

33. *The Sane Society*, p. 161.

34. *Ibid.*, p. 209.

35. For a broader statement of this theme, see Glenn Tinder, "Human Estrangement and the Failure of Political Imagination," *Review of Politics*, Vol. 21, October 1959, pp. 611–630.

36. Thomas Hooker, "A True Sight of Sin," quoted from Perry Miller, ed., *The American Puritans: Their Prose and Poetry* (Garden City, N. Y.: Doubleday Anchor, 1956), p. 154.

37. Paul Tillich, *The Courage To Be* (New Haven: Yale University Press, 1959), pp. 124, 125.

38. Albert Camus, *The Fall*, tr. by Justin O'Brien (London: Hamish Hamilton, 1957), p. 73.

CHAPTER IV

1. The following discussion draws heavily from Martin Buber, *Paths in Utopia*, tr. by R. F. C. Hull (Boston: Beacon Press, 1958), esp. pp. 1–16, 129–151. I have elaborated freely on Buber, however, so he is not responsible.

2. *Ibid.*, p. 13.

3. *The Sane Society*, pp. 282–283.

4. *Ibid.*, pp. 343–344.

5. *Ibid.*, pp. 271–272. Fromm repeats the point at *ibid.*, p. 361: "No change must be brought about by force, it must be a simultaneous one in the economic, political and cultural spheres. Changes restricted to *one* sphere are destructive of every change."

6. *Ibid.*, pp. 283–284.

7. *Ibid.,* p. 323.
8. *Ibid.,* pp. 334–335.
9. *Man for Himself,* p. 243.
10. These speculations appear in *The Sane Society,* p. 359.
11. *Ibid.,* p. 360.
12. For recent English views, see R. H. S. Crossman, ed., *New Fabian Essays* (London: Turnstile Press, 1953), especially the essays by C. A. R. Crosland, R. Jenkins, and A. Albu. See also the intelligent books by G. Friedmann, *Machine et Humanisme* (Paris: Gallimard, 1946), and *Où va le Travail Humain* (Paris: Gallimard, 1950). Fromm has borrowned much from Friedmann.
13. See Frank Tannenbaum, *A Philosophy of Labor* (New York: Knopf, 1950).
14. Daniel Bell, "Meaning in Work: A New Direction," *Dissent,* Summer 1959, p. 244.
15. Perhaps the leading work on the theme is John Kenneth Galbraith, *The Affluent Society* (Boston: Houghton Mifflin, 1958). See also the brilliant book by Percival and Paul Goodman, *Communitas: Means of Livelihood and Ways of Life* (Chicago: University of Chicago Press, 1947). The Goodmans' book is the finest recent work of utopian thought known to me.
16. I have drawn this account from Polanyi, *op. cit.,* pp. 112–114.
17. José Ortega y Gasset, *The Revolt of the Masses,* translator anonymous (25th Anniversary Edition; New York: Norton, 1957), p. 15.

CHAPTER V

1. Saint Jerome, *Select Letters of St. Jerome,* ed. and tr. by F. A. Wright (London: Heinemann; New York: Putnam's, 1933), letter 28, "Ad Pacatulam," pp. 479–481.
2. Proverbs, 20:2.
3. *Escape from Freedom,* p. 263.
4. *Ibid.,* p. 262.

5. Roy Fuller, "January 1940," in *The Middle of a War* (London: Hogarth, 1942), p. 10.

6. This and the following three paragraphs owe much to the intelligent essay by Kenneth Keniston, "Alienation and the Decline of Utopia," *American Scholar*, Vol. 29, Spring 1960, pp. 161–201.

7. Albert Camus, *The Myth of Sisyphus and Other Essays*, tr. by Justin O'Brien (New York: Knopf, 1955), p. 61.

8. Quoted from *ibid.*, p. 64.

9. Erich Fromm, "Psychoanalysis and Zen Buddhism," in *Zen Buddhism and Psychoanalysis*, p. 87. Emphasis added.

10. *Ibid.*, p. 98.

11. *Ibid.*, p. 106.

12. *Ibid.*, pp. 104, 105.

13. *Ibid.*, p. 107.

14. In addition to Conrad's *Heart of Darkness*, see on this theme the equally chilling parable by William Golding, *Lord of the Flies* (New York: Coward-McCann, 1955), and the fine treatment by J. Bronowski, *The Face of Violence: An Essay with a Play* (New York: Braziller, 1955).

15. "Psychoanalysis and Zen Buddhism," *op. cit.*, pp. 120–121.

16. Drawn from Richard De Martino, "The Human Situation and Zen Buddhism," in *Zen Buddhism and Psychoanalysis*, p. 152.

17. *Ibid.*, p. 161.

18. Drawn from D. T. Suzuki, "Lectures on Zen Buddhism," in *Zen Buddhism and Psychoanalysis*, p. 121.

19. De Martino, *op. cit.*, p. 156.

20. "Psychoanalysis and Zen Buddhism," p. 109.

21. *Ibid.*, p. 92.

22. John Burnet, *Early Greek Philosophy* (New York: Meridian, 1957), p. 98.

23. *Psychoanalysis and Religion*, p. 1.

24. Ralph Waldo Emerson, *Journals*, entry of March, undated, 1843. Quoted here from Bliss Perry, ed., *The Heart of Emerson's Journals* (New York: Dover, 1958), p. 196. By quoting Emerson on this point I do not mean to suggest that his

vision was always clearer than that of the philosophers of Fruitlands. Emerson, too, was a utopian, and suffered from the utopian blindness to the everyday. And his conception of beauty was everlastingly spiritualized and otherworldly. Perhaps he could see the shortcomings of those he criticized because he shared so many of the same ones himself, and because he tried so hard to conceal or overcome them. See, for example, the *Journal* entry for April 18, 1824, pp. 17–23.

Permissions

The author extends grateful thanks to the following publishers
for permission to quote from the indicated materials:

Harcourt, Brace and Company, Inc.: T. S. Eliot, "Gerontion,"
Collected Poems 1909–1935, 1952.

Harper & Brothers: Erich Fromm, *The Art of Loving,* 1956;
Erich Fromm, D. T. Suzuki, Richard De Martino, *Zen Buddhism and Psychoanalysis,* 1960.

Harvard University Press and Loeb Classical Library: F. A.
Wright (Ed.), *Select Letters of Saint Jerome,* 1933.

The Hogarth Press Ltd.: Roy Fuller, "January 1940," *The Middle
of a War,* 1942.

Holt, Rinehart and Winston, Inc.: Erich Fromm, *Escape from
Freedom,* 1941; *Man for Himself,* 1947; *The Sane Society,*
1955.

Alfred A. Knopf, Inc., and Hamish Hamilton Ltd.: Albert
Camus, *The Fall,* Justin O'Brien (tr.), 1957.

Longmans, Green & Co., Inc.: William James, *Pragmatism: A
New Name for Some Old Ways of Thinking,* 1907.

The Macmillan Company and A. & C. Black Ltd.: John Burnet,
Early Greek Philosophy, 1952.

Julian Messner, Inc.: Lawrence Lipton, *The Holy Barbarians*, 1959.

New Directions: F. Scott Fitzgerald, *The Crack-Up*, Edmund Wilson (Ed.), 1956.

W. W. Norton & Company, Inc., and The Hogarth Press Ltd.: Sigmund Freud, *Civilization and Its Discontents*, 1930.

Oxford University Press and The Clarendon Press: David Hume, *A Treatise of Human Nature* (L. A. Selby-Bigge, Ed.), 1897.

Routledge & Kegan Paul Ltd.: Martin Buber, *Paths in Utopia*, 1949.

Saturday Review: Erich Fromm, "Man is not a Thing," Vol. 40, 1957, pp. 9–11.

C. A. Watts & Co. Ltd.: T. B. Bottomore and Maximilien Rubel, *Karl Marx: Selected Writings in Sociology and Social Philosophy*, 1956.

Yale University Press: Erich Fromm, *Psychoanalysis and Religion*, 1950.

Index

A

Abraham, 174
abstractification, 207
abundance, 19, 115
  pleasure and, 146–151
Adams, Henry, 238
adjustment, 160
alienation, 19, 53, 220–221, 252, 256, 316, 317
  bureaucratization and, 196
  capitalism and, 186–192
  in Christian thought, 220–221
  conscience and, 198–199
  consumption and, 196–197
  Existentialist concept of, 225–233
  Feuerbach on, 185–186
  Fromm on, 173, 174, 192–199, 201–205, 211–212
  guilt and, 198
  Hegel on, 175–185
  human nature and, 197–199
  idolatry and, 194–195
  Marx on, 183–193
  mental health and, 197–199
  modern causes of, 218–220
  Nettler on, 201–202
  from others, 216–219
  in Plato's thought, 222–223
  from politics, 251–252
  productive orientation and, 134n.
  psychiatry and, 198–199
  reason and, 52–54, 198–199
  from self, 197–198, 213–216, 219
  from work, 249–250, 264–279
  (see also homelessness)
Anabasis, 157
anamnesis, 119
Anderson, Sherwood, 238
Aquinas, Saint Thomas, 83
Aristippus, 143, 154

339

Eros, 49, 50, 114, 123, 141, 157
Erotic, *see* Eros
Escape from Freedom, 45, 46n., 47n., 57, 93, 96, 97, 114, 169n., 173n., 259n.
esthetics, ethics and, 111–114
estrangement, *see* alienation
ethics
  esthetics and, 111–114
  character and, 85ff.
  humanistic, 26–32, 142–158
  pleasure and, 144ff.
  psychoanalysis and, 83–84
  psychology and, 32–33, 64–65
  religion and, 126
  sociology and, 68–69
  study of, 12, 68–69, 84
  temperament and, 86, 94–95
evolution, 30n., 43–44, 79
  Bergson's theory of, 59–60
  moral–biological, 56–62
existential condition, *see* human condition
Existentialism, 43–45, 52–54, 58, 174, 206
  alienation and, 220–235, 316ff.
  freedom and, 228–229, 231
  human condition and, 316–317
  individualism and, 224–225, 228–229
  "schools" of, 228ff.
  social reform and, 232ff.
Existentialists, *see* Existentialism
exploitative orientation, 89, 100, 102, 199n.

F

faith, 107
Fascism, 173n., 195
Faulkner, William, 239
Fear of Freedom, 302
Ferrier, James Frederick, 179
fetishism of commodities, 190
Feuerbach, Ludwig, 185–186
Fitzgerald, F. Scott, 69–70, 238
Forgotten Language, The, 46n.
Fourier, Charles, 241
frame of orientation and devotion, need for, 46n., 51–52, 53
Francis, Saint, 114
Frazer, Sir James G., 294n.
freedom
  constitutional, 299
  dilemma of, 297–298
  Existentialism and, 228–229, 231
  Fromm's conception of, 114, 298
  goodness and, 298–299
  Hegel on, 177–184
  privacy and, 302–303
Fromm, Erich
  audience of, 260–262
  basic features of his work, 6–9
  brief biography of, 3
  psychoanalysis and, 5, 7–8
  as social critic, 3–4, 8, 10–11, 12, 208ff.
Freud, Sigmund, 5, 7, 8, 16, 46n., 47, 50, 58, 59, 61, 78–79, 83, 84, 86–89, 99, 102–104, 120, 132–133,